Game of Thrones Season One Essays

Illustrated Edition

By Pearson Moore

By Pearson Moore:

Game of Thrones Season One Essays

Game of Thrones Season Two Essays Illustrated Edition

LOST Humanity
The Mythology and Themes of LOST

LOST Identity: The Characters of LOST

LOST Thought: Leading Thinkers Discuss LOST

Cartier's Ring
A Novel

Intolerable Loyalty
The Invasion of Canada 1775
(coming in February, 2013)

Direwolves and Dragons Volume 1.01: Symbolism and Thesis

Direwolves and Dragons Volume 1.02: Bran and Jon

GAME OF THRONES
SEASON ONE ESSAYS

Illustrated Edition

PEARSON MOORE

Game of Thrones Season One Essays Illustrated Edition

Cover concept and design by Pearson Moore 2012

ISBN   978-0-61-568118-4

Published in the United States by Inukshuk Press

Inukshuk

Press

For my father

Table of Contents

Introduction: Five Paths of the Direwolf 11

Instinctive Honour: The Decency of Eddark Stark 21

Episode 1.01: A Mad Man Sees What He Sees 29

Episode 1.02: Meat and Blood 39

Symbolism and Allusion in the Direwolf Scene 49

The Grotesques: The Thesis of Game of Thrones 63

Episode 1.03: Northern Blood, Southron Armour 77

Episode 1.04: Seven Bastards 91

Bran Stark: The Third Eye 103

The Nine Circles of Jon Snow 125

Episode 1.05: Family, Duty, Honour 139

Episode 1.06: The Weight of Armour and Gold 149

Tyrion Lannister: The Geography of Possibilities 163

Episode 1.07: The Seven Theses 173

Episode 1.08: Mightier Than the Sword 187

Episode 1.09: The Sword of Mormont 199

The Triumph of Eddard Stark 213

Episode 1.10: Fireborn 225

Daenerys Targaryen: I Am the Blood of the Dragon 237

The Seven Claims to the Iron Throne 247

A History of Westeros 259

Game of Thrones Season One Essays

Illustrated Edition

Young Arctic Wolves
Copyleft Spacebirdy 2012, CC-SA 3.0, Free Art License

"They were meant to have them."

These six words mark the beginning of Game of Thrones. They are the origin and locus of all plot development and character interaction in the story. The scene to which they refer serves as guidepost for the challenging and treacherous journey we will undertake in this first season of Game of Thrones: the voyage toward understanding the most compelling fantasy series ever brought to television.

The words are not new. Those of you who have not yet read George R. R. Martin's classic novels may be tempted to turn your attention elsewhere. "Big deal," you say. "'They were meant to...' has been said by every cardboard-cutout wizard and perfect hero and stereotypical old hag in every fantasy book ever written. If that's all there is to this, I'm gonna find something else to watch." If Game of Thrones were about signs and wonders and magic and fearless heroes and evil orcs and ruthless black lords, I would join you in your quest for alternatives. But Game of Thrones is no ordinary fantasy story. Some of the characters we will come to love and admire are going to be defeated. Some characters we believe to represent less than human ambitions will sit the iron throne, mocking everything we thought we understood of justice and a genre dedicated to the triumph of good over evil.

Game of Thrones does not only upset genre convention and viewer expectation. The series takes us to levels of significance rarely attempted in television. I know this because I have read the novels, and I know that GRRM has been intimately involved in production; the integrity of the story has been maintained. A Song of Ice and Fire is probably the most tightly and intricately plotted set of novels I have ever read. Rarely, a novel will work at several levels, challenging us to apply every bit of analytical and literary skill in understanding characters, plot, themes, and thesis. Game of Thrones does this, but in a silent, fearsome, breathtaking way. The understanding of most of the characters ranges no further than the two most immediate levels of the story. Some are aware of the symbolic significance of objects and events. A few have limited insights into the deeper significance of the rich history being created all around them. But not a single character in the five novels has been empowered to hold the complete truth. Even the most cherished characters are unreliable narrators of the story. Only two people can possibly understand the full story in all its depth and breadth and intricate significance: GRRM and you, the person watching the story unfold.

THEY WERE MEANT TO HAVE THEM

The direwolf scene in the first episode of Game of Thrones is central to the series as a whole. The television series is going to deviate from the novels. Vast swaths of the novel—entire chapters—will never be presented. Characters will have slightly or entirely different personalities relative to their counterparts in the novels. Some who live on in the books will die on the small screen. But I know with absolute certainty that this single scene will unfold on television almost exactly as it does in the second half of the first chapter of the novel, "A Game of Thrones." I know this because that scene holds the key to every significant event in the story.

There is much to admire in this brief scene. We will witness the compassion of a father for his children and for small animals. We will see the emergence of leadership qualities in Eddard Stark's two older sons, Robb and Jon. The direwolf cubs that are rescued will become important characters in their own right later in the story. These are the superficial plot-related elements of the scene, and giving our full consideration to their relation to events and characters will provide satisfying insight into the series. We could catalogue the many ways in which the scene propagates character arcs and multiple plotlines and analyse the symbolism of the antler fragment, the dead direwolf bitch, the colours of the surviving direwolf pups, the colours of their eyes, and so on. These multi-tiered analyses would likewise provide a fascinating knowledge of the story, though at a more profound level.

St. Francis tames the Wolf of Gubbio
The Century Magazine, 1912

The aspect of the scene that I find most attractive and meaningful to our journey is the fact that not one of the characters sees the bigger picture. Each character understands important pieces, but they are all deficient in critical facets of their understanding as well. "The men looked at the antler uneasily, and no one dared to speak. Even Bran could sense their fear, though he did not understand." Bran is only ten years old; he cannot be expected to understand the significance of a stag antler fragment thrust into the dead body of a direwolf. His father certainly not only understands, but feels the chill of it deep in his soul. But later in the book version of the scene Bran is the only one to observe that each of the five dark-haired direwolf pups is blind—they have not yet opened their eyes. We will learn soon enough that each of the direwolves—including the dead bitch—corresponds to a human character in the story. In an important sense, then, Bran is the only one of the six characters in the scene to understand that everyone—even his father—is blind.

They are blind because they do not see the fifth path. There is not a maester among the party, but even if Grand Maester Pycelle himself stood with them at the carcass he would not have eyes to see what had transpired, and what it meant. I speak here of the metastory, the unspoken unifying aspect of the story that contains the themes, the important ideas, and the thesis of A Song of Ice and Fire. It is the blind uttering of a well-worn, comforting phrase that brings drama to this scene, because Jory Cassel, Captain of Eddard Stark's guard, believes himself erudite in expressing his assessment of the grand symbolism of his house's sigil being gored by the pointy crown of another house's sigil. The true significance of the words is that he has missed the point, and that knowledge is truly unsettling. The significance of the six words to us is simple: We are on our own. No one is going to explain the story for us. We're going to have to figure it out ourselves.

FOUR PATHS

TAR Intersection
Public Domain Work, 2007

The story is the first path, and also the most intricately designed of the paths. The best and the brightest, those truly dedicated to the story, are the most worthy resource at this level. It is on this path that we find recaps and excellent analysis at websites like Westeros.org. My essays will not be considered among these. I am too easily lost in the endless details of plot and character history. As a result, I try to stay clear of the level of detail many analysts enjoy. Dozens of major characters and hundreds of minor characters fill the several thousand pages of A Song of Ice and Fire. The television series will be even more challenging to those of us infected with DDD (detail deficit disorder). If you haven't read the novels, you're going to need at least a character name cheat sheet (GRRM provides one at the back of each novel), and you're going to want to read the recaps at Westeros.org.

The sheer volume of information required to make sense of this story cannot be overestimated. You will need to understand not only characters and their relationships to each other, but the geography of Westeros and the greater world beyond the Narrow Sea and the connections to characters. Littlefinger is not just a name, but an indication of Petyr Baelish's origins, his philosophy of courtly life, and his likely political strategies. Geography influences attitudes. The Dothraki, riding their horses through the deep grasses of the hot, wind-swept plains, live for the moment, entrusting themselves to the care of an all-powerful prince, a khal, who embodies the virtues of manly strength and fearless courage. The Lords of House Stark, on the other hand, fortify the last northern outpost of regal civility, living not in the present, but preparing always for a grim future. "Winter is coming," they say in the north. It is a warning, a constant beating to arms, and a stoic, disciplined philosophy of readiness. Be on guard, alert, on your toes, for you will need every resource, every bit of physical and spiritual strength, to survive the coming storm.

The back story is the second path, and in Game of Thrones it is going to have significance nearly equal to that of the current story. It is through the back story that we learn of the multi-dimensional motivations of each of the major characters, and many of the minor characters as well. Many of you know me from my Lost essays. I wrote 63 of these starting in 2008, and most of them during the final season. If you watched Lost, you are aware of the importance of back story. We learned of Jack's need to "fix" people and things, we came to appreciate Kate's inability to stay in one place with one man. You may be surprised to learn, then, that thousands of newcomers to Lost never watched the flashback scenes. Eager to whiz through the series, they skipped the flashbacks and hunkered down to take in the spectacle on the Island. Many of these people, who fast-forwarded through fully half of the series, nevertheless have been able to construct a complete understanding of the Lost story. If you are among those happy campers who were able to condense 118 episodes into less than sixty hours in front of the flat screen, you are to be congratulated, but also warned: You will find no such opportunity to skip over back story in Game of Thrones.

The back story is essential, not only for understanding the crucial, story-defining motivations of the major characters, but also to the appreciation of Westeros itself. If you do not know how Robert Baratheon came to be ruler of the Seven Kingdoms and have not figured out Ned Stark's role in his rise to power, you will never appreciate the full ramifications of events on the Wall, the treacheries at Winterfell, the intrigues at King's Landing. This story is intense. It will demand not only your fully engaged participation, it will stretch every faculty of comprehension, in a way that will make the intellectual fervor of Lost seem the preoccupation of children in comparison. My son at twelve years old understood Lost. Now a sixteen-year-old, I doubt he possesses the maturity required to understand Game of Thrones.

We will need to understand both back story and the present unfolding of events if we are to grasp the intricacies of the plotline and character arcs, which we find on the third path. The plotline has a long trajectory, reaching ten thousand years into the past and several years into the future, beyond the beginning of the story marked by a direwolf's carcass. You can certainly take a shortcut to this path. Salon, among several other internet sites, has put together a one-page Cliff Notes for the entire four-volume *A Song of Ice and Fire* (http://www.salon.com/entertainment/tv/feature/2011/04/09/game_of_thrones_primer). You can read it, I suppose, and think you have absorbed all you need to know before you begin the adventure. I would advise against this. Lost had such a one-page primer, also, called "LOST in 8 minutes 15 seconds" (http://www.youtube.com/watch?v=QIuXZ37GQIs). It's funny to anyone, but to those of us who spent thousands of hours absorbing Lost lore over six years, the video is absolutely hilarious. There is simply no way to make sense of Lost in eight minutes, and there is no way to condense ASoIaF to a single typewritten page.

The fourth path is illuminated for us by the flickering torch of symbolism. We do not see everything in its constantly changing light, but we make out connections and meanings of which we would otherwise remain ignorant. This is the realm of the powerful sigils and objects whose utility is only the lowest indication of their greater significance. Knives and swords and rings wrapped around maesters will come to carry an import we could never imagine without experiencing them. Colours and odours and streaks of light in the heavens will come to be portends and signs and wonders in our minds' eye. After you have soaked in just a few episodes you will think back to this pre-season essay, and you will wonder why I decided to tell you there were five paths. You will have learned of the supreme symbolic significance of a different integer, a slightly larger number, and you will come to believe I was leading you astray in saying there are five paths. But do not fear. I do know of the tremendous significance of that symbolic number, and you will, too. But there are five paths, and only the fourth path alludes to symbolic knowledge. There is a fifth path, and it is the path I prefer to walk.

THE SEED

The metastory is the fifth path. It is the aspect of fiction I seek to uncover in my essays. This is not any sort of noble undertaking. I concentrate on metastory because it is the easiest of the five paths for me to follow. The first and second paths are long and winding. They meander about this way and that, sometimes in circles, zigging and zagging from one situation to another, almost always with characters and motivations and destinies and unforeseeable outcomes rushing toward each other in a mad dance, an unbelievably chaotic game of thrones.

I am a scientist. Worse, I've been a scientist for thirty-five years. For the last ten of those years I've run a consulting business, teaching pharmaceutical companies throughout North America how to efficiently extract and purify the most valuable and effective drugs from the most difficult and unforgiving biological matrices. These companies are always battling the clock, and I need to render my advice quickly, before their competitors beat them to market. I've learned the only way for someone like me to make sense of anything as complex as pharmaceutical development is to simplify. "Our yields are all over the board, sometimes sixty percent, sometimes twenty," they tell me, as we look out on the vast sea of complex equipment filling the football field-sized production floor. Which of the dozens of unit operations in their process is causing the problem? I grab a hard hat, stretch the plastic booties over my shoes, don gloves, and walk out onto the floor. "Ask them to stop for a moment," I say, pointing to a rotary evaporator. The director does so, but I know he's not happy about it. Thanks to me they'll probably have to start their run over again. They stop the machinery and I open the port at the cooling coils. I grab a swab, dunk it inside, and smear the liquid on my glove. I bring it up to my nose, breathe in the sharp odour, wave my hand about, and take another whiff. There's no odour this time, but there's still liquid on my hand. It's water, as tests will later prove. Their process is supposed to be anhydrous, meaning no water, but their evaporators are full of water. I solved their problem. Best part of it, though, is that the director isn't frowning anymore. He's laughing.

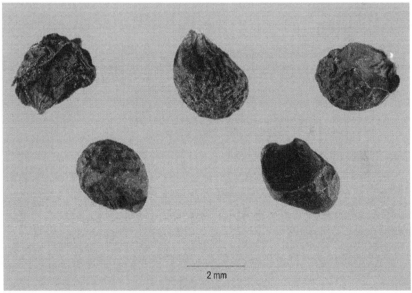

Allium tolmiei seeds
Steve Hurst, USDA, 2007

There's nothing magical about knowing where to look for problems in a production process. It's a matter of simplification to basic ideas. The strategy is the same in the analysis of television drama. Storytelling operates according to a few basic principles, so simple in structure that even someone like me can make sense of them. I seek the seed of an idea, for the seed contains all the elements of the idea, without the embellishments and complications that obscure the primary thought that went into fashioning the thesis and themes of the finished novel or screenplay.

A dragon egg, simple in form, will produce a dragon in all its majestic strength and complexity. I prefer to ponder the egg, to contemplate the paths it is likely to follow as it becomes young hatchling, growing lizard, and finally mature, fire-breathing monster. I prefer to start at the beginning, and from there to travel a fifth path which acknowledges the primacy of theme and thesis over every subsequent event. Here is how the Wiki of Ice and Fire (http://awoiaf.westeros.org/index.php/A Song of Ice and Fire) describes the seed that became A Song of Ice and Fire:

After *Beauty and the Beast* ended in 1989 Martin returned to writing prose and started work on a science fiction novel called *Avalon*. In 1991, whilst struggling with this story, Martin conceived of a scene where several youngsters find a dead direwolf with a stag's antler in its throat. The direwolf has several pups, which are taken by the youngsters to raise as their own. Martin's imagination was fired by this idea and he developed it into an epic fantasy story..."

THIS PUP ALONE... OPENED HIS EYES

Canis lupus pup closeup
US Fish and Wildlife Service, 2006

If we are to understand, we need eyes to see. In the novel, there was a direwolf pup among the survivors whose eyes were open. He did not have a dark coat, but fur as light as snow. The significance is that there is among the men and boys in that first scene one person who understands the event in a way no one else ever will. All his eyes are open.

If we wish to see, we must begin here, at the site of a terrible tragedy, where six young pups lost the mother who was their only hope of survival in a harsh and unforgiving place. We must study this scene, know its every nuance, feel every texture of blood-spattered snow and fur-covered flesh. This is the cold and wonder-filled beginning of a song that pits ice versus fire, snow versus sigil, man against nature, wolf against lion, stag against dragon.

Study well. Whatever else may be true, winter is coming. The direwolves await

Eddard Stark
copyright Dalisa 2011
used with permission

"If you would take a man's life, you owe it to him to look into his eyes and hear his final words. And if you cannot bear to do that, then perhaps the man does not deserve to die."

He is Lord of the North, successor to kings of old, father to six children, Hand of the King. More than that, he is the story's anchor, the person we can trust to deliver the truths of a harsh and unforgiving land to our minds and to our hearts. "Winter is coming," he warns us. He, with us, is a stranger in this strange land of Westeros. He is humble, loyal, faithful, and decent—qualities of his forebears, qualities which have no place in the Seven Kingdoms. Eddard Stark is the rock, the sure and steady centre around which those of lesser virtue play their Game of Thrones.

There is decency, for Eddard Stark lives. But in a land of deceit and vainglory and lusts for privilege and power, does decency suffice?

VIRTUE

Hercules Between Virtue and Vice
Emmanuel Michel Benner circa 1890

The qualities that define a hero are not solace to his spirit, but hardship to his existence. Virtue does not call us to something greater, for true virtue is not on display to our casual eye. It is integral to the hero, no more welcome than a headache or a pain in the side, but necessary to his life, to his destiny. Not something summoned, but something endured.

"Can a man still be brave if he's afraid?"

Bran's question makes sense to us. He speaks as a six-year-old child, but he articulates the same fears we all carry in our hearts. His father's response reveals experience and character:

"That is the only time a man can be brave."

Fear, for the hero, is not a condition from which one must flee, to seek refuge in safety or warmth. Fear, for this rare category of human being, is a summons to action. Ordinary men flee burning house and thundering storm, seeking protection from elements that harm, seeking remedies to remove discomfort. The truly fearful man—the humble, obedient, and faithful man—enjoys no safe harbour. He rushes into the building to fight the fire, he endures the storm to carry others to their salvation.

The hero is brave because he fears. He is decent because he knows the callous and loathsome nature of his own heart. He is humble because he must live every day with his own thoughts of glory and self-aggrandisement. "If only I could muster the courage, I too could rush into that burning building," we tell ourselves. The hero tells himself no such thing. He does not struggle to summon courage. Rather, courage already owns his wretched soul, and *it* summons *him* to perform his duty, to exercise the faculties that define his person.

Such is the difficult plane in which Eddard Stark lives and moves and bears all burdens. His is a world of duty, responsibility, the continuity of expectations as old as the most ancient weirwood.

LOYALTY

Protocol demands that a mere lord, and especially one whose recent ancestors were kings, must physically demonstrate fealty to king and queen. Kissing Queen Cersei's hand, Ned provides the necessary demonstration of loyalty. Despite his deep distrust of the queen, I believe we correctly imagine that Ned would kiss her hand even in the absence of onlookers. For Eddard Stark, loyalty is not a matter of protocol. He is not loyal by choice, but by nature. His loyalty does not depend on the weather, or his mood, or the advantage that might obtain from situations playing in his favour. He is loyal because this is the stuff of which he is made.

In short order we will learn much of the relationship between the Hand of the King and the King's wife. Queen Cersei is of House Lannister, and Eddard Stark has good reason to suspect her motives. Her twin brother, Ser Jaime, had the audacity to occupy the Iron Throne after Robert's victory over Rhaegar Targaryen on the Trident, surrendering the throne only after Ned and his bannermen rode in to proclaim Robert of House Baratheon king of Westeros and the Seven Kingdoms.

The loyalty of Eddard Stark is not dependent upon his estimation of the worth of the person receiving his obedience. This is an important observation to make of the man, for we will also learn of his deep affinities for those closest to him in his youth: his beautiful sister, Lyanna Stark, and his best friend, the man who became king, Robert Baratheon. Inclinations of the heart are important factors in any life, whether hero or mere mortal, but they rarely form the sole basis for thought or action. For the hero, whose instincts are ruled not by passion but by principle, the most enduring feature of friendship is commitment.

FAMILY

Familia 777
copyright Yesenia603 2010, CC-SA 3.0

If a hero's friendship is best described as a form of commitment, the supreme expression of emotional bond is found in the unwavering devotion to parents, spouse, and children. It is in the context of family that loyalty and commitment attain their deepest and truest resonance.

The fact that devotion to family cannot be compromised is an interesting proposition. The hero, of course, cannot compromise that which is most important, for the principles imbedded in the fabric of his being are those that determine his decisions and actions. Yet loyalty and commitment are not the only virtues serving as determinants of Eddard Stark's volition. Honesty, bravery, fortitude, justice, and a host of other, sometimes competing perfections, at one time or another will lay claim to Ned's conscience, his voice, and his sword. The Lord of House Stark will not be given an easy road to navigate.

Family is not an intellectual abstraction, and it is this truth that will complicate the final challenges to Eddard Stark's being. He will face threats to his family, threats to the kingdom, threats to his person. He will become aware of unholy alliances and unclean relationships that will threaten not only the kingdom, but humanity and civilisation—in fact, all of human life in Westeros. His decisions will have immediate, life or death significance for himself, his children, the king he serves, and the kingdom entrusted to his care. Which loyalties will gain ascendency over the others? Which virtues will determine his deeds? We are compelled to serve as intimate witness to a most engaging drama, when Eddard Stark will be called upon to make unfair and cruel choices. The story of the last Lord of Winterfell made an excellent novel. It will surely provide the basis for a grand and memorable television series.

THE HEART OF A HERO

Two Knights
James Baldwin and Ida Bender
Reading With Expression 5th Reader, 1911

Ned and Robert Baratheon grew up as brothers, fellow wards of Lord Jon Arryn, Defender of the Vale. Both were heirs to their respective lineages, House Stark and House Baratheon. King Aerys Targaryen must have understood the boys as threats, and he commanded Lord Arryn to turn them over to the Crown. Lord Arryn refused, and instead incited his house to arms, called the banners supporting his line, and led the early revolt against House Targaryen.

Lyanna Stark was Ned's only sister, a fair maid of sixteen when Ned's best friend, Robert, fell in love and became her betrothed. After Rhaegar abducted Lyanna, she died "in a bed of blood." It was the abduction of Robert Baratheon's fiancée that enflamed the original revolt and ended with Robert killing the heir to the crown and ascending the Iron Throne to end the rule of the House of Dragons.

Family and friendship were the crucial components of Eddard Stark's childhood growing up in the Eyrie under Jon Arryn's care. The same ties to sister and adopted brother were the considerations that led to the overthrow of House Targaryen and the installation of Ned's closest friend as ruler of the Seven Kingdoms.

The motivations behind the rebellion are crucial. Did Ned and Robert act out of love for Lyanna, or was justice the deeper motivation? Did Robert have his eye on the throne from even before the days of the rebellion, or did he merely seek retribution for Lyanna's death at the hands of the king's son?

The novel is not entirely clear on this point, though some quite poignant scenes took place. I have developed my own conclusions, but I will not share them here. I believe the most important consideration, as we prepare for the launch of this television series, is the fact that the question has been posed. What were the motivations of Eddard Stark and Robert Baratheon in rebelling against the Iron Throne? We are not served at all by declaring that these motivations were good or pure, for the intention in unraveling the histories of these men is not a determination of their morality, but rather an indication of the likely course of future events.

BASTARDS, DWARVES, AND LOYALTIES

The question of loyalty is further strained by the nitty-gritty realities of social divisions and their effects on the calculus of self-worth. Jon Snow, son of Eddard Stark, has no claim to Winterfell or the north, even though he is Eddard's first-born. He is illegitimate, born out of wedlock not to Catelyn Stark, but to a woman Ned never identified.

He is the House Stark reflection of Tyrion Lannister, arguably the most interesting character in A Song of Ice and Fire and one of the most challenging figures in fantasy fiction. Both Jon and Tyrion are capable men, both rejected for faults not of their making. Jon is a bastard, Tyrion is a dwarf. That they can be rejected for reasons having nothing to do with elements of their character calls into question the validity of any notion that those in their families are motivated predominantly by loyalty. If these people are not loyal to their own family members—or refuse membership in the clan even to their own biological children—this high level of disrespect must be taken as strong indication that some virtue other than loyalty is the supreme value guiding House Stark and House Lannister.

One naturally rebels at the idea that social convention has greater sway than the principle of loyalty, but the cases of Jon Snow, Tyrion Lannister, and Robert Baratheon's many bastard children tend to strengthen the validity of any such hypothesis. The plight of these men opens the field to any number of valid hypotheses. Perhaps love or justice are, after all, more important to the rulers of these clans than any fealty to king and country. In fact, perhaps these ill-defined principles are the very causes of the first rebellion against House Targaryen.

Perhaps in our present story, these amorphous affinities will cause even greater instabilities than those that led to the fall of King Aerys.

ORTHOGONALITY OF CHARACTER

In the end, Eddard Stark is not only Lord of Winterfell, Warden of the North, and Hand of the King. He is father to six children, soldier, husband, leader, capable administrator, descendent of kings. He is equally at ease with a kind word and with a steel sword. All of these are important to his character, to the decisions he makes, and all were explored in the 674 pages of *A Game of Thrones*. His character brings fictional complexity to a new level, and in this man we have a creation of substance and gravity, one that demands our careful attention and discriminating thought.

Winter is coming, he tells us. Let us see how well loyalty, decency, and justice fare in the deep snow, in the howling wind, in places cold and evil. Let us see what comes of Eddard Stark.

The Other Girl
copyright Dalisa 2011
used with permission

The young knight leading the expedition north of the Wall saw what he saw: Nothing. The young but respected ranger in his charge told him a fanciful tale of disemboweled and beheaded torsos, of legs and arms strewn about in a strangely chaotic symmetry. "Wildlings," the young knight concluded. Free Folk from north of the Wall. They do things like that, these wildlings. No, the ranger said, shaking his head, this butchery was not the work of wildlings. The contempt in the young knight's eyes was vivid. When he investigated the site himself, he saw not a single body part. He must have congratulated himself, perhaps shaking his head as he contemplated the young mad man the Lord Commander of the Night's Watch had given him for his patrol. But the knight knew what he saw: Nothing.

Perhaps if the knight had held for himself some measure of the young ranger's madness he might have heard the approach of the White Walker. But so convinced was he of the superiority of his high-born state, of his ability to discern truth from the fearful yappings of lesser men, he heard nothing. But if he had not eyes to see, how could he be expected to have had ears to hear? What need had he of listening, of watching, when he was so very clearly the stuff of superior stock?

The knights and sellswords and bannermen of Winterfell hunted down the young ranger. He had dishonoured himself and the Night's Watch by deserting his post at the Wall. Worse, by showing himself in Winterfell, he had brought dishonour and disgrace to the realm of the one man in the Seven Kingdoms who would not abide dishonour in any form. Eddard Stark, Lord of Winterfell and Warden of the North, descended of a long line of men who lived and died by their duty, their word, and above all, their honour. Whatever the young ranger said in his defence could amount only to a sorry justification of unthinkable cowardice. Does a just man need eyes to see anything beyond the glaring facts of a deserter's disgrace of his oath? "I saw White Walkers," the ranger said. A deserter, Ned Stark must have thought to himself. A deserter and a mad man. There were no White Walkers, not for thousands of years. Surely he was a mad man and nothing more.

Perhaps if Ned Stark had held for himself some measure of the ranger's madness, of his willingness to trust his own senses...

Tonight we saw many instances of men who knew themselves to be above the fray, who treasured the virtues to which they had entrusted their offices, their high positions, their very lives, and their families' lives, to such an extent that virtue itself became their means of discerning truth from madness, knowledge from fear. A mad man does indeed see what he sees. But in truth, he sees. Can we say the same of Ned Stark? Of King Robert? Of Viserys Targaryen? Perhaps without the eyes of mad men they have all become blind.

FOUR HOUSES

Such are the conceits of men destined to play this game of thrones. Winter is coming, but even those who live by these words have not the common sense or humility to know their own weaknesses and blindnesses. The strong, the far-seeing, those whose conspiracies have already succeeded in bringing down the Hand of the King, Jon Arryn, are those who give into their weaknesses and their madnesses, who plot and scheme in silence, or in upper rooms during incestuous trysts of unrestrained fornication—a great overflowing stream of sensory madness. Certainly Ned Stark would count Cersei's adulterous perversions as something beyond the worst imaginable dishonour. But she and her twin brother are the ones with eyes to see, while he and Robert remain blind. Let Robert believe Viserys Targaryen stands as the supreme threat to the Iron Throne, Cersei must be thinking. Allow him to take pleasure in servant girls and whores. Seeing her husband pull the voluptuous wench onto his lap seemed to bring satisfaction to Cersei's thin smile.

Four Houses
copyright Pearson Moore 2012

"Mountain lion?" one of the men asks.

Ned shakes his head. "No mountain lions in these woods."

There is in this scene no coincidence in the deaths of a stag and a direwolf. The direwolf and the stag are the sigils of House Stark of Winterfell and House Baratheon—the King's house—respectively. Is the mention of a lion in this scene coincidental, or does this apparently innocent invocation of the sigil of House Lannister—Cersei's house—have bearing on the scene, too? Was a stag brought down by a direwolf, or did the stag succumb to a lion? Will Cersei manage to disembowel her husband, the King, or will something Eddard Stark does—perhaps something noble and honourable—lead to the King's ruin?

The direwolf scene references three of the four houses in the drama we will witness unfold this season. Perhaps the fourth house was not mentioned because everyone except the King believes the dragon—House Targaryen—to be dead or so far removed as to be inconsequential to the game of thrones. I have to believe that if King Robert had been present at this post-execution romp through

Wolfswood he would have been searching the skies for the winged, fire-breathing beast that had eviscerated the stag.

There is no lack of virtue among these men, but no lack of vanity, either. King Robert unseated the Targaryens after they abducted his beloved fiancée, Lyanna, Ned's sister. It seems unlikely that young Viserys Targaryen could have had any role in the tortures inflicted on Lyanna; he is merely attempting to reclaim the throne he understands to have been wrongfully taken by the usurper, Robert Baratheon. Robert dreams every night of killing the Targaryens; his thirst for vengeance and unrequited grief for Lyanna are the blinders that render him oblivious to Cersei's schemes. Viserys would allow an army of forty thousand, "and their horses", to have their way with Daenerys if by such debauchery he could regain the Iron Throne; his lust for power is the vain desire that feeds his delusion of supremacy, and makes him unaware of his impotence in a land ruled by the khals.

WINTER IS COMING

Winter Scene at Shipka Pass, Bulgaria
copyright Psy Guy 2006, CC-SA 3.0

This is a series rich in metaphor and multi-layered meaning. The symbolism of the direwolf scene provides just one example of a brief set of images for which an exhaustive analysis might require several hours. The Stark words, "Winter is coming", are factual: The years-long summer is drawing to a close, and the deprivations of a cold, dark winter will soon be visited upon everyone in Westeros, not only in the dark and humourless north. But the words are not intended to be taken at face value. The Starks, in the middle of the coldest, deepest, longest winter will say, "Winter is coming." An outsider would protest, "Winter's bloody well here now!" But this is not what the Stark words mean. The words are metaphor: Trouble is afoot. The world is such that good and honourable women and men must be alert, on their toes, and ready for any eventuality. Winter is not a season, but a state of mind—a state of being.

We see threats in the north: Direwolves, wildlings, White Walkers. There are threats across the sea, in Viserys Targaryen, his young sister, Daenerys, and Khal Drogo, who leads vast armies. The Queen and her twin brother, possibly aided by their "Imp" sibling, Tyrion, constitute an immediate threat to the Iron Throne. Everyone playing the game is blind to some threats and overly sensitive to others. How do we assess the comparative strength and potential for any particular disturbance to lead to a shift in power? Are the threats in the north and across the Narrow Sea so far away as to merit no more than peripheral attention? Are the machinations of House Lannister so pedestrian and childish that they will be easily addressed by someone as wise and noble as Eddard Stark?

This game will play out not over a few short episodes, but over long seasons to come. Only one person, George R. R. Martin, could possibly know the definitive resolution to this story, but the final volume in A Song of Ice and Fire remains unwritten; indeed, it is possible that GRRM has not yet devised a suitable ending. Those of us who have read the first four novels have some idea of the plot and trajectory, but no one watching this series, whether first-time viewer or 16-year veteran of ASoIaF, has been privileged to know the endgame.

That is not to say that a significant investment in time is not worthwhile. Most of you, sometime during the series, are going to want to know more. The novels, of course, are the best place to start. Westeros.org contains thousands of pages of material available nowhere else, and you will certainly wish to peruse the rich treasuries there. Essays are available at my website (www.winterfellkeep.com), and many of you will wish to avail yourselves of the type of analysis accessible only in this way. You will have quite a natural desire to become familiar with at least some of these. The reason is simple: Winter is coming. The season and its dangers call for sober temperament and nimble consciousness. Even as we begin our journey, aware of the blindness of those fortified by virtues rare among men, we are ever aware of our own likelihood of failure. How can people like us, endowed with only modest levels of virtue and lacking the vision of the best characters, hope to follow labyrinthine plots and multi-dimensional characters and their competing and entangled relationships? We do so by learning from each other. We read. We educate ourselves. We prepare for the trials of winter.

GEOGRAPHY

The Geographer
Johannes Vermeer 1668

The geography of Westeros and Essos is not difficult to learn, but it is important to the story. The major ruling lineages, called houses, have their origin in particular geographical locations, and alliances between houses are likewise often geographical. Geography also determines the means of travel, the types of defences employed, and the kinds of battles that might be fought in a particular location. Some fortresses, such as the Eyrie, are virtually impregnable due to location, while other bastions, such as the Red Keep at King's Landing, are significantly more difficult to protect from outside attack. Anyone wishing to move quickly between Winterfell and the lands of Arryn in the east, near the Eyrie, would naturally take advantage of the sea route rather than taking the much slower and more dangerous route south along the Kingsroad and through the poorly protected eastern mountains.

Because of the historical and virtually unchanged importance of geography over the centuries, we can gain appreciable understanding of alliances and and plot trends simply by studying maps of Westeros. Prior to the unification of the Seven Kingdoms under Aegon the Conqueror (aka Aegon the Conquerer, or Aegon the Dragon) some three hundred years before the beginning of our story, each of the Seven Kingdoms was ruled by a separate king. Casterly Rock and the western lands were under the rule of House Lannister, The Mountains and Vale of the East were under House Arryn headquartered at the Eyrie, Storm's End and the southern lands came under the control of House Baratheon only after Aegon's Conquest. House Stark, headquartered at Winterfell, came to be in close alliance with House Baratheon several years before the deposition of Mad King Aerys II less than twenty years before the beginning of the present story. This unlikely alliance was formed when young Eddard Stark and Robert Baratheon became the wards of Jon Arryn, who was murdered only days before the story began. Ned and Robert were as close as brothers for the many years they grew up in the Arryn household, and came to regard Jon Arryn as a father. The equally unlikely alliance between House Lannister and House Baratheon came to pass when Cersei Lannister became Robert's consolation prize after the death of his beloved Lyanna Stark. We have already seen evidence that the Baratheon-Lannister alliance may not be stable or trustworthy, as Cersei and her twin brother, Jaime, apparently plotted the death of the King's Hand (second in command), Jon Arryn.

Detailed maps are available here:
http://winterfellkeep.com/MapsofWesteros.aspx

PRINCIPAL PLAYERS

The centrepiece of this story, quite clearly, is Eddard Stark. We have met several members of his household: his wife, Catelyn (called "Cat"), his daughters, lovely Sansa and tomboy Arya, and his sons, the very young Rickon, the young climber, Bran, the heir to Winterfell, Robb, and Ned's bastard son, Jon. We have already met several of the Lannisters: Cersei and her brothers, Jaime and Tyrion. House Targaryen, the former ruling clan, is represented by Prince Viserys, who considers himself rightful "King of the Andals" of Westeros and heir to the Iron Throne, and his young sister, Daenerys, who has become Khaleesi (Queen) to Khal Drogo of the Dothraki.

A list of major and supporting characters may be found here: http://en.wikipedia.org/wiki/List_of_characters_in_Game_of_Thrones

Every one of these characters is distinct, with beliefs and priorities and hierarchies of concern unique to her person and different from even her closest blood relations. Sansa Stark looks on young Joffrey and feels her heart go pitty-pat; young Arya looks on Joffrey and probably wonders if she could take him in an arm wrestling contest. Viserys is the most power-hungry of all the characters, and his young sister seems the most subdued and withdrawn—at least in these first scenes.

I find the most interesting distinctions between characters among the Stark children. We're much aware already of the 180-degree difference between boyish Arya and beauty queen Sansa, but I find even more intriguing the differences between Bran, Robb, and Jon. Robb is not afraid to assert his not-yet-bestowed authority as heir to Winterfell, as he demonstrated in the direwolves scene. Jon is more analytical and insightful than Robb, with his observation that the five direwolf pups corresponded to each of the five Stark children and that therefore the pups should be saved; they were a sign, essentially. He seems overly sensitive to his status as untitled bastard to the Lord of Winterfell, but thoughtful and reflective as he soaks in the wise words of Tyrion Lannister on their first meeting outside the Winterfell banquet hall.

And then we have Bran.

THE CHILDREN

The Children of Charles I
Sir Anthony van Dyck, 1637

I don't frequently offer wagers, but I am relatively confident in betting that of all the casting decisions in Game of Thrones, the auditions for Bran Stark were most aggravating and tension-filled for the casting director. In most productions aimed at an adult audience, and especially those created by HBO, children are at best minor characters, and more often than not serve as nothing more than background accoutrements to the main story. In this series, the children **are** the main story. Bran, Robb, Jon, Arya, and Sansa are going to carry more of this story to greater heights than all of the supporting characters combined, and with greater bearing on the outcome of the season than many of the adult characters. And of all the children, Bran's story will have the greatest and most immediate importance, and probably the greatest potential to survive into later seasons, should these be approved by HBO.

You may think I offer this wager on the basis of my knowledge of the four ASoIaF novels. If so, you would be incorrect. I will insist, in this essay and others, that the novels must be understood as distinct from the television series. Characters and situations in the novels could be slightly or enormously different from their closest counterparts in the novels. As those tracking such differences know, the television presentation has already discarded several important scenes from the novel, and has added scenes that never appeared in the novel. I am basing my judgment of the children's importance on what I understood of the critically important direwolf scene that I have already mentioned several times in this essay, and in my pre-season essay, "Five Paths of the Direwolf". Here is how the Wiki of Ice and Fire describes the seed that became *A Song of Ice and Fire*:

"In 1991, whilst struggling with [*Avalon*], Martin conceived of a scene where several youngsters find a dead direwolf with a stag's antler in its throat. The direwolf has several pups, which are taken by the youngsters to raise as their own. Martin's imagination was fired by this idea and he developed it into an epic fantasy story..."

The direwolf scene is the very genesis of ASoIaF. That foundational event and later critical scenes sprinkled through the first few episodes of GoT contain enough information to allow a tentative formulation of a thesis for this series. From the thesis we can draw up a list of characters and situations likely to be important in the final episodes of this season and seasons to come. It is my conclusion that three characters will play a crucial role in the long-term unfolding of the story: Tyrion Lannister, Daenerys Targaryen (Stormborn), and Brandon (Bran) Stark. Even now, with knowledge of Bran's contributions to the first six episodes, I am able to put together a seven-thousand-word essay focussing entirely on his character and its importance to the greater story. My analysis of Bran appears later in this book.

In coming weeks we will begin to see strange and remarkable similarities between these very different children and their counterparts in other houses. We will take note of yet stranger similarities between them and characters as diverse as Tyrion Lannister, Daenerys Targaryen, and the wildlings and White Walkers of the lands beyond the Wall. This is one of the greatest adventures ever brought to television, and without question the most multi-dimensional and fascinating fantasy production ever created for the small screen. And we've only just begun! Prepare yourselves, for next week we walk the treacherous Kingsroad. And remember: Winter is coming.

Jaime Lannister
Copyright Dalisa 2011
used with permission

What is the connection between a crippled, comatose boy and a direwolf hundreds of kilometres away? What possible connection could there be? We need not worry about "grumkins and snarks and all the other monsters your wet nurse warned you about." In the end, isn't it true that we are nothing more than "meat and blood and some bone to keep it all standing"?

Such is the wisdom of the most erudite of the Lannisters, long the conniving servants to the King of the Seven Kingdoms, and poised to take the throne. Perhaps the only knowledge one requires in this game of thrones is study of whetstone and sword, for in the end, we are but dust and dreams contained in meat and blood. Dust and dreams are taken by the wind, meat and blood fall to the sword, and what remains are the stories of old men, the songs of wash women, the cutting laughter of a prince.

"It's fantasy," you tell me. "There's supposed to be magic and spells and dragons and wolves. That's why the boy woke when the direwolf died. It's just the way these stories are told."

Perhaps. But this amounts to nothing more than Jaime Lannister's speech at the forge, reworded. If you look into Bran's eyes, though, you will find that Jaime's words fall short. Bran's eyes indicate no fairy-tale restoration of lost faculties. The connection is not magical, there is no Merlin or maester to chant incantations that bring peace and order to the realm. There are only a boy's eyes, disturbing in their ability to see. Tonight's episode was deliciously unsettling, precisely because Jaime and Tyrion are both wrong. There is more holding us together than meat and blood, more inside us than dust and dreams. We observe a simple game of thrones, but every player in this fantasy game carries in her heart a song more profound: a song of ice and fire.

FULL OF POSSIBILITIES

Mongol Horse Archer
Unknown artist, circa 1550

"The Dothraki have two things in abundance: grass and horses. People can't live on grass," Ser Jorah told Daenerys as he handed her a stick of horse jerky. We might have taken the far-off look in her eyes as mournful resignation to her sad lot as she chewed on hard leather. If not for the lusts of the Baratheons and the Lannisters she would be in King's Landing, enjoying every benefit of position and privilege due the daughter of a king. Instead, she spends her days in endless movement from one grassy sea to the next, her hands scraped and torn by the reins, her legs bruised and blistered from unforgiving days in the saddle and miserable nights at the edge of a bed.

There are so many ways to interpret a woman's eyes, or a boy's eyes, but context gives us the key. "Love comes in at the eyes," the attendant-girl said. Not only love, but every other emotion and quality and state of being. The context in Game of Thrones is sensory. The Maester's Path, as the gurus of television culture at EW or TV Guide or any of dozens of other sites will tell you, began with a great treasure trove of scents to be mixed and matched with purpose and place. And then there were sights and sounds and even tastes, as chefs patrolled the larger cities of North America in HBO vans, creating Westeros-inspired treats to entice us to experience a new type of television drama.

We need to taste that dried horse flesh in the moment Daenerys tears off a piece. We need to feel the unrelenting heat on our bare skin, the stifling hot air filling our lungs, the saddle sores covering our rump. New awareness of the strange things in the air and on the ground assaults us in an unceasing barrage of stimulation. There is no time for pity or self-absorption. Under such constant stress the best we might dream for is resignation in hopes of some future ability to cope and adapt. Perhaps the more likely outcome, we realise, is hopelessness, depression, or even an urge to bring an end to the continual suffering of days and nights.

Riding with Daenerys, experiencing the pain and monotony and sadness, we might be tempted to consider our first instinct regarding her state of mind as being correct. She is withdrawn, hopeless, depressed, and her far-off gaze is surely all the proof we require in asserting the accuracy of our assessment. But we must include in our counsels the greater context of her life. She evinced no surrender to unsavoury fate in seeking out stories about dragons, or in querying her handmaid about the art of pleasuring a man. Those eyes are not empty and resigned, they are full and engaged, analysing Ser Jorah's words, and finding them incomplete, in every way inadequate to her thoughts.

Her eyes indicated not withdrawal, but energised engagement. "Are you a slave, Khaleesi?" her servant-girl asked. The answer was swift, strong, and intentionally erotic. The Dothraki have more than grass and horses, and Daenerys has more than breasts and a vagina. She has constantly-moving thoughts, a mind made nimble by necessity and by the excitement to power. She is no longer a girl, no longer a slave to Viserys, she is becoming Khaleesi, who can "finish a man with nothing but her eyes." Her handmaid had greater wisdom than Ser Jorah Mormont. Daenerys could become the one for whom "kings traveled across the world for a night... khals burned her enemies just to have her for a few hours." This was power within her grasp, and she was more intoxicated by the handmaid's words than by the soft fingers that caressed her flesh and the full lips brought close to hers.

Few in Essos or Westeros would understand the new Khaleesi. Perhaps one who might understand is another whose eyes are always moving, reading books or reading people: The Lannister halfling—the one they call the "Imp". "Death is so final," he told his brother. "Whereas life... life is full of possibilities." This is no mere common-sense attitude or recitation of the obvious. It is a statement of intent, and an idea we will explore in future essays.

GRUMKINS AND SNARKS

Arthur Fights the Seven-Headed Serpent
Henry Ford, The Red Book of Romance, 1905

"I'm sure it will be thrilling to serve in such an elite force," Jaime said with such derisive insincerity you could almost hear the smirk spread across his face. "And if not, it's only for life."

Jon will surely play an important role in this grand epic, if only because he is truly among the elite, not of the Night's Watch, but of those characters in Game of Thrones whose eyes see things others do not. "You are a Stark," Ned told him at the western cairn. "You may not have my name, but you have my blood." This was not a joyous scene for me. Eddard Stark had no appreciation of the direwolves in Episode One. He is so sworn to duty and honour that even common sense and devotion to family seem long-neglected aspects of this noble lord. Sansa also has Ned's blood. She who called her ferocious direwolf "Lady", and was probably only weeks away from dressing the wolf in frilly dresses and hats. Having a particular set of genes is no indication of character, but neither does a desire to make the most of oneself count for much in the world of Westeros. Eddard Stark has made much of himself, and has set high standards for his family and household. But he does not see with Bran's eyes, nor even with Jon's.

The scene at the western cairn was sad because I realised it is not Ned's blood that Jon shares—it is Bran's, and Arya's and Robb's. Bran and Jon felt in themselves the great importance of the direwolves. Both Bran and Jon are always climbing, always trying to ascend to some greater understanding. Bran scaled the highest and most dangerous heights of Winterfell, and Jon will soon rise to the full height of the Wall. They are the seers, those who reject mere appearances and seek a broader vision from the highest places they can find within their world or within their thoughts.

Jon and Arya share an identity as unsatisfied bastards. Neither of them can hope for power, yet both of them are more capable than their siblings and anyone else who would assert their privilege as high-born lords and ladies. Jon is bastard by blood, Arya is bastard by gender. "It's so skinny," she said. "So are you," her half-brother responded. But they both knew there is no shame in being skinny and quick. "Sansa can keep her sewing needles," Arya said. "I have a needle of my own." I get the distinct feeling that these closest of siblings are going to need quick wits and fast swords in coming months.

We were witness to Ser Waymar Royce's death beyond the Wall at a White Walker's sword during the first eight minutes of Game of Thrones. Perhaps there are no snarks or grumkins, but there surely are Others—beings so fearful that even a sworn ranger would rather face execution than confront them again on patrol north of civilisation. We know that Jaime's sarcasm derived of centuries of general complacency, and also of the Lannister family's obsession with political intrigue and manipulation of those in power. He is, after all, the Kingslayer, whose sword proved the merits of his incestuous fornications with his beautiful twin, Cersei. The most troubling aspect of scenes focussing on the Night's Watch is that we see no indication that anyone is aware of the peril awaiting Westeros north of the Wall.

But the disquiet we feel is good. The ghosts and goblins of Westeros are not the simplistic monsters of Harry Potter or other pedestrian entertainments. There is much more in this story than the tired conventions of sword and sorcery, as we are beginning to see. The White Walkers, called "Others" in the novels, are a creation unique to fiction, perhaps similar in complexity to the Man in Black of Stephen King's "The Dark Tower" series, or the Smoke Monster of Lost. Just as the Smoke Monster was the first mystery of Lost and also the final mystery solved, we should probably anticipate that only one person in the world truly knows the full meaning of the White Walkers and that the mystery has not yet been revealed. Even with the release of "A Dance With Dragons" the last pages of the story remain unwritten. We will wait several more years before the full story of the White Walkers emerges.

THANK GODS FOR BESSIE

The truth is in the eyes.

Good drama is visually expressive, and Game of Thrones tonight was a visual feast unlike any other. We saw the truth with our own eyes, through the main characters' eyes, but more importantly, we saw the truth *in* their eyes. The truth is that King Robert is scared, and he has not a clue what he should do. Robert relieved himself at a tree then joined Ned at their lunchtime feast. "What do you say, just you and me, on the Kingsroad, swords at our sides, couple of tavern wenches to warm our beds tonight." Ah, for the good old days and the mindless, meaningless indiscretions of youth. What he would have given, he said, for another night with Bessie and her big tits.

Roman Sleeping Woman
Felix-Auguste Clement, 1859

But Robert's memory was selective. It was only when Ned refused to discuss Willa that Robert's recall improved. "We were at war. None of us knew if we were going to go back home again." The good old days were not the days of youthful abandon, but the time of Robert's greatest engagement with life. The decisions he made seventeen years ago were informed by courage, commitment, and the call to duty and honour he felt in kinship with Ned. It has been in the years since that Robert has forsaken his ideals and his responsibilities. He commits himself to wine, women, and a full belly, not to the duties of kingdom and family. There was never any Bessie, and the call to leadership was not a lusting after the Iron Throne, but a knowledge that only Robert Baratheon could bring the realm out of the chaos caused by Mad King Aerys.

There is much sadness in his eyes, for he has lost everything, and the loss is entirely his doing. King Robert used to stand for something; now he is barely king. Oblivious to the threats beyond the Wall, unaware of Cersei's schemings, obsessed by the all-but-extinct Targaryens, Robert has lost relevance to the current age. His greatest battles won, he has left behind the healthy fear that flows from courage and the questions that flow from commitment. He is left with nebulous anxieties and nameless uncertainties. "There's a war comin', Ned." It's not that his body has grown weak; he could certainly wield the warhammer in his thick hands. But his eyes do not see like Bran's or Jon's or Arya's, and he could no more formulate a battle plan than resist the next servant girl who crosses his path. His eyes are fearful, sad, and... tired. Joining the cult of hedonism has not stimulated, but rather deadened his senses. Just as there never was a Bessie, there never can be a Bessie, because there is not a woman alive who has it within her to force this man dead-to-the-world to rekindle his zest for life and his commitment to causes just and true.

There is some cause for optimism. Robert may have ceded his concerns to an earlier age, but Ned seems to hold onto the value of commitment. "You never told me what she looked like," Robert said, speaking of Willa. "Nor will I," Ned responded. Perhaps an unwavering commitment to honour might have a place in the uncertain times to come. If the Lannisters hold as much sway as they seem to possess, perhaps a man of uncompromising character can change the course of events in King's Landing. At the very least, we know from this lunch in the forest, and from Ned's active and seeking eyes, that Ned does not live in the past with Robert. He remains engaged, even if he is often blind to the meaning of events around him. Ned may indeed turn out to be the best Hand the king has ever known.

SWORD AND WHETSTONE

The Jon and Tyrion scenes have become my favourites of this series. In the Sword Needs a Whetstone scene, Peter Dinklage's face went through more than a score of rich expressions in the space of less than three seconds. It was a performance the likes of which are rarely put to film, and was certainly the centrepiece of tonight's episode. Tyrion Lannister is probably the character closest to grasping the full reality of Game of Thrones. One of GRRM's favourite characters, it would be tempting to assign Tyrion a place of precedence, perhaps as the literary embodiment of GRRM's personality or vision. I don't think we can make such an assessment, though, for reasons I will explore later in this volume.

"Things are expected of me.... My brother has his sword, and I have my mind, and a mind needs books like a sword needs a whetstone." The analogy is sound, and meaningful to our understanding of these characters. Neither Jon nor Tyrion is fully developed. Both of them require a sharpening and quickening of the mind if they are to face future challenges. To what extent will they realise the need to learn and adapt? Some of Tyrion's words indicate broad engagement, while other utterances point to a kind of cavalier complacency very much akin to that of his brother-in-law, the King.

I suspect Tyrion's understanding of his world will continue to grow. For if it does not, he will be in no better position than any of the other characters. His arrogant dismissal of "grumkins and snarks and all the other monsters your wet nurse warned you about" is not only a sign of his present ignorance, but a measure also of the degree to which he will be obliged to unlearn much of what his culture has taught him. "You're a smart boy. You don't believe that nonsense," he told Jon. He of course considers himself smart, above the nonsense of fairy tales and Night Watch superstitions. Perhaps he will one day understand that the smartest people are those who realise they know nothing, even for all the books they have read. Even the greatest of maesters must intuit and divine. The measure of a scholar is not her understanding of theories and histories, but her ability to create solutions to current problems. Tyrion remains untested; it seems likely indeed that he will soon be stretched far beyond his present erudition.

THE GROTESQUES

Six Grotesque Heads
Gaetano Gandolfi, circa 1790

What do a cripple, a dwarf, a tomboy, a bastard, and an exiled princess have in common? In their own way, each of these major characters is a grotesque—a person deemed somehow unfit to the ordinary rigours of life, a regression from the natural order of things. Yet these are the characters who carry the story of Game of Thrones. These are the most fascinating characters, and ones worthy of the full measure of our consideration.

Not everyone will feel the need to plumb the depths of these characters and their impact on the story. For those who do have an interest in reading more, rich resources are as near at hand as a Google query. In this volume, it is my hope to explore the heart of Game of Thrones. Two essays in this book will tear into the three-minute direwolf scene from Episode One with a thoroughness aimed at sating the needs of the most obsessive fan. Some nine thousand words will be devoted to the full examination of the symbolism and themes presented in those three minutes. And of course, I have devoted an essay to each episode. "Lord Snow", Episode Three, arrives next Sunday, and continues our song of ice and fire. I will be here again, agonising with you over the words characters use, the things they leave unsaid, and the truth we find in their eyes.

Direwolf (Canis dirus)
Unknown artist, circa 1900

The direwolf scene in Game of Thrones, Episode 1.01, is one of the richest, most meaningful scenes in the first part of the series. The scene sets the tone for the remainder of the season, and even sets up events that will occur far into the future. Because of the high pertinence density of this material, it has become my favourite scene in the story.

I have chosen to write two analyses of this scene. This decision may seem surprising, being that the sequence has a duration of exactly three minutes—less than three percent of the roughly two hours of the series broadcast so far. I have devoted two essays, about six thousand words, to the first two episodes. By the time I finish the analyses of symbolism and thesis I will have given over nine thousand words to this single three-minute scene. However, the emphasis I bring to the brief passage at the beginning of the story is not my own. This scene formed the genesis of the entire A Song of Ice and Fire (ASoIaF) series by George R. R. Martin (GRRM). Anyone who wishes to truly understand Game of Thrones (GoT) needs to take a close look at the events of this scene, seek the meaning behind the elements, words, and actions, and gain an appreciation for the depth of thought that is required to attain fullest enjoyment of the program.

The scene can be analysed from as many as four distinct levels: superficial and factual, symbolic and allusive, allegorical, and thematic. I am going to concentrate in this essay on the symbolic and allusive character of the scene. In the companion piece to this essay, "The Grotesques," I will hammer out a tentative interpretation of the thesis of GoT, which will rely heavily on the allegorical and thematic elements of the scene.

LITERARY BACKGROUND

The direwolf scene originated in 1991, as discussed in earlier chapters. Obviously this single scene cannot be understood as setting in stone the entire plotline for GoT. However, every plot has a starting point and a trajectory with relatively fixed orientation. We should understand this scene as the natural starting point of the series, but I believe we can also see in these brief events the beginnings of the movement of plot.

OBJECTIVES AND DIFFICULTIES OF THIS ESSAY

The Thinker
Auguste Rodin, 1902
Photograph by Andrew Horne, released to PD 2010

I aim to elucidate several of the important symbolic and allusive elements of the scene, as I believe these have bearing on future plot and character developments. In this effort I face challenges unique to GoT and new to me as an essayist.

My primary objective is to provide fertile ground for thought. I am not necessarily interested in giving a factual account of events, but very interested in approaching scenes in such a way that readers may be liberated in their thoughts and enlivened to new ideas. I am not necessarily interested in revealing future events, but quite interested in describing what I feel to be trends or trajectories. The facts we see on the screen will speak for themselves, but we are free to think about them in any way we might like. My aim is to influence thought, not to make predictions or provide spoilers.

Of course, the difficulty in writing about GoT is that I have read the novels. In theory, this should not be a problem. Since my intention is to stimulate thinking and not to regurgitate factual information, I don't need to rely on my knowledge of the novels in writing the essays. A complicating factor is that the television series is hewing close to the novels, in just about every respect we might wish to consider: character arcs, plot, order of scenes, and so on. In addition, I have been trusted with certain privileged information regarding later episodes. It is tempting, indeed, to extrapolate from events on the small screen to later events I know to occur in the novels and later in the season. However, I have two solid reasons to shun this temptation.

First, revelation of events is not my objective, as already stated. More importantly, though, I have an abiding and consuming interest in the flavour and tone of the events, not in their factual content. The television series has already deviated from the novels in small ways and even in some ways I consider to have major impact on the story. Thus, I cannot rely on the television production to mirror exactly the ideas and occurrences and character traits developed in the novels. This has extreme importance, as I will demonstrate later in this essay.

Inevitably, I will discuss trends that may lead to certain unavoidable outcomes. The criterion I apply in these cases is the same I have applied in analyses of the television programs Lost and Mad Men. If I discern a likely future event based on current events and trends, I will feel free to discuss the future event. Therefore, those who do not wish to become aware of occurrences that have not yet transpired may wish to delay a reading of this essay until later in the season. This essay will reveal major information that many may consider to be "spoilers".

CONTEXT I: THE NORTH

Trouble is brewing in the north. Strange events are occurring at the Wall, and the Lord Commander of the Night's Watch is fearful for the safety of himself and his family of sworn brothers on the Wall. He asks his most trusted knight, Ser Waymar Royce, to go north, to be the Commander's eyes. Royce obeys, because he is a good knight, and he feels a call to duty. But his brothers of the Watch, Will and

Gared, are not enthusiastic about going north. Wildling activity is coming close to the Wall. People have died in mysterious ways. Were they murdered? Will, the youngest ranger, is almost killed by a White Walker, but he gets away. "I saw White Walkers," he says, whispering. He speaks softly, because he knows Lord Stark, who inhabits a world very different from his, will not believe him.

CONTEXT II: THE SOUTH

Trouble is brewing in the south. Strange events are occurring in the realm, and the King of the Seven Kingdoms is fearful for the safety of himself and his family of royal children in King's Landing. He asks his most trusted lord, Lord Eddard Stark, to go south, to be the King's Hand. Stark obeys, because he is a good lord, and he feels a call to honour. But his family in Winterfell, Catelyn and his children, are not enthusiastic about going south. Lannister activity is coming close to the throne. Jon Arryn died in a mysterious way. Was he murdered? Bran, the youngest Stark, is almost killed by a Lannister, but he recovers. "The Lannisters did this," Ned says, whispering. He speaks softly, because he knows King Robert, who inhabits a world very different from his own, will not believe him.

ALLUSION

Pandora's Box
Publicity Still, unknown artist, 1929

The foreshadowing in the prologue north of the Wall is detailed, indicating a nearly perfect correspondence to events to the south in Winterfell and King's Landing. The parallels are troubling, because the television prologue ends with the beheading of the ranger, Will. We do not yet know what will come of the southbound Starks, but everything we have seen so far indicates the new King's Hand is not going to enjoy a serene life in the capital of the realm.

The nearly perfect reflection from north to south begins with the mirror anchored in the direwolf scene. Since this is the true foundation of the story we need to use the direwolf scene as the initial reference for both the northern and southern contexts of the story. It is far too easy to follow a slippery slope from symbolism to allusion to allegory, and from that point of severe extrapolation to say things about the story that turn out to be incorrect, so we should not indulge the temptation to compare the prologue to early events in the story without locking in the reference to the foundational scene.

I will make a case for an allegorical interpretation of the direwolf scene, but I defer to the next essay in this volume, "The Grotesques", to lay the groundwork for such an analysis.

CONTEXT III: WINTER IS COMING

Ice Crystal on Post
copyright Friedrich Böhringer 2008, CC-SA 2.5

There was a general sense of unease in three distinct locations in Westeros. We could also consider Daenerys' travails in Essos, among the Dothraki, but I am going to leave the Targaryens out of the discussion for now to paint a more detailed picture of the action in Westeros.

The story began with the disturbances at the Wall. Something caused the Lord Commander of the Night's Watch to send out a small scouting patrol to report on Wildling activity. We might consider that such a ranger patrol could not have been all that unusual. After all, the brothers of the Night's Watch are plentiful enough that they must have been dispatched on regular patrols. However, the likelihood that Wildling activity was in some sense unusual seems high. The physical layout of the Wall includes a generous stretch of deforested land that must have been cleared by the rangers. This gap of several hundred metres between the Wall and the beginning of the northern forest must have been put in place to allow the rangers on the Wall to observe the appearance of any Wildlings. Ice climbing is probably not an activity unique to our own time and place, and the rangers would want as much advance warning as possible of any attempts to scale the Wall. Ser Waymar's patrol was not long into the forest before Will discovered the strange sight of apparently ritually-defiled Wildling bodies. This strange finding indicated the close presence of something other than Wildlings, and of course we later found out the blue-eyed White Walkers—probably beings not even remotely humanoid—were responsible for the massacre. But more importantly, the finding of Wildling remains so close to the Wall probably indicated an unusual Wildling activity level that precipitated the patrol we saw at the beginning of the episode.

To the unusual Wildling activity and the first recorded observation of White Walkers in several centuries we can add the unusual behaviour of direwolves. Seventeen-year-old Robb Stark said, "There are no direwolves south of the Wall." This was a spectacular statement of immense importance to the thesis of GoT, and I will be looking very closely at these words in the next essay. For our purposes in the analysis of symbolism, it is enough to say that the appearance of a direwolf bitch and her puppies was strange enough for Robb to remark on it, and for everyone in Ned's party to agree with his statement. Even though the eldest among the party had experienced many winters, none of them had ever seen a direwolf south of the Wall. Young Robb was articulating a truth that was evident to all, and would have been something he learned in his childhood. The Stark sigil was the direwolf, and Robb would have learned its significance at a very early age.

"Winter is coming" refers not only to the long, cold, dark season that has not been experienced for many years in Westeros, but it also refers to a coming time of tribulation. The unusual events at the Wall are all examples of the latter significance. We have no indication that Wildling activity is connected to seasonal migrations or behaviours. More important to our discussion, the White Walkers had not been seen in centuries. As Ned told Bran, "The White Walkers have been gone for thousands of years." We have to consider that all of the events so far associated with the Wall and lands to the north constitute a unique set of occurrences that indicate significant change is afoot, and that this change is something which no one at Castle Black is prepared to face.

The Wall was not the only locus of troubled events. The King's entourage, including his family and apparently most of his court, made the month-long trek to Winterfell from King's Landing. Under a king of House Baratheon one would have expected to see mostly the prancing, crowned stag sigil on banners and armour. But the sigil in greatest evidence was the proud gold lion of House Lannister, the Queen's house. Over the years the court has been infected and infiltrated with Lannisters to the point that hardly any Baratheons were in evidence. And with the appearance of the Lannister-led king's party came trouble for the Stark family. We learned the Lannister twins, Cersei and Jaime, were responsible for Lord Jon Arryn's death, and they have been carrying on an incestuous relationship for quite a long time. If Bran disclosed what he saw, Cersei's plan to control the throne would have unravelled and she could have faced execution. The only choice was to kill the witness to her illicit tryst. Winter arrived early in Winterfell, and things only became worse after Ned's departure, with the attempt on Catelyn and Bran's lives.

The situation in King's Landing was no less grim. The Lannisters controlled virtually all of government, they were successful in assassinating the King's Hand, Jon Arryn, and they appeared to be laying the groundwork for the assassination of the King himself. The King may not have been entirely aware of the Lannisters' moves, but his nervousness was evident, especially in his private lunch with Ned in the open field just off the Kingsroad. He felt trouble brewing. "The worst thing about your coronation... I'll never get to hit you again," Ned said in jest. Robert's reply was serious. "Trust me, that's not the worst thing." The note he passed to Ned concerned Daenerys Targaryen's wedding to a Dothraki "horse lord". As usual, Robert was ascribing his sense of unease to the Targaryens. Of course, he felt unease long before he heard of Daenerys' wedding, and it was not Daenerys Targaryen who caused Jon Arryn's death. The Targaryens were simply the usual suspects in Robert's mind, and his nervous and preoccupied mind ascribed his fear and angst and sense of foreboding to the girl across the sea. Ned saw through Robert's strange obsession and argued with him. And then the truth came out. "There are still those in the Seven Kingdoms who call me usurper," Robert said. "There's a war comin', Ned. I don't know when. I don't know who we'll be fighting. But it's comin'." He felt the evils around him. He just couldn't pinpoint the source.

All over the realm, from north to south, winter is coming.

THE DEAD STAG

The stag is the symbol of House Baratheon. Now that we have seen a couple of episodes of GoT, the symbolism of the dead stag is clear. House Baratheon is going to fall. By some means we can only guess, the kingdom will be disemboweled, torn asunder from within. The mention of mountain lions in association with the dead stag could indicate another instance of foreshadowing; the lion is the sigil of House Lannister. Ned's response ("No mountain lions in these woods.") parallels Robb's statement on seeing the dead direwolf bitch ("There are no direwolves south of the Wall."). Since the direwolf was quite obviously south of the Wall, we are obliged by the conventions of literary analysis to consider the mention of moutain lions as significant. Indeed, we are fully entitled to build upon this theory to see the direction it might take us.

The Dead Stag
Richard Ansdell, circa 1875

The antlers are the symbol of the sovereign power of the King. One of the antlers was snapped off, indicating that the King will lose sovereignty; someone outside of House Baratheon will sit the Iron Throne. Since at least one of the antlers remained, we might also surmise that a remnant of the King's former power will remain intact. To whom that power might flow or become entrusted, we cannot say, however. But the loss of an antler did not kill the stag. Nor was he killed in the manner one might expect. Instead, he was disemboweled, the evisceration possibly symbolising destruction from within, perhaps through a palace coup.

Most of the symbolism comports nicely with evidence we have already observed. House Lannister has been conniving for many years, and is perhaps close to the final stroke that will install their line as the new rulers of Westeros. There was no mention at any time of the Targaryens, the dragon sigil, or anything that might be construed as relating to dragons. There were no fires, no screeching from the sky, no beating of wings. But the scene was not limited to a gored or otherwise disemboweled stag and mention of lions. Not a minute after we were introduced to the stag, we saw the deer's most likely antagonist, and subject of the stag's anger.

THE DEAD DIREWOLF

The dead direwolf bitch poses a severe and troubling complication to our understanding of the symbolism and allusive significance of the scene. We are only too aware of the possibility of the Lannisters taking control of the kingdom, but the most likely cause of the stag's downfall was not a mountain lion, but the dead animal who bore the antler fragment, embedded deep in its throat. More troubling, the direwolf is the sigil of House Stark, and Eddard Stark has been a close friend— as close as a brother, in fact—to Robert Baratheon. It seems to me unthinkable, based on the already detailed backstory we have for Robert and Eddard, that either of them could be persuaded by some bit of information or even outright treachery to turn on the other. We know only that someone representing House Baratheon was symbolically disemboweled by someone of House Stark, and the representative of House Stark sustained a symbolic lethal goring through the throat by someone from House Baratheon. Both houses will fall.

I find no reasonable extrapolation to any particular set of future conditions that fully explains the manner in which the two houses will come to be in opposition to each other, only that such an opposition will occur. However, the identity of at least one of the participants in the drama is relatively easy to assign.

Tyr und Fenrir.

Tyr and Fenrir
John Bauer, 1911

Early in this essay I developed a strong parallel between the deserter, Will, and the Lord of Winterfell, Ned Stark. "'I saw White Walkers,' Will said, whispering. He spoke softly, because he knew Lord Stark, who inhabited a world very different from his, would not believe him." I did not record the next event in the chronology, but that event, of course, was Will's execution at Eddard Stark's blade. Will was beheaded. Minutes later, we saw the dead direwolf bitch, gored through the throat. The intimate juxtaposition of two deaths *via* neck wound was not coincidental. The head is symbolic of the leader, and we know well the leader of House Stark.

I believe there are three possibilities we might pursue in attempting an identification of the person or entity represented by the dead direwolf. The most obvious suspect, of course, is Eddard Stark. He is the Lord of Winterfell, the head of House Stark, and we know he is heading into a hornet's nest in King's Landing. Like the lone direwolf, he is going into battle alone, without the pack; that is to say, he is leaving most of his family and household behind, in Winterfell. He is running contrary to the intuitions of his line, which obey the instinct to hunt and go into battle well armed and in packs, not in single combat. Also like the direwolf, Ned Stark "don't belong down here [in King's Landing, Ned's destination]." Just as the direwolf properly belongs north of the Wall, Eddard Stark properly belongs north of the Neck, in Winterfell. Ned is heading to a place where he clearly will not belong.

But the symbolism may go farther than this. We have already heard Catelyn tell Robb "There must always be a Stark in Winterfell." That is, Robb was not permitted to leave Winterfell as long as Ned was absent. If anything happened to Ned, Robb would become Lord of Winterfell. If we look at the symbolism this way, simply decapitating Ned Stark would effect no real change in the balance of power between Baratheon, Stark, and Lannister, or even Targaryen, if we wish to include this far-away house in our calculus. Considered in the light of the realpolitik of Westeros, the symbolism of cutting off the head of House Stark may be intended to signify the fall of the entire house. Perhaps Winterfell itself will fall, or the office of Lord of Winterfell will be vested in some lineage other than House Stark.

A third possibility, more remote, is that the direwolf is symbolically female, and represents a female of House Stark. Although this possibility seems not as well supported, we can look to the direwolf pups and their significance to lend credence to this hypothesis, as we will discuss shortly. Catelyn, as we already saw, was severely wounded in her struggle with the paid assassin. Perhaps she will be called upon to make the ultimate sacrifice for her "pups", Robb, Sansa, Arya, Bran, and Rickon.

THE FIVE DIREWOLF PUPS

Five Stark children will survive the trials to be visited upon their house. This single scene provided us with the identities of two of the surviving children, and the likely identity of the third and fourth. I am less certain of the odds of survival for the remaining two. I include in my count Jon Snow, since Ned told him at the western cairn, "You are a Stark. You may not have my name, but you have my blood."

The five grey pups correspond to each of the five Stark children. More than that, we learned later that the pups correspond not only in number, but almost certainly also in gender. Sansa named her direwolf "Lady," while Arya named her pup "Nymeria," both names for female wolves. I don't think we've yet learned the gender of the pups distributed to the male children, but I'm willing to wager that all three of them are male wolves.

After only 120 minutes of air time, we have a solid feeling about the connections between the children and their direwolf pets. The direwolves follow the children around in the same way that ordinary house pets would follow their masters. And they are no less protective of their masters than the most fiercely loyal dog. We saw Bran's wolf rip out a man's throat when he tried to attack Catelyn and Bran. The wolves are certainly aware of the children as beloved companions and masters.

If the direwolves are emotionally attached to the Stark children, we have even stronger evidence of a particular child's connection to the direwolves, and not necessarily the direwolf that was given to the child. When Ned Stark killed Sansa's wolf, Lady, Bran opened his eyes for the first time after being pushed out of the window by Jaime. We do not yet know whether he was shocked into consciousness by Lady's pain or death, or awakened by some other mechanism, but we do know something interesting about Bran, a new aspect of his character associated in some way with the direwolves.

Sense of Sight
Annie Swynnerton, 1895

Bran sees now, in a way that he has never seen before. We know the change that has come over him is no simple restoration of his former self. We did not see him jump out of bed or move about in glee. We simply saw him open his eyes. There was no smile, no other acknowledgement of his sudden awareness of his surroundings. His face showed only a piercing stare, a deep grounding in full consciousness, unlike any expression we have ever seen on such a young child's face. Bran was not made whole by the direwolf's death. He was made into something **more** by an awareness that accompanied the death of the direwolf. He was aware not only of his immediate surroundings in his room in Winterfell. In some strange way we do not yet comprehend, he was fully aware of events transpiring hundreds of kilometres away. To say Bran sees is to say something qualitatively different and far richer than saying that anyone else sees.

Bran will survive the coming calamities. His new sight is significant, and will certainly not be wasted in an early death. Bran shares qualities with Jon Snow and with his younger sister, Arya. I believe these two will likewise survive future trials. I am not so confident of Robb and Sansa's ability to cope with a drastically changing world. It was Robb who said, on seeing the dead direwolf and the several young pups, "There are no direwolves south of the Wall." I will return to this strange statement in the final essay, but for now, it is sufficient to note simply that Robb was blind to the reality in front of his eyes. Sansa, likewise, wants desperately to believe in the goodness of her fiancé, and is willing to overlook even the worst defect of character to retain in her mind the concept of a noble prince who will one day rule as fair and gracious king. The direwolf, in her mind, is not a loyal bodyguard, but a "lady". Sansa has a warped and quite narrow view of the reality around her. If she survives into adulthood with her current emotional and conceptual disabilities, it will not be due to any reserved capacities for rational behaviour. If she is to survive, she will have to change, and drastically.

THE DEATH OF LADY

It is tempting to declare that the death of the direwolf assigned to Sansa is a sign of the girl's impending doom. There are several reasons to cast doubt on the strength of this allusion. The strongest of these is the circumstance that led to Lady's execution. Her death was Cersei's delicious form of retribution for the minor injury to her son's arm, but more importantly to her, it was the means by which she reduced the court's esteem for House Stark and cut away at the deep bond of friendship between Robert and Ned. All of these minor wounds served to increase her influence in the court, and the strength of her family's political currency will have great importance should she attempt to depose the King.

Although it seems likely that the death of a direwolf indicates a Stark child will die, I really believe we lack the evidence to make a determination. You who have read all four novels are laughing to yourselves right now, because you believe you know the answer. We know the answer that is correct for the novels, of course. But can we be sure that the same answer will apply in the television series? I am not so sure. Some of the children are more important than others, and their relative importance may have to change. A novel can go into as much depth as the author feels is necessary. We've already seen that a television series, which has only a limited amount of time to tell its story, must simplify and cut here and there. It is quite possible that children who survive in the novels will not survive the television series, and vice versa.

WOLVES OF THE DIASPORA

Canis lupus portrait
National Park Service, 2005

The direwolves were distributed to children who have already been scattered across the continent. The three boys remain in Winterfell while the two girls approach King's Landing and Jon Snow has reached the Wall. Nymeria is off in the forests somewhere, Lady is dead, and the other wolves are with their child masters. That the wolves were distributed immediately after their mother's death should probably also be taken as allusive of future events related to the children. If events in King's Landing overtake the Starks, it seems unlikely the children will be immediately reunited under one roof. This is not Harry Potter, after all. There is no justice, no allowance made for sensibilities around children's needs. If a child impedes Cersei's progress, we already know the fate that child will suffer. Cersei will not be as sloppy the next time she has a child executed—she'll make sure the job is done correctly.

THE ASCENDENCY OF JON SNOW AND BRAN STARK

I am very sure of the survival of Bran Stark, and equally sure his half-brother, Jon, will endure the coming tests. Bran has a special kind of vision, but Jon also has vision, as we saw in the direwolf scene. Unlike Ned, who refused to acknowledge the truth of the ranger's words ("I saw White Walkers"), and Robb, who refused to acknowledge the plain truth of direwolves' movement south of the Wall, Jon confronted and dealt with the reality before him. "Lord Stark," Jon said, calling to his father, "there are five pups, one for each of the Stark children. The direwolf is the sigil of your house. They were meant to have them." No one, not even Lord Stark's most learned advisors, knew to make all of these connections in such a short frame of time. That Jon Snow was able to do so is indicative of the rare vision he has. He is a leader, and he will soon find himself in a place desperately in need of real leadership. The white direwolf went to the man who now wears black. A colour symbolising purity married to a colour symbolising selfless duty. It is a rich combination, and it is also the end of our discussion of symbolism. For if I am to reveal the true reason Bran Stark and Jon Snow will survive, I will need to depart the province of symbolism and allusion and move whatever reasoning and analytical skills remain to me into the realm of allegory and theme.

The core of Game of Thrones is not Ned Stark and Robert Baratheon and Cersei Lannister. Their time has come and gone. The children are the future, as those who believe themselves wise are wont to say. In our story, though, the saying rings true. The children are not only the future, they are the story. The core of Game of Thrones is Bran, Tyrion, Jon, Daenerys, and Arya. A cripple, a dwarf, a bastard, an exiled princess, and a tomboy. Children all. Bastards all. Grotesques all. But they share so much more in common. I will explore every one of these fascinating characters in the next essay.

Grotesque Profile
Leonardo da Vinci, circa 1495

"Some people can read *War and Peace* and come away thinking it's a simple adventure story. Others can read the ingredients on a chewing gum wrapper and unlock the secrets of the universe."

Lex Luthor had it right. We will extract meaning from *War and Peace* or Game of Thrones only to the extent that we provide ourselves with a framework for creating connections between story elements. The richness of *War and Peace* is wasted on those who do not take the time to construct a conceptual foundation for the story.

Thesis can be a frightening word. It evokes images of hordes of sour-faced professors grilling a poor graduate student who has the temerity to proclaim a new understanding of an obscure author or a seldom-mentioned footnote in history. The professors are qualified to quiz the student in detail on the most arcane minutiae even distantly related to her topic—her thesis—because they alone possess the intellectual tools to understand any detail in the study of humanities.

This is not my understanding of thesis. A thesis is simply the main thought we take from a story, or historical event, or experiment in the laboratory. The thesis I extract from GoT may be quite different from the one you pull from scenes and episodes. There are no right or wrong theses, but I believe some theses are more suited to our greater enjoyment of the series. My intention in this essay is not to convey some maxim that must be accepted as inerrantly true fact, to be counted as cherished belief at risk of losing academic credentials or intellectual credibility. Even if my name were George R. R. Martin, I believe you would be entitled to disagree with me regarding the deepest meaning of GoT. You're equally entitled, if you so desire, to tell those arrogant, sour-faced professors to go to hell. My single intention in writing this essay is to provide some ideas—some things I noticed along the way, basically—that might be useful in expanding our awareness of connections between ideas in GoT.

As in my essay on symbolism, I am again going to concentrate on the direwolf scene of Episode 1.01 ("Winter Is Coming"). However, since I am attempting to offer my take on the thesis of the entire series, I will have to seek supporting ideas in other scenes, and I am going to refer at least briefly to material drawn from the novels. I contend that the thesis of GoT will be virtually indistinguishable from the thesis of ASoIaF. To the extent that GRRM is involved in production of the television series, this seems a valid contention. Therefore I consider reliance on supporting material from the novels to be justifiable as I build a case for my understanding of GoT.

THE DIREWOLF SCENE IN THE NOVEL

The direwolf scene in the first book of ASoIaF is considerably more complex than the version we saw in Episode One of GoT, yet the televised version contained more material. The most important differences, I believe, are found in the dead stag of the HBO version, and the greater participation of the Stark children in the novel. The scene is only four pages long, constituting the second half of Chapter One ("Bran"); I recommend that everyone carefully read this brief passage. If you do not yet own a copy of AGoT, you should be able to download the first chapter without cost from Amazon or at other sites on the Internet.

The stag is entirely missing from the original version of this scene. The scene begins with Jon announcing "Father, Bran, come quickly, see what Robb has found!" Thus, Robb and Jon were the first of the party at the side of the dead direwolf, not Ned as in the HBO version. The children owned the scene, with the major revelations coming not from Ned and his advisors, but from Jon, Robb, and Bran. Robb discovered the body, Jon identified it as a direwolf, Robb figured out that it had died from the stag antler embedded in its throat, and Robb proclaimed "We will keep these pups." The adults were united in their opposition to the children's plan, spending the better part of two pages fighting the idea of keeping them. Ned relented only when Robb said, "They won't die. We won't *let* them die." The scene ended in a strange manner, with Bran making an observation about Jon's snow-white direwolf pup: "Bran thought it curious that this pup alone would have opened his eyes while the others were still blind."

Wolf lying in grass
U. S. Fish and Wildlife Service, 2002

After Episode Two we have a strong impression of the importance of seeing with eyes. Bran has a kind of sight that no one else in the series possesses. There is no coincidence in the fact that Bran is the only one who noticed the open, observant eyes of the sixth direwolf pup. Of course, symbolically, Bran is recognising the special sight reserved for Jon. Each direwolf pup represents the child to whom it belongs, so that when Bran observes something unique about Jon's direwolf, he is really stating a quality owned by Jon. Bran's thought in this scene, coupled with the new sight we observed at the end of Episode Two, indicate that Bran's abilities are at least a level above even the most insightful of characters. Bran possesses some kind of ability we might tentatively refer to as "metasight"; not only does he see more than anyone else, he knows which people can be trusted to elucidate greatest truth from a given situation.

Jon shines most brightly in both versions of the scene. He is the one who figures out the connection between the direwolves and the Stark children. In the novel, he says, "Lord Stark. There are five pups. Three male, two female. You have five trueborn children. Three sons, two daughters. The direwolf is the sigil of your House. Your children were meant to have these pups, my lord." That Jon made this determination, and not House Stark's most trusted elders, is no mistake. In fact, the leadership Jon demonstrates in this scene is tied intimately to the thesis of Game of Thrones.

ADULT VIRTUES

Allegory of Virtue
Simon Vouet, 1634

If we weigh this scene against the earlier execution scene, we begin to see distinct differences between children and adults.

Bran: "Is it true he saw the White Walkers?"
Ned: "The White Walkers have been gone for thousands of years."
Bran: "So he was lying."
Ned: "A mad man sees what he sees."

Bran walks away from this conversation neither convinced nor satisfied in his father's response. His face carries a frown as he mulls his father's words. Later, near the end of Episode One, Catelyn confronts Ned about his intention to ride south to become the King's Hand. Not only did the last Hand, Jon Arryn, die mysteriously, but, as Catelyn reminded Ned, "Your father and brother rode south once on a king's demand." The Mad King Aerys executed both of them. Catelyn sees no virtue in Ned's adherence to honour. She and Bran both understand something important about Ned: he is blind. His unexamined deference to the demands of honour has made him blind to the reality of the ranger's words about the White Walkers, and blind to any alternatives beyond satisfaction of King Robert's call to service as the Hand.

Blindness is a common ailment among the old and wise. Jaime Lannister made fun of the "gallant men of the Night's Watch" during his talk with Jon at the forge. The wisest among the adults, Tyrion, said to Jon that the Night's Watch protects the kingdom "against grumkins and snarks and all the other monsters your wet nurse warned you about. You're a smart boy. You don't believe that nonsense."

Adults are blind. Children see.

But this is not the thesis of GoT. If it were, Tyrion could not be held up as an example for us. But he is held up for us, possibly as the key figure in GoT. Despite superficial appearances, Tyrion, Jon, and Bran share some quality that reveals to us the deeper meaning of the series. It is my intention to uncover this shared quality during the course of this essay.

THE OLD GODS

Catelyn expressed discomfort when she interrupted Ned's silent contemplations in the godswood, under the white, red-leafed weirwood tree. From the context of her words and the message she bore, it was clear she would not have disturbed Ned as he sat under the sacred tree unless she had good reason. The death of Jon Arryn, the closest thing to a father that Ned had growing up, was such a reason, but it was still not enough to reduce her anxiety in the godswood.

Catelyn: "All these years and I still feel like an outsider when I come here."
Ned: "You have five northern children. You're not an outsider."
Catelyn: "I wonder if the old gods agree."
Ned: "It's your gods with all the rules."

This brief interchange is rich with meaning. Catelyn, of House Tully, is not from the north. But it is not the north itself that bothers her, it is the godswood. She is an outsider not because she is from the south, but because she worships different gods. Yet, from the context of their discussion, the "old gods" are of the north. Catelyn's gods, probably the seven gods we have already heard in conversations (along with "seven hells" and septon and septa—priests and priestesses of the Seven), are evidently worshipped by those in the south, while the old gods are worshipped in Winterfell.

The geographical gradations established by this conversation and other tidbits gleaned from the first two episodes are fascinating. We know that the White Walkers are found only north of the Wall, but they have not been seen "for thousands of years"—at least until Ser Waymar's party chanced upon them, anyway. Beings north of the Wall, then, would appear to be among the oldest denizens of Westeros. Winterfell does not have White Walkers, and its recollections of ancient times seems to be vague. The old gods, if they are found only in the godswood, and perhaps have a most formidable presence only in the vicinity of weirwood trees, must have a weak, almost vestigial influence on events south of the Wall. They are either unknown or essentially unworshipped south of the Neck. Ned was alone in the godswood until Catelyn came in, and context seems to indicate we would be safe in assuming that few citizens of Winterfell and environs spend much time in worshipping the old gods, as the godswoods and weirwoods seem to be few and far between. Thus, ancient ways would appear to be more or less limited to the north, but even here the old practices are dying away. The south, content with its newer faith in the seven gods, has apparently long forgotten any interest in the old gods.

Isis
Tomb of Seti I, 1360 B.C.

The old gods' ways are simpler. They don't have "all the rules" that the southern gods require of their adherents. An act of worship as simple as oiling a greatsword is apparently as complicated a ritual as the old gods expect. Compare this to the incense and bells and bows and banners and measured and counted steps and geometrically perfect processions we witnessed at the funeral of Jon Arryn in King's Landing. Seven septons attended the body, of course, and they processed around him in some hours-long ritual that would have required months of preparation in the choreography of movement, chant, and symbolic rite. The faith of seven requires not a priest, but many priests. The old gods require no priests at all, only a person willing to absorb the meanings found in silence.

I don't believe GRRM is trying to make any statements about the value of one type of religion over another. I think the important lessons to be taken away from Catelyn's talk with Ned in the godswood relate to geography and the temperament associated with time and place. Westeros is not a melting pot. It consists of distinct cultures highly dependent upon geographical location. The further north one goes, the more important the old ways become. It happens that religious practice is one of the most visible signs of the old ways, but this is probably because religion is often the last remnant of culture to survive change over prolonged periods of time. I don't think GRRM is urging us to go out and worship trees.

THE VIRTUE OF SILENCE

Temperament is the deeper issue here, I believe. A duty-bound and honourable man sits silently under a sacred tree, oiling his sword, contemplating nature, perhaps praying to his gods. Observe the clanking, clunky awkwardness and cold devotion to ritual in the Jon Arryn funeral scene and compare to the soft-focus, misty beauty and harmony in the scene in the godswood. There is no coincidence in the director's decision to place this scene immediately following the funeral sequence. We are *supposed* to compare and contrast the two approaches to religion.

GRRM wants us to believe the quiet harmony we see in the godswood and reflected in Ned's calm is as desirable and worthy an attribute of character as Ned's devotion to family and loyalty to king and country. The cultivation of inner peace is a virtue in GoT.

Nouvelles Fables
copyright Abellman, 2008, CC-SA 3.0

But inner peace does not suffice. Discretion, it is said, is the better part of valour. GRRM would use a slightly different vocabulary. He would tell us that honour without the ability to see is no virtue. Ned is an honourable man, but he lacks vision. He has no capacity to exercise discretion because he has no ability to see any options beyond those indicated by honour, duty, and responsibility. Discretion is the better part of valour because the truly brave man needs to exercise good judgment and common sense in evaluating the need to take courageous action. In the same way, inner peace is wasted if it is not applied toward the resolution of real-world problems. The lesson of the godswood is that the inner inclination of a person is of paramount importance. In the context of the religion of the old gods, the imperative is to be disposed toward an attitude of attentive openness. In simple terms, the whole purpose of the godswood is to provide a place for people to *listen*.

But we know Ned is blind; could it be that he is all but deaf, too? I have to wonder whether he even hears his gods anymore. I believe inner blindness and inner deafness are the greatest of sins in GoT.

THE SIGNIFICANCE OF PLACE

Map of Utopia
Abraham Ortelius, 1595

Catelyn is not uncomfortable only in the immediate vicinity of the weirwood. She is uncomfortable just about anywhere in the godswood. She announces her discomfort when she is yet four or five metres away from Ned. The entire godswood is somehow sacred, a place set apart, and this is the cause of Catelyn's anxiety. She does not understand these old gods. She certainly does not feel their presence. Ned does not pray in the fields or in the rooms of his keep. He prays in this sacred place, because this is the place to pray.

I don't think the location is arbitrary. In the south, adherents of the faith of seven can build their houses of worship in any old place they like. The northerners, apparently, must limit their true prayers to the godswood. The southerners are attached to complex, manufactured ritual while the northerners are attached to the sacred nature of particular locations.

We already have a feeling that the older ways and the symmetries of quiet contemplation and listening are desirable attributes in GRRM's world. When we tie these virtues to the significance of ancient trees growing in ancient forests and their increasing importance as we travel north, we begin to see a gradation of virtue tied intimately to gradients of latitude and time. The older ways are preferred over the newer ways. Northern ways are preferred to southern ways. Simple and quiet ways are preferred to complex and noisy ways. Natural is given preference over artificial. Connection with place is preferred over connection with ritual.

The Old Ways

Virtue	Vice
Old	New
North	South
Forest	City
Simplicity	Complexity
Quiet	Noise
Natural	Artificial
Inner sight	Inner blindness
Inner hearing	Inner deafness
Connection	Disconnection

If simplicity is truly a virtue, perhaps some effort to pare down this list would provide yet deeper insight into the meaning and value of the old ways.

I'm going to begin by removing "old" versus "new" from the list. The old ways do not appear to have virtue in the sense of having preceded the new ways, but only to the extent that they allowed for connection to place and the expression of preferences for simplicity, quiet, and the other virtues. I think we can also strike the preference for north over south from the list. Geographical distinctions were useful in elucidating the preferences for various virtues, but it does not seem to me that latitude is an inherent selector for virtue. If it were, and if the local population invariably represented virtues present at that latitude, we would expect White Walkers to bear greater amounts of virtue than anyone else in Westeros. This seems entirely unlikely. Much more likely, it seems to me, is that the old ways simply died out more quickly in the south than they did in the north, not by random coincidence, but by the fact that in colder climes people are more dependent upon each other for survival, and less inclined to reject old and trusted ways of doing things. Thus, the relationship between the old ways and latitude is really a third-order connection. The true connection is with the primary virtues further down the list.

BONDING

I cannot identify a solid rationale for exclusion of "forest" from the list of virtues. At least for the present time, I will leave this virtue on the list, but I will seek means to corroborate the legitimacy of its placement.

Grouse Grind Trail, Grouse Moutain, British Columbia
copyright Chris Stubbs 2007, CC-SA 3.0

Returning to the direwolf scene of Episode One, we know that the children's identification with the direwolves was seen as desirable to those with inner sight. Bran was most insistent that the direwolves not be killed, and their impending executions inspired Jon to make the logical connections that virtually forced Ned to spare the pups' lives. We have seen that the direwolves have not only an emotional attachment to the children, but at least in the case of Bran and Lady, some sort of deep, spiritual or psychic bond also exists. This bonding is also held up by GoT as a virtue.

If bonding with direwolves is a virtue, and if connection to particular forests is likewise a virtue, a reasonable common denominator would appear to be nature itself. Game of Thrones, it seems to me, asserts that deep connection between human beings and nature is a primary virtue.

Simple connection to nature is clearly not the only theme of Game of Thrones; in fact, I don't believe connection to nature constitutes the full expression of the primary theme or thesis.

THE GROTESQUES

The characters that seem best grounded in reality are those in one way or another rejected by greater society. The bastard, Jon Snow, is the one who made the most sense of the complex situation at the side of a direwolf bitch's corpse. Daenerys Targaryen, the vagabond princess who fled for her life to Essos, who looked forward to a life of prostituting herself to Khal Drogo and anyone else her brother specified, is instead learning to bend the Khal to her wishes. Tyrion Lannister, who should have been a meal for wolves, is instead the most learned member of House Lannister. Arya Stark doesn't suppress her natural talents so that she can pursue the sewing and needlework for which she is all thumbs. All of these social rejects, in ways that matter, are able to see and hear things to which others are blind and deaf. They accept and embrace the truth. They listen and learn.

The children have so far been the greatest exemplars of attentive openness, bonding with nature, and ability to learn and improve. In this light we should understand Robb's pronouncement during the direwolf scene to have possibly grave consequences for his future. "There are no direwolves south of the Wall," he said, even as he looked on at the direwolf's corpse. Robb, like his father, refuses to acknowledge the truth before his eyes. This is a dangerous tendency. I fear there may be little or no hope at all for Eddard Stark, and precious little hope for his first-born son. Robb is surrendering too easily and too quickly the openness and simplicity of youth for the artificial complexities and blindness of adulthood.

Tyrion is as yet blind, but very early he acquired the habit of being open to learning. Perhaps his propensity for study will give him eyes to see and ears to hear. Of all the adults, he seems most likely to embrace a life "full of possibilities".

The Children of the Duc de Bouillon
Pierre Mignard, 1647

Ser Waymar Royce said, in flippant response to the ranger, Will, "It's a good thing we're not children." We now understand this was no coincidental, throwaway remark. The arrogant young knight said these words precisely because his adult wisdom was fatally flawed. In the dangerous world of Westeros, in a world which values most of all the artificialities of politics and the game of thrones, the state of being most useful to any of us is that of a child. If Ser Waymar had cultivated an attitude of child-like openness to the truth that was all around him, he might have lived. Instead, he arrogantly insisted on the greater value of adult blindness, and he was cut down in an instant.

The fullest expression of the superiority of the grotesques will become evident in the experiences of the boy with the greatest physical disability of all. If the television series mimics the novels, Bran Stark will not be able to physically move on his own. But his sight and his ability to move about in the world will be virtually unconstrained by time and place. We will learn in vivid and powerful scenes of his unique abilities. It was not an accident of physics that saved him after his fall, it was his openness to new sight that prevented him from succumbing to death. After all, "Death is so final. Whereas life... life is full of possibilities." Bran

74

represents the pinnacle of those possibilities, and the full richness of Game of Thrones.

THESIS

Those most likely to succeed in life are the ones who align themselves not with the artificialities of human society, but rather who seek full communion with nature as the most desirable spiritual state. Attaining to this state is possible only if one embraces a child-like attitude of openness toward and acceptance of the quiet whisperings of forest and fauna, direwolf and dragon. The song of ice and fire is best sung and most appreciated in a quiet place, beside gentle stream, in the shadow of a weirwood, in forest calm, by children who know the old ways, who see and hear, listen and learn.

Edward VI of England, 1546
"The Boy King"

Form defeats substance, a high-born woman says. "Someday you'll sit on the throne and the truth will be what you make it," Cersei tells Joffrey. Others disagree: Substance penetrates and defeats all, they say. "Fear is for the winter," Old Nan tells Bran. Fear is the nameless, penetrating chaos of White Walkers. Formless fear approaches from the north. But pure form without substance comes together in the south. Should we fear northern blood, or southron armour? Jon Snow hears the answer in Benjen Stark's harsh words. Arya Stark feels the answer in Syrio Forel's hard blows. We will come to know the answer, too, but only if we stand with Jon to face the gales seven hundred feet above the frozen forest, only if we give ourselves to the Bravo's dance of water and wind. Winter is coming. Let us join the dance...

SOMETHING MORE APPROPRIATE

The men on the Wall don't change their clothes until they wear out. Citizens of Winterfell wear clothing appropriate to the season. The court of King's Landing, on the other hand, dons apparel consistent with station and occasion. Ned Stark's drab, utilitarian garments from the unimaginative north have no place among the bright colours and happy embroideries of King Robert's southern city. "Perhaps you'd like to change into something more appropriate," the servant suggests to Ned.

If clothing made the man, Eddard Stark would have fit in perfectly among the nimble-tongued denizens of the royal court. But the artificialities of form extend far beyond the flatterings of silk and lace and bejeweled fingers and wrists. There are protocols and expectations of attitude and assertion, words to be spoken, and words to avoid. Lord Varys, master of spiders and whisperers, has survived two kings, not through prowess of sword or wit, but through the pretensions of a well-trained tongue. He knows what to say to whom, how to say it, and where. We prayed to the gods for Prince Joffrey's recovery, Varys says. Ned replies with stern, northern words: "Shame you didn't say a prayer for the butcher's son."

Ned expresses irritation in every scene. We see his seething contempt for the slimy, lilac-drenched flatterer, Lord Varys. When he grabs the neck of Littlefinger, Lord Petyr Baelish, it's hard to know whether Ned is more disgusted by the coin master's forked tongue or the desire in Littlefinger's eyes when he speaks of Ned's wife, Catelyn. "Oh, the Starks," Littlefinger says when Ned releases him. "Quick tempers, slow minds." But it is not wits Ned Stark lacks.

Eddard Stark's second confrontation with Jaime Lannister is much like the first, but we see a bit more of the inner attitudes of these princes of the realm. Jaime is leader of the enormous tide of Lannisters that seems to fill every crack and crevice in the court. He stands in his armour, facing down his northern nemesis, as if barring him from the Iron Throne. He invokes recent Stark family history, telling the story of the death of Rickard and Brandon, Ned's father and brother. The story is meant as bald intimidation, matching Jaime's arrogant, smirking stance. But there is something authentic in his words. "Nobody deserves to die like that," he says. "Five hundred men and this room was quiet as a crypt."

Jaime's attitude changes before our eyes, becoming something compassionate, something whole and just. Five hundred men could allow injustice to be visited on the most noble house in the kingdom, but not Jaime Lannister. When he claims to have killed King Aerys as retribution for the mad king's massacre of Starks, we get the feeling that perhaps Jaime speaks the truth, that he did have a sense of honour and justice. But Ned knows what he knows. He knows Jon Arryn is dead. He knows his young son lies comatose in his bed, and will never walk again. Perhaps Jaime, in taking Mad King Aerys' life, felt himself a defender of the Starks and their honour. But oath and loyalty, for Ned, transcend even the bonds of lineage and blood. "You served him well," Ned said of Jaime's service to the king. "You served him well, when serving was safe."

We think we know why Eddard Stark does not fit into this world of flattery and form, but there is more here than a simple mismatch between ambitious, back-stabbing Lannisters and honourable, forthright Starks. To find the true nature of the problem, we need to consider other moves in this dance, we need to turn our ear to other voices in this song of ice and fire.

WHAT DO YOU KNOW ABOUT FEAR?

The Scream
Edvard Munch, 1893

"Don't listen to it," Old Nan says. "Crows are all liars."

The chilling introduction to this scene has nothing to do with listening, though. For the next image in this scene is not about listening, it's about **seeing**. Bran sees the crow. If we recall anything at all from Episode Two, we must at least remember there is something in Bran's eyes—something in the way he **sees** now—that distinguishes him from anyone else in Westeros.

"Deep into that darkness peering, long I stood there wondering, fearing, Doubting, dreaming dreams no mortals ever dared to dream before—"

The raven was a sign of dark, mysterious foreboding long before Edgar Allen Poe wrote his most famous poem. Ravens in Game of Thrones are messengers. "Dark wings, dark words," they say in Westeros. Ravens carry messages no one wishes to hear, words from far away, from beyond the range of human sight. Words from beyond. And Bran **sees** them.

Bran hates Old Nan's stories, he says. "I know a story about a boy who hated stories," Nan responds. Humour, and not even dark humour. She's trying to steer us away from the raven. But Bran will have none of it. Tell me the scary stories, he says. Ah, we think, the childhood fascination with claws and fangs and bumps in the night. "Fear is for the long night, when the sun hides for years. When children are born and live and die, all in darkness." There is much indeed to serve as fuel to our fear, our fear of darkness, our fear of things beyond our sight. Fear from beyond. Perhaps a juvenile fascination with the terrors of the night is the only thing motivating Bran's choice of bedtime story. Perhaps.

If I were to loan you my copy of any of the ASoIaF novels you would find occasional jottings in the margins in red, blue, and black pen, in a half dozen languages. It's a kind of eighteen-colour highlighting system for an old crank too cheap to go out and buy eighteen pens. But when you arrive at one of the brief chapters titled "Bran," the jottings become so dense as to obscure GRRM's prose. I write notes on notes, and footnotes to notes, and when I run out of space I continue my ramblings on the blank Appendix page at the end of the book, and beyond. The Bran scenes are short, but they are so dense, so packed with information at so many levels, they cannot constrain themselves to the two or three thousand words Martin allots.

I'm going to say more about this multi-tiered density of thought at the end of this essay, because I believe the way we approach the HBO interpretation of Martin's masterpiece is possibly the determining factor in our enjoyment of the series. More importantly, the way we look at complexity tends to shape our friends' and acquaintances' ability to derive equal pleasure from taking in the program.

I believe Bran is a central figure in GRRM's story. The second-longest chapter in this book will treat this single character in detail, and I hope in such a way that stimulates thought. For now, we have much to consider in the mind-boggling way the scene ended.

"One time she told me the sky is blue because we live inside the eye of a blue-eyed giant named Macombe," Robb told Bran.

Bran did not smile. He did not frown. "Maybe we do," he said.

Bran was not simply acknowledging his brother's words. He was neither angry nor amused, neither agitated nor calm. Bran was dismissing his brother's words. But it was not the simplistic dismissal of negation, the impishness of a younger brother eager to assert his uninformed opinion over an elder's wisdom and knowledge. It was dismissal for the sake of displacement; Bran was replacing Robb's interpretation with his own. Old Nan's stories, Bran said, are true. Bran was telling Robb, and anyone with ears to hear, that we must commit every faculty of reason to these old stories, for there is in them some truth that we may sometime be able to glimpse—if ever we gain eyes to see.

"You still don't remember anythin'?" Robb asks.

Bran shakes his head.

"Bran, I've seen you climb a thousand times. In the wind, in the rain, a thousand times. You never fall."

This is a story, too. A stiff wind and strong rain would turn the stones slicker than ice. No boy, not even the most experienced climber, could prevail against such conditions. But the story is Robb's, drawn from long experience, and Robb's story contains the same truth Bran finds in Old Nan's stories. Are we entitled to selectivity in our analysis of this scene? Can we soak in and nod in agreement with the wisdom of Old Nan's stories, but in the same moment discount as uninformed the truth Robb brings in his story?

Bran sees. He knows the stories, remembers every morsel of every story Nan ever told him, even the stories he learned years before he woke up in a bed unable to move. He doesn't remember, he says. Bran, he of sight beyond sight, knowledge beyond the constraints of logic and science, says he does not remember anything about the fall.

Now here's the most chilling idea of all from this most chilling of scenes. Bran sees everything, but he did not see his fall. We saw his fall, but we know we see far less than Bran sees. The question, as you have probably by now guessed, is very simple: Did Bran really fall?

THREE EGGS

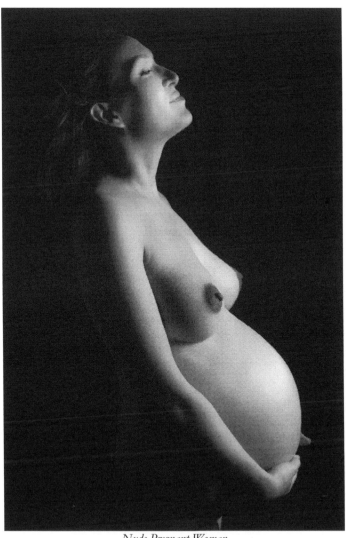

Nude Pregnant Woman
copyright Laura Benvenuti 2011, CC-SA 2.0

The Great Stallion has blessed the khaleesi with a baby, the handmaid says. Change is overcoming her, preparing her, creating new life inside her. Perhaps this new life is the greatest threat of all to the King of the Andals, Lord of the Iron Throne. Could the events playing out across the Narrow Sea in Essos, in the land of the Dothraki, vindicate Robert's crazed obsession with the Targaryen menace?

Khal Drogo's seed has found a fertile place in Daenerys' womb. She has fewer saddle sores of late, and the khal is adapting to her, enjoying her sexual desire and assertiveness. Their relationship grows strong. Is there any reason to believe the prince gaining form and substance and strength inside the young queen will not share in every quality of his unyielding, unmatched father and his insightful, intuitive mother?

I will extend myself a bit here and say I don't believe this is the case. I have said in previous essays ("Meat and Blood: The Competing Cultures of Game of Thrones 1.02") that Daenerys Stormborn Targaryen is among the Grotesques, Tyrion Lannister's shorthand for those among us considered not to measure up, but who nevertheless delight in life's "possibilities". She, along with Bran, Arya, Jon, and Tyrion, define a quinquevalence expressed in five distinct voices, each of whom points to the thesis of GoT, as I argued in "The Grotesques" (Chapter 6).

The more dangerous seed is not the one growing inside Daenerys, but Daenerys herself. Emotionally and intellectually she was nothing more than a child when she arrived in Pentos. She was an unformed seed—an egg. Now, she tests her power, not only in the khal's tent and as she squirms about over his loins, but beyond the reach of sensual charms, outside on the endless, green Dothraki sea, commanding the khalasar horde itself.

"You're learning to talk like a queen," Ser Jorah says in admiration.

"Not a queen," Daenerys says, shaking her head. "A khaleesi."

She is adapting perfectly to the expectations of everyone around her, proving her ability to embrace Tyrion's position that "life is full of possibilities". Indeed. We might expect that those who are most aware of the gift of life, who live every day surrounded by those who consider these grotesques in some way undeserving of life, would also enjoy the greatest success in expanding the range of life's possibilities. Daenerys was only a seed. But now, in the khalasar, she has cracked the protective shell, to her brother's shock and incredulity. No longer an egg, she is her own person, growing, changing, but most of all, *learning*.

I said there were three eggs. Probably you guessed I am not referring to the dragon eggs to which the directors have been drawing our attention in almost every scene focussing on Daenerys. I have mentioned two eggs: Daenerys and her unborn son, heir to the khalasar. I am aware of a third egg, though—something which may, in the end, prove to contain within itself a power more awesome than that wielded by the new khaleesi. And, yes, that egg is there, present in the khal's tent, though of course, it is not the khal I'm thinking of. We will return to this idea in later chapters.

FORM WITHOUT SUBSTANCE

"You fought off a direwolf," Cersei told her son.

"I didn't fight off anything," Joffrey responded. "All I did was scream. And the two Stark girls saw it, both of them."

"That's not true." The queen's voice was sure and true. "You killed the beast."

The words make no sense to the boy, but only because he is imposing Baratheon sensibilities on a situation that required Lannister thought.

Cersei explains by way of example: "When Aerys Targaryen sat on the Iron Throne, your father was a rebel and a traitor. Someday, you'll sit on the throne and the truth will be what you make it."

We understand this idea, that princes and potentates can so direct our thoughts as to create something that has never existed, to so captivate our imaginations that we believe it is there. These are stories, too, you see, no less powerful, and no less true than the ones spun by Old Nan. There is nothing inherently evil in such stories and dreams.

THE LANNISTERS' LEND/LEASE PROGRAM

Franklin Delano Roosevelt, circa 1940

In our own time—well, in our grandparents' time—Franklin Delano Roosevelt had us believe in something not there. He called it the "New Deal". But because people believed in it, it came to be true. Pierre Elliott Trudeau asked his people to see before their eyes a "Just Society". Forty years were required, but in the end, every element of his vision came to form the strongest yarns of the grand mosaic we know as Canada. Martin Luther King had a dream, too, and forty-five years after he expressed his vision of an unobtainable state of mind, the people of the United States judged a man by the content of his character, not by the colour of his skin, and elected him their president.

But there are dark visions, dreams that are false, not true. We see this grim and evil darkness in the "weapons of mass destruction" that provided the single rationale for a superpower to invade a sovereign nation, kill its people, and depose and imprison its leader. Those of us who remember, recall vividly the 1980s promise of a new kind of economics, "trickle-down economics", that would bestow greatest wealth on those already blessed with financial abundance. The powerful and wealthy few, we were told, would invest in us, in our labour, and in that way provide jobs and prosperity. Wealth would "trickle down". Oh, we were trickled on, all right. But there was nothing salutary in the increased unemployment, the stock market crash of 1987, the Savings and Loan fiasco, the quadrupling of the national debt, or any of the other destructive events that were the natural outcome of bestowing selfish people with virtually unlimited ability to control the economy.

In the end, if your story is good enough, if you are a skilled actor, you can convince your people of anything. Roosevelt did it. He compared the Lend/Lease program, which gave hundreds of billions of dollars of support to the UK during the Battle of Britain, to lending one's neighbour a garden hose. "You wouldn't make your neighbour pay for the hose now, would you? You'd just ask him to bring it back when he's done." From that point of view, the United States wouldn't go into debt. And Roosevelt wasn't breaking any of the numerous laws that prevented him from becoming involved in the Second World War. He was just being a good neighbour to Great Britain.

The reality was something else entirely, of course. Not only did Roosevelt send Churchill hundreds of billions in weapons and supplies, he used the United States military to escort the matériel across the Atlantic. He risked an attack on a U.S. military vessel, which would have required immediate response, which would have brought the United States into the war. Roosevelt's action was illegal, against every law Congress had passed. But was Lend/Lease ethical?

Roosevelt's action was not selfish. At risk to his own presidency, he acted out of concern for the welfare of a less powerful country. We know Cersei's vision of a world in which Joffrey can snap his fingers and cause every one of his subjects to believe the most ridiculous and self-serving of his utterances is not intended to serve the interests of anyone except her and the most loyal of her family. In fact, as we will soon learn, she does not trust anyone in House Baratheon—anyone at all among Robert's relatives—to obey her. Cersei shares her twin brother's vision.

"And my husband?" she asked.

"I'll go to war with him if I have to," Jaime said. "They can write a ballad about us... The boy won't talk, and if he does, I'll kill him. Him, Ned Stark, the King, the whole lot of them, until you and I are the only people left in this world."

This isn't a fabrication of weapons of mass destruction to justify control of Middle East oil. This isn't some fairy tale about "trickle-down economics" to put a few thugs and cronies in charge of a country's economy. This is outright war against all of humanity. It is the purest form of selfishness. It is the clearest expression we have yet heard of the Lannister ideal.

Cersei's dream is one of form without substance. The king fabricates a rigid and impervious suit of armour around whatever falsehoods he wishes to proclaim from the throne. It matters not a bit that his proclamations are devoid of any particle of substance, honesty, or truth. It matters only that they serve the maintenance and strengthening of the empty and evil shell that is House Lannister.

SUBSTANCE WITHOUT FORM

"I'm ready," Jon said. "I won't let you down."

"You're not going," Benjen said. "You're no ranger, Jon."

"But I'm better than every other—"

"Better than no one!... Here, a man gets what he earns."

The courtyard trainings and jousts led by the Master of Arms, Ser Alliser Thorne, serve only his own nebulous, perverse pleasure and Jon Snow's formless anger and resentment. The pickpockets and thieves and rapists Ser Alliser are given are pathetic and useless in his eyes. "Well, Lord Snow, you're the least useless man here." Jon, of course, is no lord, but he is next to useless, and certainly no leader. A leader does not lord it over others, as Ser Alliser would have Jon do. "Lord Snow here grew up in a castle, spitting down on the likes of you." He didn't tack on the phrase "you worthless, vile scum," but he might as well have. It was certainly a phrase held firm in his mind's eye, and no doubt the most respectful thought he could muster for the pitiful recruits in his charge.

A ranger, given responsibility for less experienced men, could never have anything less than complete respect for those joining him on patrols beyond the last structures of civilisation. He had to be in all ways a leader. He could never exude the visionless, near-sighted, self-centred, formless, unpredictable anger and energy that defined Jon Snow. A ranger needed direction and purpose, he had to bring form and objective and responsibility to his plans. Most of all, a ranger had to bring dignity, respect, honour, and humility to every human interaction. Jon lacked all of these.

Jon is not the "useless man" Ser Alliser would have us believe, though. He is a bastard, one of Lord Tyrion's "grotesques", who searches the grim narrowness of life for every possibility. He exploits every potential for learning and growth, coming to find deepest affections for the man who most insults him. Tyrion is an exasperating and unsympathetic little man who cares little for anyone else's emotional state. But he has quickly become the best teacher Jon has ever had, and Jon, with Daenerys, has an unquenchable desire to learn, to push against the limits imposed by those considering him in some way less than a complete man. Respect and admiration of teachers is a corollary virtue in one such as Jon, and he extends this respect to his Uncle Benjen, even when the man says things Jon would rather not hear.

The outcome of Benjen's rough words ought to have been predictable. But Jon surprised us. He figured out what he was doing wrong. Rather than obeying Ser Alliser's sadistic, destructive call to embarrass and beat into the ground every challenger, Jon used the daily duels as a way of teaching and supporting and encouraging his brothers in black.

Jon begins to acquire the skills we consider part and parcel of the frame of mind and habit of character we call leadership. But leadership is not the goal of Jon's learning. To understand that goal, we need to turn to a man named Syrio Forel.

THE WATER DANCE

"This is the Bravo's dance. The water dance. It is swift—and sudden. All men are made of water. You know this. If you pierce them, the water leaks out, and they die."

Mifune
The Seven Samurai, 1954

Not elegant, certainly not yet with the style of a Bravo. But she reached out and grabbed the sword from its midair flight—and only on the second try. Arya has significantly more skill than I possess; I had to repeat this scene eight times before finally grabbing the frame that showed Arya nailing the catch.

What is the Bravo's dance? I believe it is nothing less than the perfect marriage of function and form, substance and style, desire and purpose. It is what Arya and Jon and Bran and Daenerys are learning. It is the goal of all their grotesque, world-expanding yearnings, because it is the ultimate tool in addressing and finally manipulating to one's liking a world that is continually in flux. Men are water, always flowing, always changing. But so too, the world around these bastards and tomboys and dwarfs is eternally in flux. The only way to obtain firm footing is not to acknowledge some distant or objective or academic awareness of the flux. No, the only way to obtain firm footing is to abandon it, to mock it, to dance around it. The only way to get a firm grip on the world is to become the flux, to become master of the dance. The grotesques of Game of Thrones are receiving their first dance lessons.

SUBSTANCE AND PURPOSE

By now, if you have read a few of these essays, you notice some peculiarities. I rarely endeavour to persuade you of my point of view. I just come out and give an interpretation of a scene or a facet of a character's personality. I may support the statement with two thousand words of observations and logical deduction, or I may simply allow it to hang out there in midair, unexamined, unanalysed in any way.

These are not episode recaps, and they're not academic treatises. My single intention in these essays is to throw out ideas that contribute in some way to your own thinking about the episode, the characters, or the series as a whole. I may briefly mention GRRM's novels, or some bit of history (this week, for example, it was the World War II Lend/Lease Program) or culture, but my focus is always the television drama itself.

If you could comment on this text, you would find I encourage open discussion, and I single out for praise anyone who adds new ideas. I genuinely embrace diverse, open discussion, and you will find I often use second person address in my essays. I really see myself writing one-on-one to each person reading this essay. Those who are interested will not have any difficulty confirming my love of discussion among the 900 or so responses I left for the thousands of people commenting on the over 60 Lost essays I published on the Internet last year. They're all still there at SL-Lost and Dark UFO.

I believe your ideas are as valid, useful, and valuable as anyone else's. I know we do not live in an egalitarian world. Many in the Lost community hold me up in ways that are frankly embarrassing. I have my detractors, too, of course, but these are not nearly as embarrassing or as personally difficult for me as some of the more over-exuberant fans. I enjoy fans, of course, but I enjoy much more a robust, open, and honest discussion.

AN ESSAY NAMED SUE

If at times you feel your blood pressure rising during a section or two of my essays, this is all to the good, and quite intentional. You will understand that I tied fiscal conservatism to the discussion about the Lannisters, and I ended the section anointing House Lannister as the abode of purest evil, and by association indicating the evil of fiscal conservatism. The intention again, is not to point to some truth or fact, but to stimulate your thinking about House Lannister. If you tend toward the politically liberal or socialist plane of the political sphere, you may find the association useful, and not expend any more thought on the matter. If, on the other hand, you are variable or conservative in your politics, you may find the association rankles. Certainly even the worst conservative political leaders over the last fifty years could not be considered "purest evil". Therefore the association cannot stand. What I really hope is that you will go to the next step, and discover in the episodes to date those evidences that strongly indicate House Lannister is not

pure evil, that in fact, many redeeming and positive qualities are to be found in healthy distribution among the characters. The occasional high-blood-pressure sections are, essentially,
the Boy-Named-Sue style of essay composition. (see the Johnny Cash recording:
http://www.youtube.com/watch?v=T678ic45k98&feature=fvst)

ADVENTURE, ANALYSIS, AND INCLUSION

You need not share my beliefs or agree with my interpretation of any aspect of the series. In fact, I find most interesting those comments in which readers bring their own ideas and contribute them to the discussion. If you believe GoT is a fascinating adventure story, and that this in itself has greater meaning to you than any of the symbolism or other features of the story I sometimes invoke in my essays, I say bully for you. If you believe GoT is best understood through the epistemological lens of Jürgen Habermas as interpreted by the Jean Baudrillard school of sociological criticism, well good! Have at it. If we were all at a party, I would enjoy talking with each of you, to learn your ideas about adventure stories, your thoughts on psychology- and sociology-based literary criticism, gradient systems of symbolic reference, and anything else you deem relevant to the television drama.

The Conversation Piece
Solomon Joseph Solomon, circa 1895

Some of you who, with me, enjoy the adventure story that is Game of Thrones may find yourselves occasionally bullied and brow-beaten by others who insist on somewhat more arcane interpretations. I find myself enjoying those arcane discussions just about as much as I derive pleasure from the adventure story conversations. However, I do not find academic exclusivity and intellectual triumphalism to be useful to open discussion. In fact, bullying is, in my mind, a species of social intolerance that has no place in civil discourse. If you wish to prove to others the superiority of your intellect or your interpretation of an artist's work, I would ask you to kindly use some venue other than my essay. This is a place for inclusion, not exclusion. Everyone's ideas are welcome here. And if someone is brow-beating or bullying you, well, just tell 'em to lighten up. It's a television show, not a graduate course. And if they don't like my essay, well that's fine. I'm a chemist, not a brick layer (http://www.liveleak.com/view?i=5a2_1298092824). Or did McCoy say "I'm a chemist, not a literary scholar"? I'm forgetting my ST-TOS already.

We're having fun here, friends. That's all. It's supposed to be fun! And that is all it is, in the end. Game of Thrones is entertainment of the first order. Next week, we'll take a look at one of my favourite subjects: Cripples, Bastards, and Broken Things. 'Til then, on behalf of the DeGroots, Alvar Hanso, and everyone at the Dharma Initiative... oh—wrong essay! 'Til then, remember Catelyn's words: Family, Duty, Honour. See you next week!

*Jean, Comte de Dunois, "The Bastard of Orleans" 1402-1468
engraving by Mariette d'Enghien, 1680*

What is a bastard? Lineage without title? Innate ability denied social and creative outlet? If Gendry the journeyman armourer does not know himself to be the son of King Robert, is he a bastard, or merely a talented young metalworker? Can Tyrion, who says he is a "bastard in his father's eyes", but enjoys lineage, title, and innate ability, be considered truly a bastard? Tonight we saw not fewer than seven bastards, each of them illegitimate in his own way.

THEON GREYJOY

Tyrion Lannister's parting words to Theon Greyjoy, ward of House Stark, were typically biting. "Tell me, how do you think Balon Greyjoy would feel if he could see his only surviving son has turned lackey?"

Tyrion is the fearless defender of House Lannister, but he is equally unafraid of expressing his well-considered opinion on any matter large or small. In this case,

Tyrion seems to believe Theon's servile behaviour merited a lengthy dressing down prior to departing Winterfell.

Tyrion's speech is curious, given the circumstances of Theon Greyjoy's status as unwilling house guest to the Starks. The Greyjoy Rebellion resulted in the destruction of Tywin Lannister's fleet at Lannisport. It was, in Tyrion's words, "a stupid rebellion", since House Greyjoy was outnumbered ten to one by forces loyal to the King. Why would Tyrion care that the heir to an enemy house was debasing himself by surrendering to the whims of House Stark?

We have seen that House Lannister is apparently intent on taking the Iron Throne. House Stark is the primary obstacle in the Lannisters' path to the crown, due to Ned Stark's close relationship to King Robert. Both Jaime Lannister and Queen Cersei have made veiled threats on Ned Stark's life, in tense, face-to-face encounters. Even from the first episode of the series, we were aware of deep animosity between the two houses. With each episode we learn a bit more about the manoeuvrings of House Lannister to reduce the political standing of House Stark.

From the Lannister point of view, House Stark appears to be engaged in its own political posturing. Ned Stark, once a far-off threat ensconced in the northern territories controlled by Winterfell, is now king in all but title, ruling the Small Council and even serving as administrator of King's Landing. Despite every attempt of House Lannister to distance competing houses from the throne, House Stark continues to move increasingly closer to the seat of power. "Why are you here, Ned?" Cersei asked. Ned Stark is more than an irritation or temporary inconvenience in the queen's mind. His close relationship to the king is a steadily strengthening barricade, denying her pursuit of power.

Viewed from House Lannister, then, Theon Greyjoy, who has lived most his life in close proximity to House Stark, could become not only a valuable asset, but potentially a means of reducing the Stark threat to Lannister designs. If Tyrion is able to plant in Theon a seed of dissatisfaction regarding his house's servitude, perhaps Theon, or all of House Greyjoy, will become an unpleasant distraction requiring Ned Stark's attention. Anything that forces House Stark to expend energy in far-away corners of the realm will serve Lannister attempts to concentrate power in King's Landing.

I believe we can legitimately look at Tyrion's belittlement of Theon Greyjoy as a political manoeuvre. We might think Tyrion the scholar of House Lannister, but the fact is, due to his status as "bastard in his father's eyes", Tyrion has to work harder to promote Lannister interests than anyone else in his family. "Things are expected of me" (GoT 1.02).

However, I do not believe that this is the most complete interpretation, because it does not give proper weight to other factors we know to carry importance to the Imp. I believe we can consider Theon Greyjoy to be this episode's first instance of a bastard, for reasons I intend to illuminate during the course of this essay.

JON SNOW

Jon Snow's bastard status has been a dominant theme in Game of Thrones. Tonight's episode finally gave us a definition of the term "bastard", and demonstrated the sturdy foundations of Jon Snow's steady growth into a leader of men.

Jon Snow is a bastard in the standard, historical sense of the word. A bastard, according the Canadian Oxford Dictionary, is "a person born of parents not married to each other." Jon Snow is Eddard Stark's son, but not Catelyn Tully's son, and therefore he has no claim to any privileges or titles of House Stark. His lowly status is inconsistent with his evident innate abilities. His talent with the sword, and his ability to motivate people is being wasted, going unrecognised among the nameless rabble of horse thieves, petty criminals, and social rejects who constitute the Brotherhood of the Black.

Peasant Village
Johann Peter Orth, 1843

Being a bastard means being separated, cut off from the nurturing and enabling connections that normally define human interaction. It may or may not be true that "it takes a village to raise a child", but at the very least, one man and one woman are required to initiate the chain of events that results in the birth of a child. The term "bastard" is an indication that, in most societies, satisfaction of biological requirements does not suffice to attain to full personhood.

Being born a bastard means that biological function was the single connective factor in the child's upbringing. Marriage, in pre-twentieth century cultures, is a social structure geared toward the bearing and raising of children. It is a state requiring the highest levels of commitment and responsible behaviour from both mother and father, sustained at least over the course of their offspring's childhood.

A bastard is one who lacked the commitment of a mother and a father, and is therefore deficient in social connections. In fact, a bastard is the product of a ruptured relationship. A bastard is the result of brokenness between two people.

Jon: "What's my name?"
Sam: "Jon Snow."
Jon: "And why is my surname 'Snow'?"
Sam: "Because you're a bastard, from the north."
Jon: "I never met my mother. My father wouldn't even tell me her name. I don't know if she's living or dead. I don't know if she's a noble woman, or a fisherman's wife, or a whore. So I sat there, in the brothel, as Ros took off her clothes. But I couldn't do it. 'Cause all I could think was...was if I got her pregnant...if she had a child...another bastard named Snow. It's not a good life for a child."

In at least one important respect, Jon long ago came to terms with his illegitimacy. He has not accepted the social limitations imposed on him due to his status, but he has demonstrated a level of personal responsibility few people, especially teenage boys, possess. Years before he came to the Wall, he had the marks of sober, sensible, and responsible leader, and he acquired those distinctive attributes of character specifically in his capacity as a social reject, a "grotesque".

There is another important sense in which Jon Snow is a bastard. We began to gain a new appreciation of this second way of understanding bastards through the history of the Wall's newest recruit, Samwell Tarly of Horn Hill.

SAMWELL TARLY

Samwell Tarly was heir to his father's title and lands. But he never rose to his father's expectations. "On the morning of my eighteenth name day, my father came to me. 'You're almost a man now,' he said. 'But you're not worthy of my land and title. Tomorrow you're going to take the Black, forsake all claims to your inheritance, and start north. If you do not,' he said, 'then we'll have a hunt. And somewhere in these woods your horse will stumble, and you'll be thrown from your saddle to die. Or so I'll tell your mother.'"

Sam was cut off from title, land, and inheritance by fiat of his father. If, as I wrote in the previous section, "a bastard is the result of brokenness between two people", Sam meets the definition of a bastard. In fact, Sam's predicament is virtually the same as Jon's. Both young men were born to the lord of a great house, but due to circumstances not of their choosing, both have been denied the privileges of high birth.

Perhaps Sam's father was unnecessarily cruel in rebuking and rejecting his own child. But, based on Sam's aversion to every aspect of nobility, and his inability to develop the attributes of character expected of even the lowest of peasants, we might understand and perhaps even support Lord Tarly's decision to deny inheritance to his son, and to make arrangements for a younger child instead to carry on House Tarly's name, title, and properties. Is it not best that anyone as incapable as Samwell Tarly be denied the privilege of marrying and starting a family? If he falls short of every proof of manhood, how could he possibly serve as husband and father? In what way would he offer his progeny even the most elementary example of human worth?

I believe this is one of the central questions of the episode, given depth in several important scenes throughout the evening. The most subtle but probably most effective appearance of the theme occurred at the armourer's forge.

GENDRY, JOURNEYMAN ARMOURER

I am tempted to call him "Gendry Waters", though we don't learn his surname during the episode, and if I remember him correctly from the novels, only his common name is ever used. The fact that he is not identified as a bastard, that only Jon Arryn knew the boy's status before his death, is critical to the story.

The Village Blacksmith
Estelle Hollingsworth circa 1839

All of the essential elements are now in place to solve one of the grand mysteries of the series. I am going to say little about this, because the mystery Jon Arryn solved, the devious plot Eddard Stark is about to uncover, does not have direct bearing on the argument I make in this essay. My experience in serial analysis began with Lost, which was arguably the most challenging series ever brought to the small screen. From a brief first-season scene in which two characters listen to 1940s-era music on the radio and a couple instances of eerily-repeated actions during Season Two, some of the leading Lost analysts were able to predict that time loops and time travel would figure into the show. We became adept at analysing every scene for the smallest clue and considering dozens of possible outcomes. Of the major mystery alluded to in this scene, I will say only that visual clues are more important than any information in dialogue, and that the clues have been far more obvious than those meted out during Lost. That Gendry is King Robert's son only scratches the surface of the greater mystery. If you have not read the novels, and wish to throw out theories, I believe you ought to be permitted to do so. If you have read the novels, I urge you to hold your tongue.

This scene is expertly placed and has critical importance to several themes, including several sub-themes related to bastardy. At least two sub-themes are given forceful prominence in Ned Stark's parting words: "If the day ever comes that that boy would rather wield a sword than forge one, you send him to me."

INNATE WORTH

In everything he does, Gendry demonstrates the character and bearing of a king. Not only is his work at the forge superlative in every sense, but he himself recognises the quality. Most of all, he refuses to yield to any authority other than his own.

Tobho Mott: "Show the Hand the helmet you made, Lad."
[Gendry hands the helmet to Ned]
Ned: "This is fine work."
Gendry: "It's not for sale."
Tobho Mott: "Boy, this is the King's Hand! If his Lordship wants the helmet—"
Gendry [shaking his head]: "No. I made it for me."
Tobho Mott: "Forgive me, my Lord."
Ned: "There's nothing to forgive."

Gendry exudes the unwavering confidence and knowledge of his dignity that many might label arrogance. But it is anything but arrogance. He is a man *dans sa peau*, completely at ease in every aspect of his person. Ned examined details of the boy's face before giving voice to his conclusion that the boy was King Robert's illegitimate son. But the visual examination was only the confirmation of the strong evidence that exuded from every move the boy made, from every self-confident and kingly statement that flowed from his mouth. When Ned watched the boy pound hammer to anvil, he almost certainly saw in his mind's eye King Robert, wielding the grand war hammer that he used to win every battle. Gendry's muscular physique, virtually identical to that of the young King Robert, was the first of many strong indications of the boy's lineage.

Ned Stark appreciated the innate worth of those descended from superior stock. As he told Jon at the western cairn, "You are a Stark. You may not have my name, but you have my blood." Ned recognises the same royal blood in Gendry.

That Ned has an eye for nobility and breeding is testament to his integrity and his formidable leadership abilities. But I believe in this scene the writers of the screenplay, and GRRM before them, are calling us to recognition of something greater than even Ned Stark understood. Tonight's episode was a masterful exposition of the theme of innate worth. Ned grasped only part of the truth that

GoT is attempting to convey. The major lessons were given north of King's Landing, north of Winterfell, on the very periphery of civilisation, at the Wall.

INNATE DISABILITY

When Jon Snow had defended Sam from the Master of Arms' taunts and jabs, when he had fended off three of the Wall's strongest new recruits and came out of the confrontation unharmed, after he had defended a defenceless man's dignity and stood up for warrior principles, Ser Alliser summarised his evaluation of Jon Snow: "Go clean the armory. That's all you're good for."

Sword Practice
unknown artist, circa 1575

Ser Alliser Thorne has triumphed over the worst conditions ever experienced on the continent of Westeros. He survived month-long winter blizzards that killed even the best of men. We might reasonably assume that a man such as this, who has spent a lifetime evaluating the character of those hardy souls charged with defending the most dangerous wilderness in the realm, would have a fair, balanced, and pragmatic understanding of human ability. His harsh methods are necessary, and consonant with the unforgiving, deadly environment they patrol, we might conclude.

We would be entirely incorrect in any such assessment of Ser Alliser. Recall his words to Jon and Sam at the conclusion of his Winter Speech: "Soon we'll have new recruits. The new lot will be passed along to the Lord Commander for assignment. And they will call you 'Men of the Night's Watch.' But you'd be fools to believe it. You're boys still."

Jon Snow has consistently demonstrated superior ability in staged battle, even simultaneously fighting off three armed men in several rounds of Ser Alliser's exercises. He has rallied boys and men of disparate backgrounds to unite behind a single cause, thus showing an unusual gift for leadership, even under the most trying of conditions. And yet Ser Alliser, the Wall's best judge of character, and placed in charge of the evaluation of new recruits, believes cleaning the armory is "all [Jon is] good for," that he and Sam are "boys still."

From our point of view, we understand that Jon Snow is a man, that he is being prevented from exercising the full range of his capabilities due to his own anger and bitterness, but also due to the short-sightedness of men like Ser Alliser Thorne. But we also begin to see that Ser Alliser is not singling out Sam and Jon. He treats every recruit with contempt. It is unlikely that his attitude has only recently become embittered. More likely, Ser Alliser has been denigrating and belittling every recruit who ever had the misfortune to be sent to the Wall. There are Jon Snows all over the Wall, men who might have distinguished themselves in any number of ways, but were instead mocked, beaten, shamed, and broken into adherence to Thorne's brand of submissive mediocrity.

This is where even Ned Stark falls short, and where we must exercise discretion as holders of truths escaping even the best informed of characters. The Wall is rife with men holding inside themselves deep and untapped potential for greatness. The lesson of Gendry at the forge is not that individuals of a certain lineage are destined for depth of character and greatness of spirit. The lesson is that all people, regardless of parentage, carry within their souls the seeds of distinction that, if nurtured, may grow into mighty fortresses evincing strength of purpose and such bearing as to command armies.

Even the least capable among the dregs of humanity have value, talent, and innate worth. This is the truth of the bastards Jon Snow, Gendry Armourer, and Sam Tarly. It is the truth most forcefully articulated by yet another bastard, Tyrion Lannister.

TYRION LANNISTER

"I have a tender spot in my heart for cripples, bastards, and broken things."

I take Tyrion at his word. Finding time to design a horse saddle for a paraplegic boy was not an act that could have earned him the gratitude of House Stark—not in the current atmosphere of distrust and ill will. "Is this some kind of trick?" Robb asked. "Why do you want to help him?" Robb's first instinct is to suspect deception or conspiracy. He is certainly on solid ground in foregoing civilities and formalities in his direct relations with the Lannisters. But in this confrontation, Robb was not addressing a Lannister.

The Wounded Angel
Hugo Simberg, 1903

Something beyond the objectives of House Lannister had to be motivating Tyrion's thoughtfulness toward Bran. He knew he would receive only hostility and scorn from the teenage boy who too much enjoyed the power and privileges associated with temporary installation as Lord of Winterfell. Yet he took the time anyway to help Robb's crippled young brother, to allow a "broken thing" to "be as tall as any of them" when he's in the saddle.

Tyrion was not a Lannister when he designed the saddle for Bran. He was a bastard, the result of something we would perceive as a fault of nature, a physical brokenness beyond repair.

Tyrion was not a Lannister when he confronted Theon Greyjoy. His harsh words to Theon were not those of a man conniving to gain ascendency over House Stark through House Greyjoy. Tyrion had entirely different objectives in this interaction.

When Tyrion addressed Theon Greyjoy, he was confronting the man Tyrion might have become, a man whose physical brokenness is reflected in broken spirit and submissive will. He might have become the court jester, the irrelevant little dwarf whose only connection to society was through laughter at one who was less than a human being. He might have become the impish object of derision and contempt. Instead, Tyrion sharpened his mind like a sword to a whetstone, training himself to become master of virtually any conceivable situation.

Theon Greyjoy, in Tyrion's eyes, is the worst kind of bastard. His is a bastardy of choice. No one can force a person to surrender her dignity, to become broken in spirit. Theon Greyjoy, heir to one of the greatest houses of Westeros, relinquished his honour and the essence of his dignity not because Ned Stark demanded any such thing, but because Theon is weak when he might instead have made himself strong. As in the case of the fatherly and brotherly advice he has dispensed to Jon Snow, Tyrion here was giving Theon an important truth to think on. His biting words to Theon were no less an act of kindness than the saddle design he gave Bran.

BRAN STARK

Bran Stark is a bastard, too. He is a cripple, a broken thing, a grotesque. But Bran's story is becoming so complex as to defy summarisation in a brief essay. I will offer an in-depth treatment of Bran Stark later in this volume.

SER ALLISER THORNE

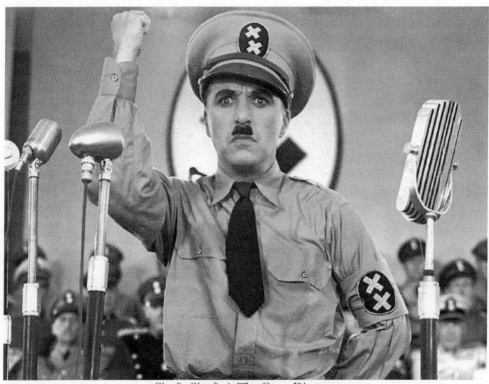

Charlie Chaplin in The Great Dictator
Unknown artist, 1940

Tyrion doesn't own the full truth of GoT. The worst kind of bastard is not the one who, like Theon Greyjoy, yields his dignity and decides to break his bonds with the rest of humanity. The worst bastards are not those who are broken inside, but rather those who train their entire energies on breaking others. People like Ser Alliser Thorne, who has single-handedly broken every man at the Wall, and Ser Gregor Clegane, who broke his own brother, Sandor ("The Hound")—for his own amusement—are the most vile of bastards. Theirs is a species of brokenness that requires dramatic intervention. A war is coming. It will make the political shenanigans in King's Landing seem as child's play in comparison. A war of bastards is coming to the Wall, and it will not be pretty. Winter is coming, they say. At the Wall, winter is already here.

Bran Stark
copyright Dalisa 2011
used with permission

"Don't look away."

Jon's advice was not necessary. Bran was as squeamish as any other ten-year-old boy. Perhaps if this were the major aspect of character at play in the boy's innocent heart he might have required his older brother's proddings just before a beheading. But something in the fifth child of Lord Eddard Stark has always needed to see things. He needs to see, not as others see, and not even as he might wish to perceive things, but he must see things as they truly are, in themselves. From even before he could walk, he yearned to see, to take in sights no one else had ever experienced.

"Don't look away."

Jon might as well have urged a raven not to give up flight, or a direwolf not to give up the excitement of the hunt. Seeing the full spectacle of life is the passion that burns inside Bran Stark, the passion that ignites Game of Thrones, the passion that animates every page of A Song of Ice and Fire. Bran has eyes that see, vision that explores and discovers. Let us, if we dare, explore the world of Westeros through the third eye of Bran Stark.

AN ARCHER'S EYE

Try as he might, Bran couldn't hit the target. His sister, Arya, even without the benefit of tutelage from older brothers, nailed the bull's eye on her first try. Bran couldn't get an arrow anywhere near the target.

Archer
Eugène Viollet-le-Duc
Dictionnaire raisonné de l'architecture française du XIe au XVIe siècle, 1856

Bran's travails on the practice range provide an important clue regarding the true nature of Bran's unique vision. We understand from context that sight is not the only aspect of experience critical to full utilisation of an archer's eye. Words of encouragement did not help. Perhaps the laughter after every one of Bran's five shots at the target was not entirely useful to the effort, either. "Which one of you was a marksman at ten?" Ned asked. But we get the distinct impression, on viewing this scene, that even the most well-intentioned encouragement could not have assisted Bran in his efforts.

Archery is not a skill brought to perfection in the mere visual identification of a target. "Relax your bow arm," Robb said. We instinctively recognise the value of Robb's advice. A good archer will coordinate every muscle in the body and every sense organ toward the goal of hitting the centre of the target. Good physical form is required for any discipline that requires a keen eye and precise orientation of muscle and bone.

Yet the degree to which Bran has tensed his bow arm is not the only indication of his lack of preparation for the release of the arrow toward its target. We see the dynamic tension in his face, the concentration in his eyes that wavers as he draws back the nocked arrow. Could it be that acuity of an entirely different type is required in this sport?

Possibly the advice he received that most accurately reflected the crux of the problem was this from his brother, Jon: "Don't think too much, Bran." If we were unacquainted with the nature of the relationships in House Stark we might be tempted to dismiss Jon's remarks as yet another attempt at polite encouragement. But we need to step back for a moment and take in the full meaning of Jon's advice, and the relational basis for his words.

FRATERNAL CONNECTION

Study the archer scene well. Consider the placement of players. Lord Stark looked on from on high. He was the High Lord of Winterfell, properly placed in a viewing stand far above everyone. Robb stood two metres away, arms folded over his chest, the very picture of the aloof heir to Winterfell, future Lord of the North.

Now consider Jon's position in this scene. He placed himself as close as he dare come to Bran without affecting the boy's physical stance. Jon was literally looking over Bran's shoulder, and at one point gently grasped both of Bran's shoulders, reminding him that "Father's watching... and your mother." Jon was physically closer to Bran, his words were gentler than Robb's, and he showed a genuine concern that was lacking in the distant attitude and body language of Robb Stark. If we interpret this scene according to the normal rubrics of cinematographic analysis, we are obliged to conclude that Jon Snow's physical proximity and gentleness of enunciation provide the visual evidence of a close emotional relationship between the two boys. The relationship between Robb and Bran, on the other hand, is more formal and distant.

Perhaps you believe I am over-reaching, bringing to the study of this scene a set of unfounded biases tangential to the true relationships within House Stark. If so, I invite you to consider the other scenes in which Bran, Robb, and Jon were present, beginning with the execution scene and the direwolf scene. In both scenes, Jon stood as close as possible to Bran. In the execution scene, Jon gently instructed Bran, "Don't look away. Father will know if you do." In the direwolf scene, Jon squatted next to Bran, and handed him the first of the direwolf pups. In both scenes, Robb stood a distant four to six metres away from his young brother. While Robb did instruct Theon to "put away your blade", his command seemed to be a misplaced assertion of authority, and not an attempt to help his brother. Certainly Theon Greyjoy interpreted Robb's instructions in precisely this manner, telling him, "I take orders from your father, not you." Consider later scenes, also, in Episodes Two and Three. In every case, Jon demonstrated emotional connection to Bran, while Robb showed emotional withdrawal or apathy.

Jon is Bran's closest brother, and in fact, he is Bran's closest friend. Now, with a better understanding of the fascinating dynamic at play in the archery scene, let's take a closer look at Jon's brief advice to his favourite brother.

VISUALISE THE TARGET

"Don't think too much, Bran."

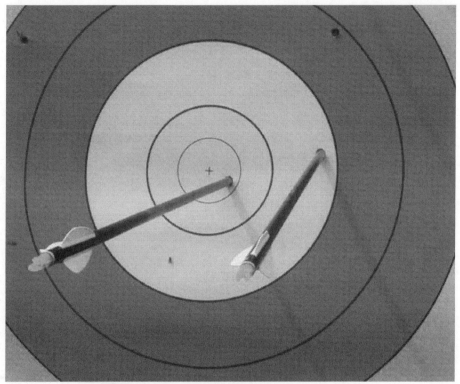

Archery Target
copyright Casito 2003, CC-SA 3.0

The advice runs contrary to everything I understand of the connection between mind and body in the optimum execution of sequential movement in sport. In my youth I pedaled some 136,000 kilometres, specialising in the century (one hundred mile race) and the double century. Even over the course of a four- or ten-hour ride I knew exactly where I had to be, the optimum body posture at every moment of the race, and the state of mind I needed to win. I visualised every single mile marker, every hill and valley and straightaway of the course. My mind was always at work, fitting my speed, cadence, gear ratio, breathing, ankling, grip on the handlebars, and every other parameter of body and machine so that I was always in peak form at every split second of the race. You might imagine my puzzlement, then, when I heard Jon utter those weird, counter-intuitive words to Bran. "Don't think too much." What could this strange advice mean?

Mental visualisation is one of the requirements of a good archer, according to Colin Wee, a top authority in archery. Wee wrote, "Visualization starts with the decision to do whatever it takes to reach your outcome. You then use tools to recreate a mental space for top performance. This helps to ground your performance to the form you have set out for yourself." It seems to me this advice could be taken to heart by just about any athlete, but it is especially important in the mentally challenging sport of archery. Tobie Hewitt wrote about visualisation in archery (http://www.tobiehewitt.com/Page_5.html):

"[A good archer] stands with the nocked arrow and bow slightly lowered, visualizing the result of his action before he lifts the bow to shoot...archery develops focus and concentration...When you are shooting bad, you can hear the flutter of a butterfly's wings. If you are shooting well, firecrackers could go off around you, and not bother you...[Good archers] shoot with the subconscious and through visualization. They visualize the arrow already hitting the target. Thoughts become things. One learns to shoot in the 'zone' a space of complete concentration and calm."

I could provide hundreds of such examples of the commonly understood need to bring complete mental immersion to the sport of archery. In my experience as a cyclist, and in the experience of every expert in archery I have ever consulted, it is simply not possible to "think too much" before executing the perfect shot or riding the perfect century. If Jon knew anything about archery, I have to believe he would have rendered quite different advice.

The problem, of course, is that Jon was a pretty good archer. He evaluated Bran's stance with a practiced eye, studying every arm and leg angle from several different viewpoints, walking a semi-circle around Bran from behind, making sure Bran was in every way perfectly aligned to deliver the best shot. How, then, could he have given advice that runs counter to everything an experienced archer would have told Bran?

DEPTH OF PERCEPTION

Jon gave his advice not as a seasoned archer, but as the person who best understood Bran's psyche. Over the first four episodes of Season One, Jon showed a deep emotional bond with Bran in every scene in which the two brothers appeared together. In fact, in each of those scenes, with only one exception (the execution scene), Jon physically touched Bran.

Physical proximity and emotional closeness must be understood as signs of a deep awareness of each other. We might easily imagine that Jon would have been able to finish Bran's sentences for him, that he would have known Bran's thoughts before he uttered words to express them.

If Jon knew Bran's thoughts, he must have been impressed by the boy's ability to express ideas in ways that resonated as no one else's ever had. Bran's thoughts ran deep. As we will see in later episodes, Jon was not the only person to recognise

Bran's abilities of perception. In fact, the depth of Bran's thought proved unnerving on more than one occasion.

The Thinker
Portrait of Ivan Ilyin, Theologian
Mikhail Nesterov, 1922

Bran thought. It was an activity entirely inconsistent with the reasonable expectation of a ten-year-old boy, but we have seen this strange ability in almost every Bran scene, and I will detail these instances as we proceed through the essay. The importance of this fact to the archery scene is that Jon was well acquainted with Bran's tendency to over-analyse things. Jon knew that Bran already had a mastery of the disciplined thought required to become an expert marksman. Other thoughts—deeper thoughts—somehow interfered with the boy's concentration. If this were not the case, and if Jon had not experienced such strange complications in the past, he would not have given Bran advice that would otherwise have been understood as running against the grain of normal learned counsel.

This state of affairs is obviously unusual in the highest degree. Bran should have been a fidgeting, undisciplined, unconfident young boy barely able to concentrate for the one or two seconds necessary to nock, draw, aim, and release an arrow. Instead, the problem weighing most heavily on Bran is a depth of thought not attained by the greatest masters of archery. In fact, as we will see in later scenes, Bran is exercising mental faculties unavailable to the most learned adults in Winterfell.

INDEPENDENT JUDGMENT

"Do you understand why I had to kill him?" Ned asked his son.

"Our way's the old way," Bran replied.

"The man who passes the sentence should swing the sword."

"Is it true he saw the White Walkers?"

"The White Walkers have been gone for thousands of years."

"So he was lying?"

"A mad man sees what he sees."

Ned's response to his son's question was curious. He didn't address his son's inquiry, but instead impugned the credibility of the ranger's testimony. From the point of view of the supreme enforcer of the law, Ned was probably forced to take such a position. The deserter was no longer a ranger, because he had broken his oath. He had to be treated as a criminal or a madman. No consideration could be given to his claim, because any such consideration would legitimise the ranger's position that he had good cause for desertion.

The clear significance of Ned's words was not legal or coercive, though. Ned didn't believe in what Tyrion Lannister later termed "grumpkins and snarks and all the other monsters your wet nurse warned you about." Ned, with Tyrion, was a "smart boy", who didn't "believe that nonsense". There were no White Walkers, and the man who said there were was insane.

This brief scene communicated well Ned Stark's blind adherence to honoured protocol and his inability to see truths beyond those that conformed to his understanding of the world. But this was not the most important fact to be gleaned from this tense interaction between father and son. There was great unspoken conflict in the moment, and it centred around Bran's reaction to his father's words. Simply put, Bran didn't believe his father.

Bran's response to Ned's statement about the White Walkers reduced the problem to its essential core: The ranger was telling the truth, or he was lying. The ranger's words could not have been true, or justice would not have been served. Since Ned was the full representation of Winterfell justice, he had to take the position that the man was lying. But he was quick to do so, without the slightest hesitation.

Bran frowned when Ned said "A mad man sees what he sees," and then he looked away, clearly not content with his father's answer. An ordinary boy, even a thoughtful young lad, would have accepted his father's words in such a matter. That Bran questioned and silently rejected his father's pronouncement is almost beyond belief. We might be willing to entertain the plausibility of such an attitude of independent thought originating in the contrary mind of a teen on the verge of adulthood. But to see a ten-year-old boy evaluate and then discard his father's words is something extraordinary. Prior to the execution scene, we had little basis to place our faith in Bran's ability to employ such depths of analysis. But subsequent scenes have rendered this interpretation of the scene entirely valid, consistent with every nuance of Bran's character.

Bran thinks. He applies a depth of discernment to his thoughts that few adults ever attain.

THROUGH A DIREWOLF'S EYES

Wolf lying
Gary Kramer, U.S. Fish & Wildlife Service, 2003

In my analysis of the direwolf scene (see "Symbolism and Allusion in the Direwolf Scene" and "The Grotesques: The Thesis of Game of Thrones") I noted my surprise that Bran's contribution to the scene had been severely abridged in the television version. GRRM brought so much depth to this scene in the first of his ASoIaF novels that it became a firm thematic foundation for the entire series. I recommend that any who are trying to follow the television series read at least these four crucial pages from the first novel, *A Game of Thrones*, because they reveal so much about the plot, character relationships, and the highly differentiated manner in which characters understand the world around them.

In the original version of the direwolf scene, Bran was by far the most observant of any of the participants. The direwolves, of course, came to have tremendous significance in their own right. Jon's observation is among the critical connections made during this brief scene: "There are five pups," he told Father. "Three male, two female...You have five trueborn children. Three sons, two daughters. The direwolf is the sigil of your House. Your children were meant to have these pups, my lord."

Jon was the one to hear the sixth pup, a snow-white runt of the litter that became Jon's. But it was left to Bran to make the most fascinating observation of the scene:

"Bran thought it curious that [Jon's] pup alone would have opened his eyes while the others were still blind."

As Jon pointed out, the correspondence of each direwolf to a specific Stark child is not coincidental. There are strong connections between the direwolves and the children they represent, as we have already seen in the first four episodes. Ghost, Jon's direwolf, in some way shows the important attributes of Jon's character. Bran's observation that Jon's wolf had opened his eyes while the other direwolves remained blind was a literary means of indicating that Jon has an ability to see not shared by others. More important, though, we take from this statement that Bran enjoys a special type of sight—a kind of "metavision", if you will—that allows him to see things as they are, and not only as a variety of limited human perception constrained by point of view. Only Bran knows that Jon sees things no one else sees. But this means Bran is aware of others in a way no one else can be. He sees in ways no one else sees, and his vision far surpasses even that of the single child (Jon) who sees better than any of the other five. It took a direwolf, and a direwolf's eyes, to enable Bran to see what he sees.

ON RAVEN'S WINGS

Go to your DVR (or Blu-Ray if you are reading this months or years after I write) and play again the scene beginning twenty-three minutes into Episode One. Listen to the majestic, soaring music as Winterfell prepares to receive its King. But take in the astounding visual display as you listen. Bran is not merely up high enough that he can see something no one else in Winterfell sees. That is true, and remarkable in itself. But the truly majestic, soaring quality of the scene is the extreme to which Bran has gone. He ascended a hundred or a hundred and twenty feet above the ground, so high that no one could even dream of following him to such rare heights.

You thought that majestic music signalled the arrival of King Robert Baratheon. You were wrong. That music heralded the fact that in our presence was one who soared with ravens. That music was for Bran.

"Bran," Robb said, "I've seen you climb a thousand times. In the wind, in the rain, a thousand times. You never fall."

Bran climbs. Everyone in House Stark knows of his rare ability to climb to heights unequalled. More than once his mother has pleaded with him to stop such dangerous activity, but she has conceded to her son this pursuit.

"I want you to promise me: No more climbing."

[Bran looked at his feet] "I promise," he said, with solemn expression.

"Do you know what?"

"What?"

"You always look at your feet before you lie."

[Bran laughed, Catelyn smiled.]

Illustration #21 from The Raven
Gustave Doré, 1884

Everyone knew Bran climbed, and Catelyn, though she would deny it, somewhere deep inside her worrying mother's heart, allowed him to do it. Why did she smile? Why did she tell Bran, in effect, it was acceptable for him to tell a lie—that his climbing could continue?

Every parent must confront difficult choices as a child grows. The inherent danger of an activity must be weighed against the activity's potential for contributing to the emotional and spiritual growth of the child. As much as most parents would prefer an environment entirely free of risks to life and limb, eventually every parent makes concessions to a child's need to grow into independent adulthood. For those parents more reluctant than average to permit inherently risky activities, nature builds in a second set of considerations to pull at a parent's desire to exploit every possible venue of a child's growth.

If a child demonstrates a special talent or an emotional affinity for a pursuit, even if the skill requires considerable risk, the parent is likely to approve. In Bran's case, the affinity he felt for climbing was so great that even the exceptionally guarded and hesitant Catelyn Tully was moved to allow Bran room to exercise his unusual desire to ascend the highest walls of the ancient castle.

Climbing was integral to Bran's spirit. If he had been denied the ability to climb, he could not have become the person he was. Reading between the lines, we come to an important realisation: Bran's vision and his climbing were the same. Climbing was the physical expression of his inner vision, and eyesight was the visual expression of his inner ability. He wished to see, and he wished to climb, in ways that moved far beyond the normal ranges of a child's desires. These were not childish wishes at all, in fact. They were the full expression of an inner disposition that was so attuned to something normally outside the purview of human understanding that the urge became unstoppable. Bran's vision and his climbing were the expression of who Bran was. Somehow, Catelyn's intuition told her that Bran could not be Bran if he did not ascend the heights of Winterfell.

THE FALL

Robb noted his incredulity at Bran's fall. No one as capable as Bran could possibly have fallen. In fact, if not for Jaime Lannister's push, Bran could never have lost his footing. Robb was correct in his assessment.

Robb's disbelief was instructive. But in order to gain the full benefit of Robb's unsettled mind, we need to look at the question of Bran's fall from more than the factual, causally necessary strictures of logic and common sense.

"You still don't remember anything?" Robb asked.

[Bran shook his head]

"Bran, I've seen you climb a thousand times. In the wind, in the rain, a thousand times. You never fall."

"I did, though."

Notice Bran acknowledged the fact of his fall only because others told him of it; he didn't remember falling. He fell, and that's how he ended up in bed unable to move or feel his legs. Or so he's been told. As I noted in my essay on Episode 1.03:

"He doesn't remember, he says. Bran, he of sight beyond sight, knowledge beyond the constraints of logic and science, says he does not remember anything about the fall.

"Now here's the most chilling idea of all from this most chilling of scenes. Bran sees everything, but he did not see his fall. We saw his fall, but we know we see far less than Bran sees. The question, as you have probably by now guessed, is very simple: Did Bran really fall?"

I do not pose the question rhetorically, and I am not seeking metaphor. In Bran, GRRM is forcing us to confront the idea of an existence that transcends the shackles of the five senses, but not in any crude invocation of the paranormal. If Bran had a type of vision unavailable to almost everyone else, could it not also be the case that he had a means of walking that transcends the five senses?

Free Climb
Dreamstime Stock Photo 2012

I have said already that, for Bran, seeing and climbing were intimately and inextricably connected. In fact, for Bran, climbing and seeing are seemingly distinct ways of articulating a single truth. That is, climbing and seeing are a single action. Bran climbed "a thousand times. In the wind, in the rain, a thousand times." His need to climb was so indelibly stamped into his spirit that even his overly protective mother was forced to relent, allowing him to indulge his passion virtually without

114

limits. For Bran, seeing and climbing are the same—they are a single activity, with the same objective, the same means, and the same outcome. He climbs things no one else can. He sees things no one else can.

We know with certainty Bran's metavision was not adversely affected by any of the events leading to his current state—whatever that state is. In fact, based on recent revelations through dreams, there seems to be a basis for believing that his sight was actually enhanced. If it is true that climbing and seeing are the same activity expressed in different ways, could it not be the case that his ability to climb was likewise enhanced by the sequence of events leading to his current state?

Bran's metavision was a more important and useful function than ordinary human sight. If Bran had lost the use of his eyes, it seems more than likely that his ability to perceive things as they are would have remained unaffected. In the same way, even though Bran lost the use of his physical legs, the intimate connection between seeing and climbing indicates strongly that he has always had "meta-legs", and these should also remain unaffected by the state of his physical legs.

Notice I am taking pains to avoid any discussion of the "events leading to his current state." I cannot say anymore that Bran fell. If his ability to see and his ability to climb were unaffected, or even enhanced, does it make sense to say the fall somehow induced the amplification of these abilities? A fall does not lead to enhanced capabilities. I am obliged to point to some cause other than falling as the origin of Bran's rare skills.

DEATH OF A DIREWOLF

Ned Stark slit Lady's throat somewhere near the Trident, hundreds of miles south of Winterfell. In that very instant, Bran woke from his coma in his bed in Winterfell. He was immediately alert, aware of his surroundings, aware of who he was and where he was.

Lady and Bran shared a connection. The connection was not diminished by distance. We know the connection was strong because Lady's death resulted in a dramatic and sudden change in Bran. He moved instantly from a perpetual comatose state into full consciousness with the stroke of his father's knife.

This was not the Lion King's circle of life. This was no Boone-Carlyle-in-exchange-for-Aaron-Littleton *quid pro quo*. The knife that severed Lady's throat was an assault on the soul of Bran Stark, and he felt the pain of it to such a degree that he was shocked out of his coma and into conscious awareness. The connection between boy and wolf was not circular, but continuous or parallel. One did not begin where the other ended, but rather they both somehow existed together.

WINTER IS COMING

For those who cannot see and climb, we have the accounts of those who can. Those who scale the heights sometimes bring back a record of their visions. We call these accounts by another name, though: We call them stories.

"My favourites were the scary ones," Bran said.

"Oh, my sweet summer child," Old Nan said, "what do you know about fear? Fear is for the winter, when the snows fall a hundred feet deep. Fear is for the long night, when the sun hides for years, and children are born and live and die, all in darkness. That is the time for fear, my little Lord, when the White Walkers move through the woods. Thousands of years ago there came a night that lasted a generation. Kings froze to death in their castles, same as the shepherds in their huts, and women smothered their babies rather than see them starve, and wept, and felt the tears freeze on their cheeks. So is this the sort of story that you like?"

Big Iglu, Kinngait, Baffin Island, Canada
copyright Ansgar Walk 1999, CC-SA 3.0

[Bran nodded]

"In that darkness the White Walkers came for the first time. They swept through cities and kingdoms, riding their dead horses, hunting with their packs of pale spiders big as hounds..."

The most fascinating aspect of this exchange with Old Nan is that Bran is already connected to these most-feared elements of ancient northern stories. Bran knows the White Walkers.

I cannot tell you exactly what he has seen. But then, neither could Bran relay to us the visions he has had. The important idea is that Bran knows the truth of the White Walkers existence—he feels it deep inside. His first-hand knowledge of the North ought to prove beneficial at some point in the future. Certainly the men of the Night's Watch could derive great benefit from the assistance of someone like Bran.

The truths of the North shared a common currency among learned adults. We learned from Ned Stark that "The White Walkers have been gone for thousands of years." From Tyrion Lannister we learned there was nothing to fear in the North. There were no "grumkins and snarks and all the other monsters your wet nurse warned you about." All of it was "nonsense". Anyone who believed in such things had to be crazy. As Ned told Bran, "A mad man sees what he sees." From Robb, staring at a freshly-killed direwolf, we learned "There are no direwolves south of the Wall."

We know direwolves have crossed south of the Wall—at least seven of them, in fact, and probably many more we have not yet seen. We also know the White Walkers were no figment of anyone's imagination, and they were not far from the Wall at the time this story began.

Bran's awareness is connected to the North because he is connected to one or more of the ancient creatures who have been there. He is connected to the ancient past, because the direwolves are so connected. In some way we have not yet fathomed, Old Nan's stories are *Bran's* stories.

FIVE LAYERS

Game of Thrones is a rich story with roots extending back thousands of years. We hear frequent references to ancient events, old religions, the three-hundred-year reign of House Targaryen, and the usurpation some seventeen years ago that elevated Robert Baratheon to the Iron Throne. We know of at least four periods in the backstory of this mythical world. As we peel back the layers, we come closer to the truths that are gathered in the person of Bran Stark.

THE FALL OF THE HOUSE OF DRAGONS

About 17 years ago

House Targaryen occupied the Iron Throne until sixteen or seventeen years ago. Two major houses assisted House Baratheon in the Sack of King's Landing: House Lannister and House Stark. Jaime Lannister, sworn protector of King Aerys ("The Mad King"), thrust his sword into the king's back, while Stark and Lannister forces killed or neutralised the remaining Targaryens and their loyal bannermen. House Stark is probably the most favoured house after House Lannister, and the patriarch of House Stark, Eddard, was raised to the most important position in the realm, the Hand of the King. Bran is second in line of succession to the Seat of Winterfell, after his older brother, Robb.

AEGON'S LANDING

About 300 years ago

Aegon I, called Aegon the Conqueror, took King's Landing, unified the Seven Kingdoms under the Iron Throne, and built the Red Keep, which remains the seat of power in the Seven Kingdoms.

THE SEVEN GODS

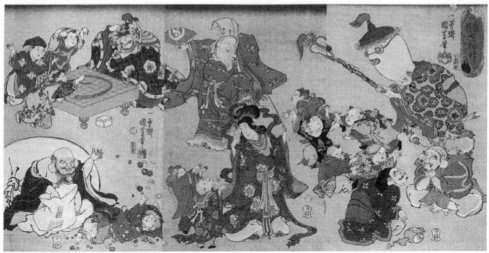

The Seven Gods of Good Fortune
Utagawa Kuniyoshi, circa 1850

About 6000 years ago

The Seven Gods replaced the Old Gods at some point thousands of years ago. The Seven have become the primary gods across most of Westeros, though many old believers remain in the North. Catelyn, originally of House Tully, follows the new religion of the Seven Gods. She was uncomfortable approaching Ned in the godswood, the abode of the Old Gods, and the place Ned preferred to worship in simple prayer.

The worship of the Seven Gods is highly ritualised, and adherents are required to follow complicated rules. It is important to note that the religion of the Seven Gods began south of Winterfell, and that the Old Gods held sway in the North far longer than anywhere else in Westeros.

THE OLD GODS

Eight thousand to twelve thousand years ago

The Old Gods were the only deities worshipped eight to ten thousand years ago. They were worshipped in forests called "godswoods", and their power seemed to be most keenly felt under the shade of the weirwood trees that were once common in Westeros.

Few in Westeros remain true to the Old Gods. The religion of the Seven has apparently all but taken over the south, and most of the remaining adherents of the ancient faith appear to be concentrated in the North. Even in Winterfell, the followers of the Old Gods appear to be few in number. When Catelyn approached Ned at the weirwood, he was alone in the godswood.

The Old Gods did not have rituals or rules. The faith of believers was simple. If we take the Episode One meeting at the weirwood at face value, something as simple as oiling a greatsword might properly be understood as an act of worship in this ancient form of religion.

The context of the religion of the Old Gods, as we have so far seen, seems to focus on a connection between humans and nature. The weirwood is the centre of attention of this religion, and seems to be the portal through which adherents communicate with the ancient gods. The weirwood is always found in the midst of a godswood, indicating the forest itself has an importance to the Old Gods.

Several events appear to have been contemporaneous with the decline of the Old Gods' influence. The Starks began manning the Wall eight thousand years ago, for instance. In fact, based on the Starks' position at the largest outpost in close proximity to the Wall, it seems likely that the Wall itself was not engineered until about that time, probably in response to the generation-long night of the White Walkers (the Others) that Old Nan referenced in her story to Bran.

It is tempting to tie together the disappearance of the Old Gods, the ride of the White Walkers, and the appearance of the Seven Gods into some type of causal relationship. I believe we need to resist that temptation for now. After just four episodes, we simply lack a reliable backstory to plot at this level of detail.

CHILDREN OF THE FOREST

I provide in this section a bit of material from the novels. Most of this is covered in the first novel of the series, *A Game of Thrones*, in the later Bran chapters. This information could be considered a "spoiler" to those who have not read the novels or seen the later episodes in Season One. However, since there has been no resolution to the Children of the Forest sub-plot, even after four novels, I don't see any reason that this information cannot be freely shared, particularly since it ought to provide useful insight into Bran's character. I intend to use this material to support certain conclusions about Bran that will not be found in the novels.

According to the Wiki of Ice and Fire, the Children of the Forest populated Westeros eight to twelve thousand years ago:

"Approximately 12,000 years before Aegon's Landing, the children ruled the entire continent of Westeros, worshiping nameless nature spirits that were later called the Old Gods... The children of the forest taught the worship of the Old Gods to the First Men, but this was largely supplanted in the South by the Faith of the Seven... Relations between the children and humans grew distant over the years, until they ceased altogether. By the time of Aegon's Landing, humans had not seen the children for thousands of years."

Near the end of *A Game of Thrones* (Chapter 66), Bran said:

"Old Nan says the children knew the songs of the trees, that they could fly like birds and swim like fish and talk to the animals."

The children's abilities seem to have been in line with our understanding of the Old Gods as providing a strong connection between nature and people. But Bran's words bring a new sort of connection, one shared between Old Nan's stories and

Bran's vivid dreams. Does Bran himself "fly like birds" and "talk to the animals"? We have ample reason to believe he is doing just that.

Merry Elves Leaping in a Ring
Florence Harrison, circa 1915

BOY'S BEST FRIEND

Summer, Bran's direwolf, has a connection to the boy we see with our own eyes, but largely take for granted.

Summer's protection of Bran and Catelyn, even to death, was exemplary of the human/dog bond that we assume as normal. But the social and psychological closeness between human and dog is unique to our world, and appears to be a feature shared with the world of Westeros. We know the bond between Bran and Lady was stronger than any such human/dog bond; it seems entirely likely that the bond between Bran and Summer is likewise stronger than anything science can understand.

My Best Friend
John George Brown, 1903

THE THIRD EYE

He had just drawn back the bow string when the raven flew in. In the fourth episode we finally had a glimpse of what Bran was seeing, and came to understand a bit better why he had such difficulty on the archery range in the first episode.

He followed the bird into a room bathed in the unearthly glow of torches. He would have needed no torches on such a bright day, but these were no ordinary torches, and in any case, he was not seeing with his two eyes. As the raven turned toward him, he saw with the full power of his inner vision the full truth of the raven. This raven saw the world, too, as it is, and not as anyone might like it to be.

"The little lord's been dreaming again," Old Nan said.

If only it were so simple. These were no dreams. These were powerful glimpses into reality. He sees them at rest, when his mind is at ease, when he has given up every bit of the complications and pretentions of his world. It is when he is relaxed and open to the simplicity of vision through the third eye that he sees and understands all.

Bran's third eye is going to become critical to this song of ice and fire. With his extraordinary vision, he peers into the past, sees the grand truths in Nan's stories, reconciles the savagery north of the Wall with the civility south of the Wall, unites the simple dignity of the North with the complex inhumanity of the South. Through Bran's three eyes, we will come to see the game of thrones as it is, and not as the Lannisters or the Baratheons or the Arryns might like to believe it is.

He is a child. He is the antithesis of Ser Waymar Royce, who said with unwitting prescience, "It's a good thing we're not children." The Children of the Forest, like the White Walkers, like the direwolves, have not been seen in thousands of years. But we have seen the White Walkers with our own eyes. The direwolves, too, have returned to House Stark. Could it be that the Children of the Forest have also returned? Could it be that one of the Children, who flies like a bird and speaks with the animals, has been born in time for the second great winter in eight thousand years?

THE OLD WAYS

As I noted in my discussion of the thesis of Game of Thrones, George Martin appears to prefer the old ways over the new:

"We already have a feeling that the older ways and the symmetries of quiet contemplation and listening are desirable attributes in GRRM's world. When we tie these virtues to the significance of ancient trees growing in ancient forests and their increasing importance as we travel north, we begin to see a gradation of virtue tied intimately to gradients of latitude and time. The older ways are preferred over the newer ways. Northern ways are preferred to southern ways. Simple and quiet ways are preferred to complex and noisy ways. Natural is given preference over artificial. Connection with place is preferred over connection with ritual."

The Old Ways

Virtue	Vice
Old	New
North	South
Forest	City
Simplicity	Complexity
Quiet	Noise
Natural	Artificial
Inner sight	Inner blindness
Inner hearing	Inner deafness
Connection	Disconnection

The children, the bastards, and the grotesques in this game of thrones are the ones who understand the forest, the simplicity in themselves, the quiet and natural beauty of the world. They are the ones who possess the inner sight, the inner hearing, and the connection to each other and to the world of ravens and direwolves and dragons and the weirwood trees in the godswood. It is not the kings and queens and usurpers and pretenders to the throne who will win the day when winter comes. Winter will belong to those who understand the real threats to the throne, who can hear it in the trees and see it in wind and snow.

It seems to me not at all unlikely that a child will lead them. A child will lead all of them. Whether the child is a crippled boy who soars with ravens, a slave girl who becomes a queen among horse lords and dragons, a bastard who commands the strength and respect of armies, or a learned dwarf who manages to overcome his peculiar lack of education and knowledge, a child will lead them all.

Someone will have to wield a sword of ice, or possibly obsidian, perhaps to put down a sword of fire, or the flaming breath of dragons. I doubt Jaime Lannister or Renly Baratheon would know where to locate such weapons. But even if they did have such rare knowledge, would they know how to wield such frightful machines? Would they have the presence of mind to summon the strength that comes from deep connection to the forests, the direwolves, and the ravens? In their prideful ignorance they will dismiss the Children, or the White Walkers, or the old ways.

A war is coming, of such darkness and terror as Westeros has not seen in millennia. Every weapon of war will be marshalled to oppose determined and ruthless enemies. Every advantage will be required. The greatest advantage is knowing the enemy, and to know the enemy, one must be able to see.

A war is coming, and when it arrives, House Stark will possess a rare and unequalled weapon. Soaring above the ramparts and turrets, above the hills and the highest clouds, is a raven who sees all, not things the enemy would have him see, but things in their completeness, things as they are. For everything in the Seven Kingdoms, everything visible to Children and direwolves and ravens, will fall under the quiet and steady gaze of the third eye of Brandon Stark.

Jon Snow
copyright Dalisa 2011
used with permission

With the training and tenacity of a tireless knight, the brilliant insight of a maester, and a passion without parallel in the north, Jon Snow has but one destiny, apparent to everyone but him. Such a one as this, who cannot lose a battle, who has greater physical and tactical skill than anyone, must have something within him possessed by few in this world. Indeed, the reward for such accomplishment must consist in a destiny only the rarest of men are privileged to experience: An early, painful, and entirely bewildering death at the hands of those who hate him. Jon

Snow is not only a bastard by blood, he is a bastard in every hateful sense of that word.

Nine concentric circles engulf Jon Snow. His odds of survival are among the worst in this dark story. If he wishes to prevail against the slings and arrows and buffets and spits he will need to rise above his own insensitivities and arrogance. He will require vision enough to understand that in the game of thrones, there are no consolation prizes: You win, or you die. Jon Snow is not winning. He is surrounded by nine concentric circles, torments of his own creation.

THE NINTH CIRCLE: BROTHERHOOD

The Ninth Circle
Francesco Bertolini, L'Inferno, *1911*

Even a cheerless, brooding, young man like Jon Snow has happy moments. The evening before the King's arrival, he and his brother Robb and their companion, Theon Greyjoy, have their dark tresses shorn to look their best for the royal visitors. We see no animosity between these three boys, only a playful competition and jokes about gaining the Queen's attention. Robb instructs the barber to "shear 'im good" when Jon's turn arrives. "He's never met a girl he likes better than his own hair."

Jon shows a thoughtful affection for his brothers. When Bran pleads with his father to spare the lives of the direwolf pups, it is Jon who scrambles to think of a reason to keep the young wolves. The context of the event seems to indicate that

Jon would never have made the connection between the five direwolf pups and the five Stark children if not for Bran's strong desire to prevent their deaths at Theon's knife blade.

Jon has a better sense of his brothers' and sisters' dreams and desires than even their own parents. When Ned wishes to make Sansa feel welcome in their new residence inside the Red Keep of King's Landing, he gives her a doll. It is quite possibly the worst present he could have presented to a thirteen-year-old who thinks of herself as the future queen of the realm. "I haven't played with dolls since I was eight," she says in disgust. But when Jon prepares a special keepsake for his favourite sister, Arya, it is the best gift anyone could ever present her, for Needle is the expression of everything she is, and everything she wishes to become.

Jon's relationship with his father is distant, but he is close enough to Robb that they embrace as brothers before Jon's departure for the Wall. But there are signs of formality, of a separation that cannot be bridged, even by good will. When Robb asks about his mother's treatment of Jon, he responds "She was very kind." That her only words to him were "Just Leave Now," was not a truth Jon could ever share with his brother.

I find it difficult to imagine Jon being constrained in such a way with his soul-sister, Arya. If she had asked about her mother's comportment, I don't believe Jon would have responded by saying "She was very kind." At worst, he would have pointed out that Catelyn was consumed by fears over Bran's health. They are so close, I imagine he has already had several heart-to-heart talks with her about his predicament, and hers. Both Jon and Arya have had to give up much of who they are because of the expectations of society.

If Arya is Jon's closest sister, and closest female friend, there is yet one person for whom Jon feels greatest affection and closest attachment. Jon feels hemmed in on all sides. His own father treats him not as a son, but as a distant and unwanted relative. Jon is obliged to forego even the most formal acknowledgement of connection to his own father, forced by protocol to address him as "Lord Stark", while the five other children simply call him "Father". Jon feels himself a prisoner in a jail created by Catelyn and all of Westeros society.

Jon's deepest affections are reserved for the one who, in his experience, shows the kind of freedom he wishes he could enjoy. Bran Stark climbs the highest heights of Winterfell—to the rarefied sanctity of wind and air—where only ravens and eagles fly. He climbs without fear, without constraint. Even Catelyn knows Bran lies when he says he will never climb again. Bran cannot not climb. One might as well tell the raven not to fly, the direwolf not to hunt, the eagle not to see.

In brotherhood there is freedom to be oneself, to share in common amusements, to feel nurture in the common bonds of family. As much as Jon yearns for the freedom Bran finds skipping along the highest stones of Winterfell, there can be no brotherhood for Jon Snow. He is not Bran's brother, but his half-brother, and nothing he or Bran or anyone else says or does can change this fact. There will always be distance between Jon and Robb, even if social constraints magically disappear. As much as he loves Arya, he will never be able to claim her as sister.

"You don't know what you're giving up," Benjen tells Jon when he implores his uncle to take him to the Wall. But Jon does know. He knows exactly what he is giving up. Through Bran and Arya he has felt the vicarious excitement of unbounded expression, the lightness of spirit that only larks and eagles know. It is an excitement he will never enjoy in his own life.

THE EIGHTH CIRCLE: BASTARDY

With single sword, without shield, he can take on three determined men and vanquish them, slicing, kicking, and punching them into submissive defeat. He is skilled with sword and bow, well versed in the manly arts, more gifted than anyone his age. But he will never have the opportunity to apply those rare skills, for Jon Snow is a bastard.

While he was raised amongst the Stark children, he was never treated as one of them. In fact, the young ward, Theon Greyjoy, who is essentially a high-born prisoner of House Stark, is nevertheless shown the kind of deference that is the normal expectation of the heir to a mighty house. That a prisoner is extended courtesies and accorded a level of respect Jon has never known can only serve as bitter salt to unhealed and hurtful wounds.

He has no claim to titles, land, or any aspect of inheritance accruing from proper lineage. He cannot even acknowledge his father as such, but must address him and refer to him as "Lord Stark". Lady Stark wants him as far away as possible, and would shed no tears at any misfortune that might befall him.

"Seventeen years ago," Catelyn told Ned, "you rode off with Robert Baratheon. You came back a year later with another woman's son."

In what way does Jon's standing as brother to the five Stark children serve him or his desire to make something of himself? We may speak of Jon's brotherly ties, but he is not more than half-brother to any of Ned Stark's children. In fact, would it not be closer to the truth for us to speak of Jon as being a half-person? Even if a person possesses rare capabilities, can his talents bring benefit to anyone if society rejects the bearer of unusual skill? Jon's familial relationships are just another source of spiritual torture and embitterment.

In a truly just world, a father's sins would not be paid with a son's eternal penance, but unjust suffering in satisfaction of social expectation has been the sad story of Jon Snow's painful existence. Jon's situation is all the more skewed in warped injustice for his innate talents and abilities. Jon Snow could have become by now a prominent leader of warriors. Instead, he languishes at the Wall, and the highlight of each day consists in accepting whatever torments and degradations Ser Alliser Thorne deigns to hurl at him.

Can we fault Jon, in light of so many injustices piled one on top of another, for railing against the world? He is better than everyone around him, but he will never be given the opportunity to demonstrate superior abilities and intrinsic talents. Everything he is and could have been destined to become will be wasted as the laughing stock and object of derision of a sadistic and frustrated master of arms in a far-off corner of the world forsaken and forgotten by all. His lot is by far the most difficult of any in Westeros.

THE SEVENTH CIRCLE: HOUSE STARK

The Barque of Dante (Dante and Virgil in Hell)
Eugène Delacroix, 1822

"You are a Stark. You may not have my name, but you have my blood."

Ned Stark would not have taken the time to say this to the boy he loved unless he meant it. For years he had been obliged to remain silent in his affections for his bastard son, but now, with his son about to commit his life to the Night's Watch, he communicates an essential truth to this most capable of his children.

Blood is thicker than water, they say. Familial ties endure all things, even the socially inconvenient fact of bastardy. Regardless of anyone's feelings on the matter, Ned Stark is Jon Snow's father, and he supports his son with affection and with the full respect anyone bearing the name Stark is due.

Ned is telling his son that even in his status as bastard there is a firm basis for carrying himself with dignity. Jon is pursuing a vocation that has long been the special province of House Stark. "There's great honour serving in the Night's Watch. Starks have manned the walls for thousands of years. And you are a Stark." Looking on at his brother, Benjen, Ned brings profound significance to his parting words. Ned is comparing Jon with Benjen, one of the most accomplished first rangers at the Wall. By association, he is placing Jon as equal to himself and all the honourable men of House Stark.

Ned is also telling Jon that his standing as son is not affected by the fact he was not born of Catelyn Tully. "You're always welcome at the Wall," Benjen said.

"No bastard was ever refused a seat there." Ned knows that at the Wall there are no class divisions. A man can become whatever he wishes to be. Every report Ned ever received from First Ranger Benjen Stark spoke of the honour and selfless dedication of the strong and determined young men who wore the Black. Looking on at his own brother, whose every action at the Wall has brought honour to House Stark, Ned must have felt a deep sense of pride in his son's choice of vocation.

THE SIXTH CIRCLE: LORDSHIP

"Ah, rapers," Tyrion said, eyeing the prisoners Benjen brought to their camp. "They were given a choice, no doubt: Castration or the Wall. Most choose the knife."

Jon looked on in silent contempt.

"Not impressed by your new brothers?" Tyrion asked. "Lovely thing about the Watch. You discard your old family and get a whole new one."

Perhaps Jon continued to hold fast to the illusion that the Night's Watch was an elite force comprising the strongest and the brightest from among the Seven Kingdoms, but it could not have taken long for him to recognise the truth. The Wall was the least desirable outpost in the world. Even criminals usually preferred the most severe punishment to a sentence of banishment to the furthest outpost of civilisation for a lifetime of enforced celibacy. The most capable among this ragged band of social rejects were the murderers and thieves. The others were so devoid of even minimal skill that they seemed beyond reach of even the most pessimistic assessment of force strength.

"Everybody knew what this place was, but no one told me. No one but you," Jon said to Tyrion. "My father knew. And he left me to rot at the Wall, all the same."

"Grenn's father left him, too," Tyrion said. "outside a farmhouse, when he was three. Pip was caught stealing a wheel of cheese. His little sister hadn't eaten in three days. He was given a choice: His right hand or the Wall. I've been asking the Lord Commander about them. Fascinating stories."

"They hate me because I'm better than they are."

Everything about the Wall seemed geared to make life as difficult as possible for Jon Snow. Ser Alliser called him "Lord Snow", because it was the one title a bastard could certainly never have, and therefore made the perfect appellative for insults, jabs, and slurs. If Jon was not murdered by his colleagues, he knew he stood no chance of advancing in the Night's Watch—not with vicious and cruel men like Ser Alliser Thorne in charge.

Jon enjoyed no standing as a Stark. If he bore his uncle's great name, he must have believed he would have been treated differently. Even at the Wall, the only thing that mattered was that he was a worthless bastard. No amount of talent, even if it was greater than the skill possessed by anyone else, would ever allow him to overcome the unjust restrictions society had placed on him.

Life is not fair for Jon Snow.

THE FIFTH CIRCLE: THE GROTESQUERY

Eight-Legged Kitten
The Bramber Museum, circa 1900

There must be some cathartic assurance in thinking oneself unique to the world, even if that uniqueness seems to have accomplished nothing more than focussing the worst imaginable injustices to a single point of perpetual torment. But uniqueness is a point of view.

"Let me give you some advice, bastard," Tyrion said. "Never forget what you are. The rest of the world will not. Wear it like armour, and it can never be used to hurt you."

Jon bristled at the dwarf's presumption. "What the hell do you know about being a bastard?"

"All dwarves are bastards in their father's eyes."

Those who think themselves unique will never have eyes to see the suffering of others, will never understand themselves to be the cause of that suffering. Jon Snow is fortunate to have been given a glimpse into the grotesquery of Westeros, where he spies the dwarf, Tyrion, the cripple, Bran, and the tomboy, Arya. Their designs are unique, too, and will never conform to the patterns society creates for them.

But in the grotesquery their uniquenesses are commonplace. Arya and Bran are bastards as much as Tyrion and Jon. Every one of them has deficits of character and defects of physique considered unforgivable by society. They are to be shunned, mocked, held in contempt. They are to be denied honour, respect, inheritance, social standing. Jon discovered he is not unique; the grotesquery is filled with people of every dimension and background. Anyone who falls short of social expectation is granted admittance.

Tyrion's primary vocation seems to be designated face slapper. He slapped his nephew, Prince Joffrey, three times. He has figuratively slapped everyone with whom he speaks, and Jon more than any other. But then, Jon needs those slaps in the face more than anyone else. He has been pitying himself far too long, coming to be so infatuated with the myth of his suffering that he is unable to learn. But Tyrion's hard slaps to Jon's puffed-up pride accomplished their primary objective. Jon Snow is ready to move into the fourth circle.

THE FOURTH CIRCLE: THE CLASSROOM

By acknowledging the fact that he is not unique in Westeros, in understanding his membership in the grotesquery, Jon is ready to accept his status as student. "Life is full of possibilities," Tyrion says, and it is in Jon's new classroom, on the Wall, that he is to receive the lessons with greatest bearing on his future.

The curriculum is tailored to him, with precisely those lessons he needs to advance to the next circle. If the courses are made for him, however, no provision has been made for his emotional sensibilities, and he has not been given discretion regarding the time and manner of instruction. He has to absorb the course material in whatever format it is presented.

The first lesson is simple, but possibly the most difficult to absorb: Jon Snow has lived a rare life of exceptional privilege. Tyrion pointed out that every one of Jon's colleagues in the Brotherhood of the Night's Watch has been given a far more wretched life than his. For instance, Grenn's father abandoned him at his third name day, and Pip's family was so poor he had to steal just to feed his younger sister. Jon has been so pampered in his life within the walls of Winterfell he has never had to worry about survival. He experienced the advantages of any son of a lord.

"It's a lucky thing none of them were trained by a Master at Arms like your Ser Rodrik," Tyrion said with unusual restraint. "I don't imagine that any of them have held a real sword before they came here."

Tyrion was attempting to instill a second lesson, in response to Jon's insistence that he was "better than they are." The only reason Jon is "better" with sword and bow is because of long training at Ser Rodrik's hands. The lesson didn't seem to take hold, and Jon would require a repeat lesson, this time with a more forceful professor.

"I'm ready," Jon said. "I won't let you down."

"You're not going," Benjen said. "You're no ranger, Jon."

"But I'm better than every other—"

"Better than no one!... Here, a man gets what he earns."

No man at the Wall is "better" than another. Benjen did not become First Ranger because he is the younger brother of Lord Stark. He earned the position by applying the hard lessons learned at the Wall, by serving as example to those less diligent, and by teaching and tutoring. Hardships are not meted out as punitive obstacles to the worthy. Everyone at the Wall shares in hardship, and everyone has hard lessons to learn. Leaders are those who, in the midst of their ongoing lessons, somehow manage to provide consistent example and also help others along. There are no shortcuts to becoming a teacher.

It is in this circle that Jon is expected to put together all the other lessons of life. He is a bastard, but his status as brother to Robb, Sansa, Arya, Bran, and Rickon is no less important, nor does his standing as primary recipient of Ser Alliser's ridicule in any way affect the truth that he is a descendent of House Stark.

A crucial lesson in this circle is the truth that being a bastard can become not a badge of shame, but a badge of honour, and a springboard to new levels of understanding and accomplishment. This is an idea that merits broad exploration, and I have taken on the assignment of fleshing out the important nuances of the concept in the essay on Tyrion Lannister. For now, it is sufficient to note that everything in Jon Snow's background can be construed in quite different ways, depending on point of view. If Jon thinks on his life in positive and productive ways, he can begin to understand everything in his experience as a source of strength, not only for himself, but for others. In this way, he can begin to take on the challenges of the Third Circle, which centre on teaching.

THE THIRD CIRCLE: PROFESSORSHIP

Michael Faraday, Christmas Lecture, 1856
Alexander Blaikley, 1856

The proof of successful learning is in the teaching. Jon proved himself a resourceful and unusually motivated student. Within days of Benjen's tough words, Jon was out in the practice yard, not dealing out random blows, but teaching proper swordsmanship to the cutthroats, thieves, and rapists who were his new brothers.

"Don't stand so still," Jon says. "It's harder to hit a moving target. Except for you." He points to another of his brothers. "You move too much. I can just hold my sword out and let you do the work for me."

The professor is only as useful as the learning on which lectures are based. It is in this circle that Jon must call on every lesson he has ever received. Even the darkest of days can become the starting point for lectures that change lives. Sufferings become a distinct advantage, because they are unique to person and circumstance. Jon can tap his unique experience in teaching others how to make best use of the skills they have.

Jon: "... why is my surname 'Snow'?"
Sam: "Because you're a bastard, from the north."
Jon: "I never met my mother... So I sat there, in the brothel, as Ros took off her clothes. But I couldn't do it. 'Cause all I could think was...was if I got her pregnant...if she had a child...another bastard named Snow. It's not a good life for a child."

Few people in Westeros are capable of giving such a lesson to a new recruit. Fewer still can call upon the courage to put aside emotions and desires and basic human needs in favour of a child who will never be born. Jon is teaching at a level rarely trod by the best professors. This is so because Jon is not just teaching in this heart-to-heart talk with Samwell Tarly. He is moving beyond the realm of objective knowledge into the hard-won arena of personal experience to impart wisdom that is useful to all. He is able to do this specifically because he is a bastard.

Such teaching is no mere relaying of facts. In the deeply personal nature of this disclosure about his own past, there is a hope and expectation of something grand. Jon is not seeking tenured professorship. Nor does he seek Sam Tarly's friendship. In teaching from painful personal experience, Jon is preparing the way to the second circle, which is leadership.

THE SECOND CIRCLE: LEADERSHIP

True leadership is sought not out of desire, but out of necessity. The rigours of leadership more often than not are taken up by those most reluctant to enjoy the benefits and perquisites attached to title and position. The freedoms and privileges of leadership are transitory, but the responsibility and commitment to cause are unrelenting. Leadership is solemn dedication to a purpose greater than self.

The quality of men sent to the Wall and the weaponry at their disposal are not the only aspects of life in the Night's Watch that have suffered over the years. Leadership at the Wall is only as good as the men recruited, and Ser Alliser Thorne is a prime example of the problem that has been festering and spewing forth vile puss over many decades. Other than Lord Commander Jeor Mormont and a few old men, the Night's Watch has no true leadership, and no means of imparting knowledge and instilling discipline among the pathetic and defeated men who have taken the Black.

When Samwell Tarly appeared in their midst, the first instinct of beaten and hopeless men was to share with this grotesquely overweight, cowardly man a generous portion of derision and contempt, to prepare him for the feast of insults and beatings that will become his daily lot at Castle Black.

Jon did something that hasn't been seen on the Wall in many winters.

"Prince Pork Chop," one of the recruits said. The other recruits laughed. "Where is he?"

Jon took a seat opposite them. "He wasn't hungry."

"Impossible." The boys laughed again.

"That's enough." Jon's tone was firm. He grabbed a bowl and looked the boys in the eye. "Sam's no different from the rest of us. There's no place for him in the world, so he's come here. We're not going to hurt him in the training yard anymore. Never again, no matter what Thorne says. He's our brother now, and we're going to protect him."

Jon had been training the boys for weeks. He gained their trust and admiration, and they were willing to obey his command, even if it meant disobeying the Master of Arms. The only dissenting voice was Rast. "You *are* in love, Lord Snow. You girls can do as you please. But if Thorne puts me up against Lady Piggy, I'm going to slice me off a side of bacon."

Jon stared daggers at Rast.

The stakes were as high as they could be. Discipline, order, and leadership were not abstract concepts in this situation. If only one person disobeyed Jon, the consequences would include fracturing of the alliance he had worked so hard to attain. More important, a man's spirit and possibly his life were in the balance. No one could possibly derive any benefit from Sam's death. Alive, and in good spirits, he would eventually find a way to contribute. Even if his contribution were small, his donation of labour would nevertheless make the other men's lives easier.

A leader cannot always demonstrate by example. Sometimes the alternatives to discipline, order, and respect are too destructive of morale to allow. Sometimes threats must be employed.

The important part of the scene in which Rast faced a snarling, red-eyed direwolf is not the fact that it was the only remaining means of ensuring uniformity and obedience to Jon's will. More important than the direwolf's threat was the human reality: Every one of the fresh new recruits has lined up behind Jon.

Rast is the least of those who ought to feel discomfort at Jon's ascendency to leadership. Ser Alliser's face seethed with anger when he confronted Jon over his success in gaining control over every boy in the practice yard. But behind the raw anger in his burning eyes and clenched teeth, I thought I discerned yet a second, yet more powerful emotion. Only the Lord Commander of the Night's Watch remains to hold up the Master of Arms; he has lost the support of everyone in his charge. He has every right to be afraid.

Jon cannot usurp Ser Alliser's power, and I don't get the feeling this is his objective, in any case. It may be that leadership is Jon's highest calling. However, I feel there is adequate reason to believe Jon will eventually ascend to the highest circle.

THE FIRST CIRCLE: VISION

The Vision of St. Francis of Assisi
St. Francis Meditating with Skull
Francisco de Zurbaran, 1658

Leadership is not the great ability to which all aspire in the world of Westeros. The game of thrones is played at this second level, and the primary players believe the Iron Throne their object of greatest desire. Perhaps the crown is their primary objective, but it is not the ultimate goal of this grand multi-part harmony we know as a Song of Ice and Fire. Abilities far surpassing the quotidian capacity to sit the Iron Throne are in play. Daenerys Targaryen is drawing strength from some source that transcends anything as ordinary as the leadership of a horse lord's queen. Arya is exercising a breathtaking freedom of mind and body that begs to be explored.

136

And then there's Bran.

He sees, not through his eyes, but through some other sense we are only coming to understand through dreams and visions and tense awareness of relation and story.

Vision of things as they are is the power above all others, and this rare ability is found in greatest abundance in the brother to whom Jon is closest. Jon and Robb share capacities for leadership. Jon and Arya share natural talent with the sword. It seems to me not at all unlikely that Jon and Bran likewise share some special talent virtually unique to the two of them.

A Song of Ice and Fire is not more than two-thirds written. No one—save possibly GRRM—knows what Jon Snow and Bran Stark will accomplish. But I'm willing to guess that together they will achieve some of the greatest milestones in this song of ice and fire. I am convinced that Bran Stark is not the only person in this story with eyes to see, with vision that transcends place and time. His older brother, the bastard, will ascend the full height of the Wall. There, far above river and forest, his cheeks buffeted by the roaring gale, he will turn his eyes northward—and he will see.

Catelyn Stark
copyright Dalisa 2011
used with permission

"Family, Duty, Honour. Is that the right order?"

The question Bran Stark posed to Maester Luwin should have been on the lips of every character this evening. If even a few high-born officials of the Seven Kingdoms had given consideration to proper allegiances, the continent might have had a chance to avoid war. At least they might have taken the example of Sandor Clegane, the Hound, as a guide in their thinking: The Hound got it right, even if the glory went to an unworthy knight.

The most powerful representatives of every house showed unswerving devotion to family, duty, and honour. Even Jaime and Cersei, whose motivations are not entirely clear, demonstrated uprightness of purpose in their deeds. If only they had thought out their priorities. Family, Duty, Honour. Is that the right order?

DUTY BEFORE HONOUR

Duty Honor Country
Sargeant Dakota Meyer receiving the Congressional Medal of Honor
photograph by Sgt. Jimmy D. Shea, U.S. Marine Corps, 2011

Ser Barristan Selmy is presented to us as virtually the definition of the noble knight. His authentic and easy rapport with Ned Stark, who was his enemy in the Battle of the Trident, is offered as proof of the man's virtuous heart and desire to serve. He laboured in King Aegon's Kingsguard with fierce devotion, killing many of Robert Baratheon's knights. But the purity of the man must have been evident, even to Robert, whose ability to judge character ought to be otherwise in question. King Robert raised Ser Barristan to Lord Commander of the Kingsguard, where he serves with wisdom and distinction.

A special place must be reserved in the annals of every empire for those who surrender all to the service of king and country. Loyalty independent of ideology is a rare commodity, and it is rightly lauded. Ser Barristan serves his king without question—regardless of who that king is. But therein we see the problem. Devotion to king and commitment to duty are noble and praiseworthy virtues, but they are not the defining qualities of a leader. Duty must be informed by a sense of justice and propriety, and personal commitments must figure into any determination to serve.

Every civilisation is blessed with Ser Barristans. The desire to serve is a quality most often nurtured and celebrated. But when duty is severed of its proper ties to honour, unthinking devotion can be exploited to serve nefarious ends.

The most common defence at the Nuremberg Trials was the call to duty. Even the highest of the Third Reich's leaders were merely following orders, they told the court. If we admire Ser Barristan for his selfless devotion to the crown, we are obliged to find Goering, Goebbels, Hess, Himmler, and Bormann likewise to be honourable men worthy of our respect and adulation. Just as Hitler's lieutenants performed acts that any court would have considered illegal, so too Ser Barristan carried out the insane and illegal desires of King Aerys, even helping to arrange the unlawful executions of Lord Rickard Stark and his eldest son, Brandon.

An awareness of justice must serve as the basis for any action taken on behalf of king and country. The Nuremberg Court established that a soldier is obligated to refuse any illegal order. Nuremberg Principle IV says "The fact that a person acted pursuant to order of his Government or of a superior does not relieve him from responsibility under international law, provided a moral choice was in fact possible to him."

The debate around Principle IV makes for fascinating reading, but we need not split legal hairs to understand the basic idea. A sense of right and wrong must accompany any devotion to duty; we have been given no such moral sense in the actions of Ser Barristan.

The Seven Kingdoms are filled with women and men of virtue and commitment. Tonight's episode showed us quite convincingly that even the most deeply held virtues may be insufficient if they are not supported by a dense framework of balanced probity. Characters of deep integrity are not those who demonstrate perfect adherence to a single virtue, but rather those who cultivate a broad diversity of moral excellence. A healthy civilisation depends on the moral enlightenment and discernment of its citizens. Very little enlightenment was in evidence tonight. Westeros is soon to be at war, and it will be the direct result of a culture-wide inability to construct a secure foundation for ethical action. Worse, the assertion of uncoordinated, unshared virtues has helped foster an atmosphere of distrust, and provided corrupt but convincing justification for the deadly game of thrones now underway.

POLITICAL MARRIAGE

Family is an essential consideration in the decision making matrix of any morally balanced leader. A family is not anchored exclusively in the realm of personal discretion. As the Queen noted, the only thing holding the realm together is her marriage to Robert. The stability and strength of their marriage is the primary factor determining the health and vigour of the Seven Kingdoms.

Long ago, Robert Baratheon was a man of conviction and purpose. He was driven by many virtuous impulses, and among them was a devotion to the love of his life, Lyanna Stark, Ned's younger sister. The deep, fierce emotion in his face whenever her name is invoked is testament to the passion that was once his in all matters.

I have to wonder what the Seven Kingdoms might have been like had Lyanna evaded capture by House Targaryen. King Robert noted the sad fact that the Kingdom has become a realm of "back stabbing and scheming and ass licking and money grubbing." But all these faults are nothing more than the organisational extension of his marriage to Cersei. The Kingdom is in its sorry predicament because Robert surrendered the desire for a real family to instead build alliances within the far-flung realm. Robert's Hand, Jon Arryn, advocated a marriage with Lord Lannister's daughter because he saw a merger with the richest house in the land as a prudent alliance.

Cleopatra Before Caesar
Jean-Léon Gérôme, 1866

But Robert never loved Cersei. "Was it ever possible for us?" Cersei asked. She had loved Robert once, had loved their first child, had mourned their son's death, not only because he was her own flesh and blood, but because he was Robert's. That dark-haired infant had been her hope of a true marriage, and his death was therefore a cruel double blow. Robert confirmed her fears: They never had a chance, because Robert had never felt anything for Cersei. Seventeen years later, Lyanna remains the only woman worthy of filling his thoughts.

The result of King Robert's infatuation and his inability to care for anything of value is reflected in his court. He has no patience for financial administration, which he calls "counting coppers". He can't even be bothered to make appointments or ensure the proper defence of his own lands. Virtually every kingly duty is delegated to subordinates. His lack of emotional connection to Cersei is perfectly reflected in his complete lack of interest in the most critical aspects of government. Those parts of his life that ought to have highest priority in his thoughts and words—his wife and his realm—are demoted to a second- or third-tier indifference that has naturally led to the back stabbing and scheming and fracturing of affinities between advisors and lieutenants.

Family ties constructed for political ends are not family ties at all. Strategic alliances that subsume emotional bonds to political expediency can only serve to sever connection to the ethical foundations upon which any legitimate government is based.

NOBLE WARRIOR

Sandor Clegane, the Hound, bears the wounds of a broken family relationship. We might interpret his noble defence of Ser Loras Tyrell as the predictable result of the hatred he carries for his brother, Ser Gregor Clegane, "The Mountain That Rides". We might also find some justification in the Mountain's attack on Ser Loras, whose choice of a mare in heat was aimed at unnerving Ser Gregor's stallion. I don't believe either of these mitigating factors can survive a balanced scrutiny of this scene, however. Sandor Clegane's defence of a dishonourable knight was motivated by empathy, not by any call to retribution or revenge.

Ser Gregor had enough sense to realise his horse's behaviour was the result of Ser Loras' despicable provocation. But the knowledge unhinged him, causing him to decapitate his mount and attack the man who had defiled the tournament with his trickery. The Hound's intervention was the act of a man whose brokenness was rendered whole by the situation. It was as if the wounds of Ser Gregor's childhood attack had been inflicted specifically so that Sandor might prevent Ser Gregor from attacking other defenceless people in a similar manner.

We saw proof of the Hound's true motivation when the King commanded the men to stop. Sandor immediately fell to one knee, genuflecting to His Grace. He did this even though he knew his brother was well past the point of reason. He risked his life out of duty to his king, just as he had risked his life seconds before out of honour.

MOTHERHOOD AMOK

Mother Jeanne Nursing Her Baby
Mary Cassatt, 1908

Ah, the deranged mother. It is a common enough theme in literature, but it seems an especially potent device in television drama. Last year, out in the South Pacific, we had Claire of the Jungle and her "squirrel baby", as well as Rousseau and her traps. This year, in Westeros, we have Lysa of the Eyrie and her perpetually lactating mammaries.

Family obligations may be paramount in a well-ordered life, but if they are pursued without regard to the complex needs of family members, they become deranged. The need to nurture and protect must be weighed against a child's need to grow into autonomous strength and independent will. Lysa, with a ten-year-old leech permanently affixed to her nipple, is not raising a child so much as she is creating a symbiont.

Catelyn should have brought with her to the Eyrie not the Imp, but the autobiography of Theodore Roosevelt. Roosevelt was sickly as a child, like Lysa's son, Robert. His mother pampered him and kept him close, always concerned about his frail health. But children are more resilient than a mother can know. By the time Theodore was a teen, he was boxing and running and climbing mountains. Roosevelt's name eventually became synonymous with physical health and indomitable fortitude. In 1912, giving a campaign speech in his bid for a third term as president, he was shot in the chest at close range. The wound would have killed an ordinary man. Roosevelt staggered a bit, but he resumed the podium and continued his speech. Some accounts say he spoke for 48 minutes. Others put the time at 90 minutes. "Friends," he said, "I shall ask you to be as quiet as possible. I don't know whether you fully understand that I have just been shot; but it takes more than that to kill a Bull Moose." Doctors finally convinced him to go to hospital. The bullet was never removed.

At a time when Catelyn and the realm were in dire need of calm deliberation and well-rounded leadership, they instead were given Lysa Arryn. Gods help us all.

KNOWLEDGE WITHOUT WISDOM

Pallas Athena, Greek Goddess of Wisdom
Franz von Stuck, circa 1920

He has greater knowledge than any other character in the series. He sees things no one else can ever come to know. As you may have guessed from my 7000-word essay on Bran Stark, I am fascinated by this character. Tonight we saw an entirely new though not entirely flattering view of his inner self.

Bran: "Family, Duty, Honour."
Maester Luwin: "Those are Tully words. Your mother's. Are we playing a game?"
Bran: "Family, Duty, Honour. Is that the right order?"
Maester Luwin: "You know it is."
Bran: "Family comes first."
Maester Luwin: "Your mother had to leave Winterfell to protect the family."
Bran: "How can she **protect** the family if she's not **with** the family?"
....
Maester Luwin: "She will be home soon."
Bran: "Do you know where she is now, today?"
Maester Luwin: "No, I don't."
Bran: "Then how can you promise me she'll be home soon?"

Bran not only thinks on his own, he puts his thoughts over those of Maester Luwin, and even over his father's. We accept this; after all, Bran sees more than his father sees. But both Bran and his father lack understanding. Comprehension of a situation requires not only raw knowledge, but a cognitive basis for synthesising facts and observations into a relational context. That is, understanding must be based on wisdom. If Bran is going to contribute his unequalled knowledge of the world toward some greater objective, he is going to have to gain some appreciation of the wisdom of others, and he will need to incorporate that wisdom into his own thoughts.

"Sometimes I worry you're too smart for your own good." Maester Luwin assessed the situation well. Bran has deep knowledge, a keen analytical mind, and he is ruthlessly logical in his approach to every problem. Perhaps at some point he will realise his ability to gain knowledge is not properly his own. He is connected with the birds of the air and the wolves of the field in a way that no one else is. If ever he gains an appreciation for the debt he owes the ravens and the direwolves, perhaps he will come to realise that he is likewise dependent on others in gaining the wisdom—the ability to put knowledge into context—that no one has ever been able to create out of nothing. Bran needs context. Most of all, he needs to acquire humility. Family, Duty, Honour will have no intrinsic meaning until he finds both of these qualities within himself.

MASTERS OF THE GAME

Lord Varys and Lord Baelish, the Spider and the Littlefinger, Master of Whisperers and Master of Coin, the eunuch and the pimp. Their throne room discourse was deliciously impenetrable. A casual observer might have discerned nothing more than a negotiation over terms for a night of pleasure in Baelish's bordello. What I heard—after playing the scene a half dozen times—was the first signs of an exploration of common interests, perhaps aimed at a merged effort toward the fulfilment of those goals.

But what are those interests? Does Varys' dungeon meeting with Magister Illyrio indicate support for Daenerys Targaryen, or an exploitation of her weakness for the benefit of King Robert? Does Littlefinger's assistance in House Stark's investigation of the attempt on Bran's life indicate a hope to benefit from Stark ascendency, or is he acting entirely out of loyalty to the king? And if, as it now seems, both men are aware of the crude assassination attempt as a catalyst to war between the Starks and the Lannisters, fomented by those loyal to House Targaryen, could it be that they are already acting in concert, not to protect, but to depose the King?

Even if their motives are pure, the accretion of so many arrangements and clandestine meetings, the communication of half-truths, and the maintenance of veiled and conflicting agendas ought to be so corrupting as to overwhelm even the most honourable of intentions. Do they truly serve the King in any of these complicated and cloaked manoeuvres? Is there honour to be found in any of this?

FAMILY, DUTY, HONOUR

Ned Stark truly was the honourable fool at Small Council, risking his entire family over the life of a young woman in a far-off land who is no longer a child. There was no honour in risking his family. Before he was ever Hand of the King, he was Lord of Winterfell, and father of six. But on the field of battle, facing Jaime Lannister, he acquitted himself with the full dignity and integrity of his person. He faced an honourable opponent, who sought only to rectify the wrong House Stark had inflicted on the Queen by taking her brother hostage.

Jaime Lannister's primary intention was justice. If his goal had been retribution, he would have ensured Ned's demise. He might still have slugged the guard who had the audacity to interfere with the fight, but he would have finished Ned rather than allowing him to live. But because justice was the objective, wounding him was enough. Taking him into custody would have sufficed. In Jaime's eyes, there was no justification for holding Tyrion, as he could not possibly have made any attempt on Bran's life.

Perhaps at some point cooler heads will prevail. But with almost everyone on every side rallying to family, with no regard given to duty or honour, I am not optimistic.

Tonight's episode was the richest and most powerful display of conflict so far in this series. It made for riveting, engrossing television. I wait impatiently for the next   episode!

Cersei Lannister
copyright Dalisa 2011
used with permission

"You don't fight with honour," Lysa said.

"No," Bronn agreed. Pointing to the open moon door, he said, "He did."

Ser Vardis Egen fought with honour. Prince Viserys Targaryen wore his golden crown with honour. Theon Greyjoy urged Robb Stark to defend his house's honour. Honour was much in evidence tonight, and golden crowns were

149

plentiful. But in the end, it was the golden crown worn by a thirteen-year-old boy that mattered most—to the honour of a king, and to the honour of a Stark.

Only one crown matters, because there is but one god. Is not the one who wears the crown empowered to call upon this god? Kings rule through wealth and fear, as Viserys pointed out, and who does not fear Syrio Forell's one true god, Death?

A KING'S HONOUR

King Robert showed a side of himself we have not yet seen in the five previous episodes. He cared about his image, but more than that. "I should not have hit her. That was not... that was not kingly." Actually, it was one of the most kingly actions we have seen Robert Baratheon take in these six episodes. He finally put his wife and "those yellow-haired shits", the Lannisters, in their place. He restored Ned to his rightful place at Robert's side, as his Hand.

He had no patience for his wife, her family's shenanigans, or Catelyn Tully's unilateral move to take Tyrion. He had no interest in justice—only in stability and the maintenance of the King's Peace. "I'm the King," he said. "I get what I want." Same old Robert.

Still, he seemed a changed man in at least one respect. His ill-considered words at Small Council were taken back, and Ned was reinstated as Hand. He certainly had solid, practical reasons for wanting Ned to administer the Seven Kingdoms, but the tenor of their meeting, and Robert's words, indicated a deeper rationale. "I never loved my brothers. Sad thing for a man to admit, but it's true. You were the brother I chose." Ned is much more than the King's closest advisor; he is the King's truest friend, closer to Robert's heart than even his brothers.

Robert appealed to Ned's friendship, and his honour, and felt comfortable leaving the throne and the city to Ned while he went hunting. Ned was no longer the "honourable fool" of the last Small Council meeting. Robert respected his brother, even if they disagreed on important matters.

The respect between the two men was mutual. Ned felt no need to make ill-founded comparisons between Robert and Mad King Aerys. Hyperbole on both sides gave way to a mature recognition of the strengths and acceptance of the weaknesses of both men. With their relationship back on solid ground, prospects for the Seven Kingdoms seemed brighter than ever.

A FEAT OF EXPERT ENGINEERING

Most readers will complete *A Game of Thrones*, the book upon which Game of Thrones is based, in twenty or thirty hours; only speed readers could digest the novel in less than ten hours. HBO is tasked with the obligation of presenting the main plot points and character attributes and developments in less than ten hours. The producers cannot depict every scene of the novel, for to do so would require thirty hours or more of screen time.

COMPLETION OF THE PACIFIC RAILROAD—MEETING OF LOCOMOTIVES OF THE UNION AND CENTRAL PACIFIC LINES: THE ENGINEERS SHAKE HANDS.
[PHOTOGRAPHED BY SAVAGE & OTTINGER, SALT LAKE CITY.]

Completion of the Transcontinental Railroad
Harper's Weekly, 1869

Scenes must be discarded on converting a section of the novel to a one-hour screenplay. In almost every case, though, the discarding of scenes means stripping away important parts of the plot or character developments essential to understanding motivation or ability. Since the loss of pivotal plot points or character attributes would adversely affect the finished work, the necessary elements must be added back into retained scenes. The Attack of the Wildlings scene in which Bran was nearly killed is an excellent example of a scene containing essential character development not present in the original passage in the novel. In fact, dialogue and action were created specifically for the screenplay. This condensing of material into one scene had two important effects.

First, necessary background was provided for Robb's future story. There are few coincidences in novels, and fewer yet in television productions. Robb was not left alone in Winterfell so that he could play at being Warden of the North but without the full authority vested in that office. Even if you have not read the novels, you know that at some point Robb is going to have to exercise true leadership. He demonstrated leadership skills during the confrontation with the wildlings, particularly with regard to his decision to spare Osha's life. He considered getting information from her more important that extracting retribution for the attack on Bran. Robb showed a balanced, mature sense of practical leadership that will unquestionably play out in future episodes this season.

Second, this scene demonstrated one of the pitfalls of cinematic adaptations of literary works. With insufficient time to explore every nuance of character development, the television version was obliged to cut out some of the development unnecessary to the bare-bones advancement of the plot. This short-circuiting of the novel is often achieved through expository development, which only serves to further detract from the richness of the novel. This scene fell short of the novel, but it enriched the teleplay in a way the novel never could, using a brilliant technique that brought visual complexity to the events.

The power of the novel was slightly diminished, but Benioff and Weiss used demonstrative storytelling to excellent effect, exploiting visual imagery and powerful motifs to bring strong coherence to this scene.

TWO CATHEDRALS

Martin Sheen as President Josiah Bartlet
Chief Journalist Daniel Ross, U.S. Navy, 2004

Exposition is the simple relating of facts, often in dialogue. The other way to obtain plot advancement is through demonstration, which is more often achieved visually, both in novels and in cinematic creations. Sometimes an expository/demonstrative hybrid is used. In "Two Cathedrals" (The West Wing, Episode 2.22), Mrs. Landingham, who becomes President Bartlet's personal secretary, counsels an eighteen-year-old Jed Bartlet in 1960s New Hampshire to

become an advocate for underpaid women
(http://www.youtube.com/watch?v=jwaQExqyGUk).

Mrs. Landingham: "You're going to do it."
Jed Bartlet: "Aw, I didn't say that."
Mrs. Landingham: "Yes, you did."
Jed Bartlet: "When?"
Mrs. Landingham: "Just then. You stuck your hands in your pocket, you looked away, and smiled. That means you made up your mind."

At the end of the episode, the embattled President Bartlet, who is mourning the death of Mrs. Landingham and also under investigation for withholding the facts of his medical condition, must decide whether or not to run for a second term. The ending is rich with emotionally charged demonstrative force. A fierce tropical storm is bearing down on Washington, and President Bartlet is standing in the pouring rain outside the Oval Office.

His handlers come for him, and the motorcade makes its way to the site of the press conference. He is soaking wet. "Brothers in Arms" (Dire Straits) plays in the background as the President approaches the podium to begin the conference (http://www.youtube.com/watch?v=uaUPDYXQUtw).

His staff knows he's emotionally distraught, and they advise him to choose the one reporter who will not ask him whether he will seek a second term. Of course, he ignores the reporter, chooses another, and receives the big question: "Mr. President, can you tell us right now if you'll be seeking a second term?"

President Bartlet, rain water dripping from his perfectly tailored suit, takes his hands off the podium, puts them in his pockets, looks away, and smiles.

The scene was powerful because it picked up on dozens of motifs that had been sprinkled throughout the earlier minutes of the episode, and it did so without a word of exposition. If Bartlet had responded to the question, no words could have conveyed the same majestic force as the powerful imagery. Even if he had said, "Damn right I'm running for a second term. I'm running because there are injustices that must be corrected. I'm running because I am brother in arms with the downtrodden and forsaken of this land—" it would have been true enough, but it still would have lacked the power of Mrs. Landingham's funeral, Bartlet's "Eas In Crucem" speech (http://www.youtube.com/watch?v=FScv89J6rro), the numbers he ran with Mrs. Landingham, and every other element of the episode and the season. The final scene at the podium brought them all together—without a single word.

AUTHORITY WITHOUT RESPONSIBILITY

I loved the powerful use of demonstrative storytelling in the two Bran scenes in the forest. The first scene sets up Robb's choice, and the second scene forces him to make a single decision.

Theon: "Blood for blood. You need to make the Lannisters pay for Jory and the others."

Robb: "You're talking about war."

Theon: "I'm talking about justice."

Robb: "Only the Lord of Winterfell can call in the bannermen and raise an army."

Theon: "A Lannister put his spear through your father's leg. The Kingslayer rides for Casterly Rock where no one can touch him—"

Robb: "You want me to march on Casterly Rock

Theon: "You're not a boy anymore. They attacked your father. They've already started the war. It's your duty to represent your house when your father can't."

Robb: "And it's not your duty, because it's not your house." [Looking around] "Where's Bran?"

Theon: "Don't know. It's not my house."

The implication of Bran's disappearance, based on the context of this dialogue, is that Robb is still behaving as an irresponsible boy. Robb needs to assume the full authority of the Lord of Winterfell, but he cannot even keep track of a single child. Far from being fit to assume the authority of a lord, he does not even possess the ordinary skills required of any adult. Watching over Bran and calling the bannermen are both duties which fall under Robb's purview. Robb claims the authority, and chastises Theon for lecturing him ("And it's not your duty, because it's not your house."). When Robb cannot even supervise Bran, Theon throws the chastisement back in his face: "Don't know. It's not my house."

Barbarian King
Alaric of the Goths, 370 to 410 A.D.
unknown artist, circa 1875

This scene is wonderfully engineered. It forces Robb to assume authority ("It's not your [Theon's] house" necessarily implies that the house is Robb's—that is, that he has authority over the house), but it also demonstrates his inability to assume responsibility for Bran or anyone else in House Stark.

In The Attack of the Wildlings, Robb again chooses to assert authority without demonstrating full leadership. He comes up in front of the wildlings gathered around Bran. Standing a good five metres away, he draws his sword and says, "Drop the knife. Let him go, and I'll let you live."

He expects the four wildlings to recognise his authority. A mature assessment of the situation would have called for quite a different approach. Robb is inevitably forced to lay down his sword when one of the wildlings brings a knife to Bran's throat. Even Bran could have predicted the outcome. Without a weapon, and standing too far away to make any difference, Robb would have watched as they slit Bran's throat and then came for him. Of course, the scene did not progress in that manner.

Theon knew, even if Robb did not, that one does not negotiate or wield authority when confronting forest outlaws. The only proper response is stealth, sudden attack, and recovery of hostages. Theon, never one to stand on authority, seems to have known these things instinctively.

Robb: "Have you lost your mind? What if you'd missed?"
Theon: "He'd have killed you and cut Bran's throat."
Robb: "You don't have the right—"
Theon: "To what? To save your brother's life? It was the only thing to do, so I did it."

Fans of ASoIaF will not like what I am about to say, but here it is: This aspect of the scene is more compelling than the one portrayed in the novel, in which Robb chastises Theon, and Theon merely shrugs his shoulders.

Now, I need to say that the scene as drawn in the novel adds much more to the plot and character development than this scene from the television episode. The teleplay is lacking rich elements present in the novel.

However, as I said above, not everything presented in the novel can be rendered on the small screen; sacrifices must be made. But sacrifices can be made in a crude manner, or in artistic ways. The storytelling one sees in formulaic shows like "Law and Order" and "CSI" and "NCIS" is heavily expository, usually single dimensional, and quite boring. On the other hand, creations like "The West Wing" and "Lost" are deeply demonstrative and multi-dimensional, sometimes to the point of posing difficulties for even the most dedicated analyst.

Theon points out that the action he took was "the only thing to do." He is correct, of course, and Robb cannot refute his logic. The beauty of these two scenes, what I have termed a "feat of expert engineering", is that Theon has shown Robb that he has but one choice: He must give up his childish lusting after authority, and instead approach the challenges of life in a mature, responsible, adult manner. If we are allowed to interpret these two scenes in a literary or cinematographic manner, we are almost obliged to draw this conclusion from the scenes: Robb will end up acting in precisely the way Theon argued he must. Just as the prep school Jed Bartlet put his hands in his pockets, indicating he would fight the good fight for Mrs. Landingham and the prep school's women employees—and also served as foreshadowing of his decision to seek re-election—so too, Theon's appeal to Robb in the first forest scene will not go unheeded. At some point, a Robb Stark who has accepted responsibility and has tried to apply mature judgment will come to the realisation that he must call the banners. At some point—maybe even this season—Robb will raise an army. This scene in a lonely forest provided all the proof we need.

There is no honour in vacuous assertions of authority, no virtue in claiming power without judiciously applying its effects for the good of all. Theon called Robb to honour and virtue. Blood for blood is the honourable route. It appears to be the only route left to Robb. But is Theon's choice truly the only option left to Robb? Perhaps even Theon is basing his counsel on assumptions that have no bearing on the game of thrones. Let us look at another situation to see what truths we may glean.

THE BRAVO'S DANCE

Syrio: "You are troubled?"
Arya: "Yes."
Syrio: "Good. Trouble is a perfect time for training. When you are dancing in the meadow with your dogs and kittens—this is not when fighting happens."

The honourable thing to do at a time like this—when a beloved member of the household—the man who protected Arya for years—has been killed—when her own father was nearly murdered—is to take time to mourn and grieve. One cannot say that grieving is not honourable. What better way to mourn the passing of a brave and trusted servant? But it is not the bravo's way. It is not the way of the First Sword to the Sealord of Braavos.

Syrio: "Do you pray to the gods?"
Arya: "The old and the new."
Syrio: "There is only one god, and his name is death. And there is only one thing we say to death: Not today."

Syrio's lesson is even tougher than Theon's. He pities Arya, but he is not going to show pity, for he knows that the enemies of House Stark will show no mercy. They will not wait until the time is convenient or mutually agreeable to plan their attack on Arya. They will attack her and kill her at their pleasure, not hers. If

Robert debated but rejected Ned's pleas to forego killing "the child", Daenerys Targaryen, the enemies of House Stark would bear no scruples in the murder of a twelve-year-old girl. All of it is part of the game, and in this game, you win or you die.

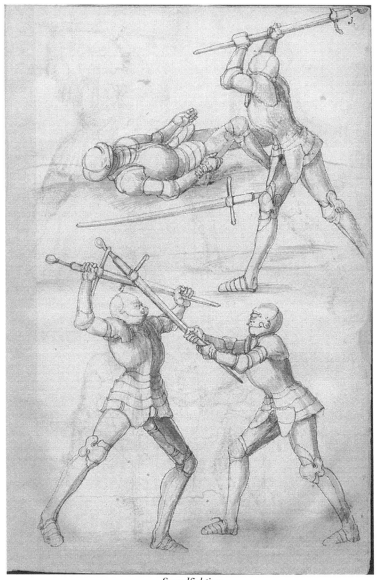

Swordfighting
unknown artist
Der Fechtkampf, *16th Century German fighting manual*

STRENGTH AND HONOUR

Daenerys had to eat the entire horse heart. But if she did not?

If she vomited it up, or if she refused, we might simply say she had dishonoured the khal and the khalasar. But anyone who truly understood the implications of not ingesting the entire horse heart would be aghast at any such simplistic interpretation. In fact, even though one might be formally correct in declaring that the inability to eat the heart would bring dishonour to the khal, we would be within the bounds of proper analysis in saying that any such declaration misses the point. So much rode on the eating of the heart that it would have been impossible to imagine her continued placement as the khal's queen. If she had not eaten the heart without retching, she would have called into question the khal's authority. The khalasar would have become agitated. Other khals might have seized an opportunity to attack the now-weakened khal.

In the same way, we cannot simply say that Daenerys rose to the challenge, that she showed courage in taking on something so difficult. If she needed to demonstrate honour beyond honour, she also needed a species of courage that transcended any of the normal limits on strength of character.

She needed to become fully integrated into the khalasar as its queen, and the only way to do that was by demonstrating unequivocal surrender of self to the Dothraki world.

This is the honour-beyond-honour to which every character is called. It is nothing less than the complete integration of self with the greater world. Not just with peers, or a royal court, or an entire society, or an entire race. This is integration taken whole: Integration with horse hearts, with ravens, with direwolves, with wildlings, and yes, with even White Walkers and dragons. It is in this scene that we begin to get a glimpse into the breathtaking vision of GRRM. He is calling his characters to something grand, something to which we are only permitted the most tangential of glances now, in this early part of the epic. The audacity of this is challenging to us, and ought to be so. This goes way beyond trite formulations such as, "The Force is an energy field created by all living things. It surrounds us, penetrates us—it binds the galaxy together." I first heard those words in the summer of 1977. Well, to be honest, I heard those words seventeen or eighteen times during that summer; after the 12th time, the ushers let me in for free. I thought Obi-Wan Kenobi was just about the wisest guy I'd even seen in cinema. Before the age of DVDs—even before the age of VCRs—maybe Obi-Wan Kenobi was wise. But GRRM is giving us something much richer than the Force.

RENLY'S CHALLENGE

Renly Baratheon tried to equate Robert's actions with those of Mad King Aerys. We've heard such talk before—at the Small Council in Episode 1.05. But young Renly's words don't carry the same force as they did when they came from between Eddard Stark's lips. And the power of the words is dispelled and dispersed by King Robert's new-found sense of purpose. He may have spent his time in the woods speaking of the days when he "made the eight", but his purposeful stride through the forest matches his renewed vigour as king. Renly's challenge is that of an impotent pretender. He poses no threat, and the King knows it. Neither are the Lannisters in the entourage any threat to the King. We know this because Ser Barristan is with the King. Ser Barristan is more than a match for any Lannister squire who might attempt anything untoward while the King is vulnerable in the forest.

The Wild Boar Hunt
Frans Snyders, circa 1640

But something about this scene remains disquieting. If singing a song of ice and fire requires of its performers a surrender of self, an integration of self with environment, we see no evidence of any such surrender in the hunting scene. King Robert is not integrating himself into anything. In fact, the very reason he is able to enjoy the hunt is that he has dissociated himself from most of the duties of king. While he is off gallivanting in the woods, House Lannister is plundering his kingdom and Ned Stark is protecting the realm. While those in the entourage are intent on a hunt, the King is telling stories of youthful conquest and taking long draughts from a wineskin. The King is isolated, not because of any manoeuvring of the Lannisters or the powerlusts of his younger brother, but due entirely to his own desire to make himself aloof. If we read GRRM's story correctly, especially in the context of Daenerys' complete surrender to her own environment, we should feel a high degree of discomfort in this hunting scene. There's something rotten in the state of Westeros—you can almost smell it in this scene.

FIGHTING WITH HONOUR

Lysa: "You don't fight with honour."
Bronn: [Shrugging] "No. He [Ser Vardis] did."

Lysa's statement, as with anything we might have said about the dishonour of failing to eat the horse heart, was irrelevant. Nothing in the rules required Bronn to fight in any particular way. He gave himself fully to the effort to fight on Tyrion's behalf. In a sense, he behaved exactly as Daenerys did. Probably an even better comparison would be with Syrio Forel. "Remember, child, this is not the iron dance of Westeros we are learning: the knight's dance, hacking and hammering. No. This is the bravo's dance, the water dance, swift and sudden." Ser Vardis, weighed down with thick armour plate and an enormous, thick shield, was dancing the awkward, heavy, lethargic dance of plodding armour and hacking sword. Bronn, wearing nothing heavier than boiled leather, could dance after the fashion of the bravos. His dance was light, fast, and brilliantly effective against the sixty or one hundred pounds of armour Ser Vardis had to lift every time he took a step or swung his arm.

We've seen this appeal to the good effect of simplicity in previous episodes. We recall, in particular, the comparison of the complicated rituals of the Seven at the funeral of Jon Arryn with Ned Stark's simple oiling of a sword in the godswood at Winterfell. But we see it, too, in Daenerys' eagerness to go with the flow, to empty herself so as to become one with the Dothraki. We see it in Arya's light bravo's water dance and in Bran's ability to commune with ravens and direwolves.

The important question we need to ask is simple: Are the principal players in the game around the Iron Throne dancing the bravo's dance, or are they wearing the heavy armour of an honourable knight?

CROWN OF HONOUR

"You shall have a golden crown that men shall tremble to behold."

The authority and splendour of office is all Viserys ever wanted. His desire for authority was no different than Robb's, really. When Khal Drogo told Viserys that his request would be granted, that he would wear a crown of honour, Viserys must have felt a kind of elation that he had never known before. Purest gold, fit exactly to the contours of his scalp, would be his forever.

The golden crown and the suit of armour bedeck the owner in majesty, splendour, and honour. Steel is heavy, and gold is heavier than steel. But this is fitting, since the golden crown confers greater honour than the steel helmet. Can anyone in the game of thrones bear the full weight of a crown of honour? Should those who play the game be seeking the weight of honour, or should they train their energies on something else?

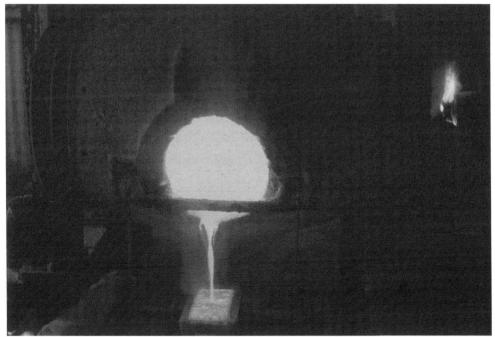

Pouring molten gold into ingot mold, La Luz Mine
Allen Drebert, 1957, released to PD 2008

Daenerys' maid servant looked at her burned fingers, then glanced at the Queen's unblemished hands, untouched by fire. "He was no dragon," Daenerys said. "Fire cannot kill a dragon." Apparently, fire does not harm Daenerys. She has never sought a crown of honour, never wished to be weighed down by gold.

Perhaps there are yet other ways to play the game of thrones. Perhaps there are those in the game who shirk authority and privilege, who seek responsibility and duty. Perhaps there is a way to sit the iron throne in boiled leather and not plate armour, to wear a crown of service, not a crown of honour. Perhaps there is one player, who, when confronted by the god who rules the game, will be able to say, "Not today. Not today." Perhaps we will find no honour in those words. But such a player can look to Prince Viserys Targaryen, rightful heir to the Iron Throne, wearing his crown of honour. "No, you're right," the player might say. "I did not fight with honour." Pointing to the Prince, his dead eyes shocked and glazed, his mouth open for all eternity, the player could honestly say, "He did."

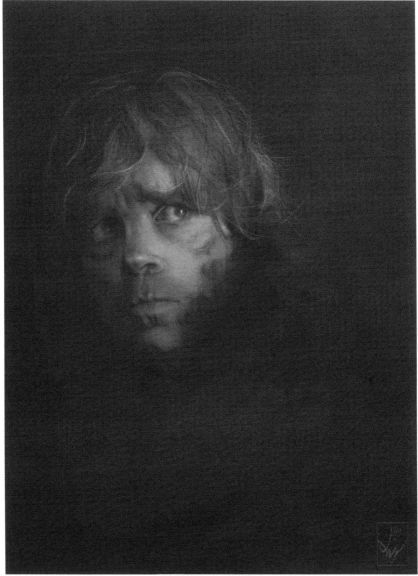

Tyrion Lannister
copyright Dalisa 2011
used with permission

How easily those of virtually limitless potential would relinquish opportunity.

Jaime: Even if the boy lives, he'd be a cripple, a grotesque. Give me a good clean death any day.
Tyrion: Speaking for the grotesques, I'd have to disagree. Death is so final. Whereas life ... life is full of possibilities.

163

Tyrion appreciated not only life itself, but the rich potentials, the heady pleasure of engaging every facet of intellect and will to thwart the malevolent forces that threaten not position and privilege, but existence. More than anyone, he is aware that life is a precarious state, subject to forfeiture at any moment, without warning. Study is the key to preparedness. "I'm told he reads all night," Lady Stark said. Indeed.

If the possibilities of life are without limit, the studies employed to attain awareness of life's infinite paths are subject to practical constraint; a library may contain only so many books, and no more. Tyrion enjoys unlimited wealth. He may read from any library in the realm. But his studies are limited by geographies physical and conceptual. We think his wit refined, his intellect sharp, but he will need more than erudition to survive the coming winter, for it is to be the coldest, darkest winter of all.

THE GROTESQUE

It is one of the central themes of Game of Thrones, and Tyrion is the category's most visible and vocal representative. I believe others within the fellowship of the damned may have greater powers or insights, but certainly no one among the despised of Westeros is more aware of his lowly status than is Tyrion.

There is nothing inherently good about living in a state of physical, social, or psychological disability. The novels frequently convey this truth, telling of the pain in Tyrion's legs, especially when he climbs stairs or mounts a horse or takes any other action that requires him to utilise conveniences built for people twice his size. Yet we know that Tyrion and Bran, as physically challenged as they may be, are held up to us as examples.

The good that derives of status as a grotesque is not a matter of physical bearing, but of spiritual orientation. To the extent that Jon Snow accepts his position as a bastard, he enjoys advancement and success; conversely, when he claims to be anything more than a bastard, or rails against the injustices to which he has become cruel subject, his status and abilities diminish. "Never forget what you are. The rest of the world will not. Wear it like armour, and it can never be used to hurt you."

Tyrion offered Jon good and useful advice, but steeling oneself against the derisions of those more fortunate is only the feeblest of beginnings of the heightened and exemplary state that George Martin holds as an ideal. "I'd rather have Franklin Roosevelt in a wheelchair than Ronald Reagan on a horse," Jesse Jackson said at the 1984 Democratic National Convention. Jackson's praise of Roosevelt was not a result of the great president's mere graceful acceptance of his state of physical paralysis. Nor was Jackson praising the overwhelming nature of Roosevelt's personality and force of character, even though they were so strong that most people were unaware of his handicapped state. Jackson looked past the accidental character of Roosevelt's existence as a cripple, and elevated the nobility of his character, which in Jackson's mind was far superior to anything Reagan achieved, even when he rode high on a horse.

But Tyrion is going far beyond the kind of moral superiority to which Jackson alluded in his speech. Many players in Game of Thrones will evince nobility of character, but "in the game of thrones, you win, or you die." Few will survive this long tale, but Tyrion, son of Tywin, seems better equipped than most to endure to the very end. Not because he is well learned, nor even because he is the intellectual leader of the grotesques. Rather, he will live when others die because of his exceptional knowledge of the geographies of Westeros and the geographies of the mind.

GEOGRAPHIES OF THE MIND

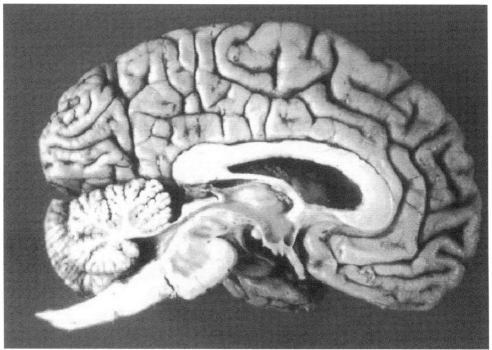

Human Brain, Midsagittal Cut
copyright Dr. John A. Beal 2005, CC-SA 2.5

"Listen to me," Tyrion begged his jailer, Mord. "Listen to me. Sometimes possession is an abstract concept." (Second Sky Cell scene, Episode 1.06)

The conversation between the Lord of Lannister and the turnkey of the sky cells was the most humorous exchange in Season One. "Abstract concept" is not a phrase taught in kindergarten, and we know the expression is not among those to be found in Mord's perhaps 500-word vocabulary. That Tyrion would even attempt to reason with Mord in this manner is hilarious. That he chose these particular words in an attempt to bribe the most intellectually challenged member of Lady Lysa's guard very nearly had me falling out of my chair laughing.

We laugh, but we are aware, too, that despite Tyrion's vast wealth of academic learning, he remains in some respects ignorant of the practical application of knowledge. The geographies of the mind include the rare mountaintop of extraordinary erudition, but they encompass deep valleys of ignorance and vast plains of indifference and neglect as well. The one who would become master cartographer must possess unequalled skill in navigating and mapping out both vale and knoll, both mountain and prairie. In this respect, we know Tyrion's skills in conceptual cartography are at best rudimentary. In ways that will certainly gain importance as the story progresses, Tyrion's ability to apply knowledge to real-world problems remains largely untested.

Supporters of Tyrion will point to his success in the Vale of Arryn. Tyrion's manipulation of the Stone Crows, Black Ears, Burned Men, Painted Dogs, and the other tribesmen of the Vale, not only to ultimately serve his will, but to become his willing soldiers in battles against powerful House Stark, must be taken as proof, they would say, of his ability to practically apply abstract knowledge.

But recall the meeting inside Tywin's tent. Shagga, son of Dolf, considered Tyrion his prisoner, even in Tywin's presence. "Until we hold the steel he pledged us, the little lion's life is ours." Tywin did not dispute Shagga's claim. Shagga would release Tyrion only if House Lannister provided the weapons Tyrion had promised, and he would consider the Lannisters' debt paid only when the Vale was delivered to them. Tyrion's negotiations did require a bit of imaginative thinking, but they were not founded on rare bits of knowledge or unusual synthetic skill. No advanced studies of the history of the Vale were required to piece together the idea that the barbarian tribesmen would gladly accept any plan that proposed their ascension to rightful lords of the East. Tyrion was merely appealing to basic greed. He relied on his father to consummate the contract. It cost nothing for Tyrion to promise gold, weapons, and land, and he knew his father would be willing to pay if it meant not having to worry about the Vale of Arryn.

I do not wish anyone to infer from my words that I consider Tyrion less than capable. He is certainly among the most capable members of the Sisterhood of the Damned. But membership in the elite corps of cripples, bastards, and broken things does not in itself confer extraordinary capability or exemption from the dire effects of slings and arrows. What is required of those who would win the game of thrones—that is to say, those who will survive this most deadly of diversions—is a meeting of mind, place, and time. The geographies of the mind must match the geographies of Westeros.

THE DISABILITIES OF WEALTH AND POWER

As a Lannister, even though he is the least of that house, Tyrion enjoys privilege, power, and wealth beyond reckoning. "A Lannister always pays his debts" because House Lannister is the virtually inexhaustible treasury to all of the

Seven Kingdoms and to the Iron Throne itself. To be a prince of House Lannister is to be born with a silver spoon in one's mouth, servants at one's side, and the promise of a life free of hunger, want, and misfortune.

Hoard of Ancient Gold Coins
photograph by Swiss Banker, released to PD 2005

But freedom from want is not necessarily a state to be sought after. Those who are satisfied in station and being have no reason to seek something greater or more complete. In fact, we might consider the fulfillment of every desire to be the state closest in essence to the nirvana of death. Tyrion seems to have understood this upon meeting Shagga of the Stone Crows:

Shagga: "How would you like to die, Tyrion, son of Tywin?"
Tyrion: "In my own bed, at the age of eighty, with a belly full of wine and a girl's mouth around my cock."

With Syrio Forel, Tyrion is quite adamant in refusing the entreaties of the god called Death. "Not today," Tyrion says. Not only does he reject death, but he instinctively recoils from any of the false satisfactions that might be attained through scholarly pursuits. He does not spend his time reading so that he might be lauded as a learned man. He does give his mind to diverse studies for the sheer pleasure of the acquisition of knowledge. He knows any guarantees that privilege and power may grant are only temporary. Influence and wealth are crutches that weaken rather than strengthen.

A popular television commercial for the 2011 Nissan Quest, currently running in the summer of 2011, depicts a woman in the parking lot of a shopping mall, carrying in her arms a five-metre-high load of items she has just purchased. As the Shirelles sing "Mama said there'd be days like this," the woman miraculously loads all her loot into the Quest, with room left over. Mama said there'd be days like this, when a woman's patience is stretched to the limit, when the fates seem to conspire against her, giving her more goods than could ever be expected to fit into an ordinary minivan.

The Nissan commercial presents us with the full range of difficulties one might expect to encounter in modern suburban America. If this is true, one shudders to consider the reserves of emotional strength such a woman might be able to call upon if circumstance forced her to confront a real crisis. Such a woman would have no reserves. She would have no capacities for addressing a true emergency. In its conspicuous excess, the commercial points to a second important truth regarding a state of wealth and power: Riches and privilege are not only debilitating crutches, they are, in fact, deadly in themselves.

This truth was made evident to us in the fight between Bronn and Ser Vardis Egen. Bronn's only weapon was a sword, his only protection a boiled leather breastplate. Ser Vardis, on the other hand, wore full plate armour and carried a long shield. With every step, Ser Vardis was obliged to lift eighty or a hundred pounds of steel. Bronn had only to outwalk the heavily-weighted knight, and when the man in armour was completely exhausted, run his sword through the knight's unprotected underarm.

The unnecessary accretions of wealth and power are useless and debilitating baggage. They cause the owner to become not only contented and unguarded, but slow and dull, weighed down with concerns that share nothing at all with the most important business of survival. Tyrion would never drive a Quest, because such a vehicle is unnecessarily large. In fact, a vehicle such as the Quest becomes more hindrance than anything else. One can no longer fit into small spaces. One must always be seeking the wide berth, the generous parking space, and frequent fills at the gas pump to satisfy the monster's unquenchable thirst for fuel. In fact, one does not drive a Quest; the Quest instead drives the owner. Wealth and power, Tyrion would tell us, are instigators of their own downfall.

THE GEOGRAPHIES OF WESTEROS

But Tyrion is not the unerring font of all wisdom and knowledge. In fact, we know at the very least on occasion his pronouncements have been incorrect. But in Westeros, incorrect thinking can lead to utter destruction. The most damning of Tyrion's statements, the proclamation that most fully revealed his ignorance, occurred during his discussion with Jon *en route* to the Wall:

Jon: "The Night's Watch protects the realm."
Tyrion: "Ah, yes, yes, against grumkins and snarks and all the other monsters your

wet nurse warned you about. You're a smart boy. You don't believe in that nonsense."

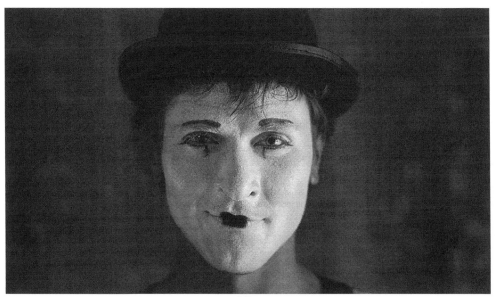

Mime
copyright *Nikita Kapranov 2011, CC-SA 3.0*

Tyrion's facial expression at the time he recited these words to Jon Snow indicated a playful sense of joy. Tyrion obviously felt his book learning and vast knowledge of the real world entitled him to a measure of intellectual satisfaction in understanding something that had evaded the young man taking the Black. Tyrion's sense of superiority rested equally on his understanding of the particulars of the case (his information-based belief that the Wall was unnecessary) and a feeling of intellectual triumphalism. In extracting from his master/pupil discussion with Jon Snow a feeling of academic and real-world superiority, Tyrion was falling prey to the same species of self-satisfaction and complacency that are the deadly result of wealth and power. By succumbing to intellectual pride, by allowing books to become virtually his sole source of trusted information, even to the point of dismissing cultural wisdom (in this case as passed on by "wet nurses"), Tyrion was markedly compromising his ability to survive the coming dark days.

I consider Tyrion's dismissal of "grumkins and snarks" to be of the same variety as Robb Stark's dismissal of the direwolf. In Episode One, as Robb looked at the dead direwolf and her living pups, he said, "There are no direwolves south of the Wall." It didn't seem to matter to him that he was staring at five living, breathing direwolves, and they were indeed south of the Wall. His life experience and the wisdom he absorbed from others told him again and again that direwolves were not to be found on the summer side of the Wall. Even when he saw proof that his knowledge was incorrect, he nevertheless stubbornly adhered to his incorrect understanding.

In the same way, Tyrion had intellectual proofs of the existence of "grumkins and snarks", or at the very least, the reality of entities just as deadly, but in his stubbornness he refused to acknowledge the legitimacy and veracity of the proofs. A particularly strong proof was posed by the very presence of the Wall. Thousands of years before, the greatest engineers and tens of thousands of workers over several generations committed themselves to the construction of the world's greatest human-made creation. Upon even cursory consideration, it ought to have become evident to Tyrion that sheer economics would have interrupted building on the Wall long before completion if the structure did not have merit far outweighing the enormous cost in time, materials, and human life. From a political point of view, rulers would not have been able to stomach the sustained diversion of massive resources, over a period of dynasties, without the strong support of the people. Economic, political, and spiritual commitment to this unprecedented, generations-long venture could only be found in the structure's intrinsic value. That is to say, the Wall really did serve to protect the Realm from White Walkers.

If Tyrion is to survive the clash of kings all the way through the dance with dragons, he must wed the geographies of his mind to the cultural, spiritual, spatial, and temporal geographies of Westeros. For Tyrion, no library is too large. If he is to survive, he will have to take the next step in his attitude toward learning, to the realisation that no library is sufficient. That is, he will have to understand that learning is aimed at filling an infinitely large void in human understanding; regardless of the amount of studying, human ignorance remains infinite. Other forms of learning, and especially learning from others and learning from the signs all around him, will have to become integral to his survival studies.

THE LIMITS OF INQUIRY

I see A Song of Ice and Fire ending with Tyrion sitting the Iron Throne as only a distant possibility. More likely, it seems to me, someone like Jon Snow, who will confront one of the most enduring threats to the Realm, will garner the political support required to ascend the courts and halls of power. There are limits to Tyrion's capacities to perceive reality. In fact, I believe the series has offered us sufficient information to construct a hierarchy of knowledge and wisdom in which Tyrion finds a place near the top, but not at the summit itself. However, this assessment depends on a couple of factors, not yet brought to bear on Tyrion's case, but which could provide him the small push required to take the throne.

First, we need to distinguish between knowledge and wisdom. Tyrion's knowledge is limited in ways not applicable to other characters. Both Bran and Daenerys have access to vast bodies of knowledge to which Tyrion will forever remain ignorant. The best Tyrion might hope for is second-hand knowledge, obtained through frank exchange with these gifted seers. He would need to have a strong basis for trust, in that the truths Bran and others like him obtain through the eyes of ravens or direwolves or other creatures could only be relayed to Tyrion through the crude and sometimes deceptive medium of spoken language. If Tyrion retained one or more seers as his closest advisors, he may have the knowledge necessary to take the throne.

Truth Escaping the Well
an allegorical painting by Edouard Debat-Ponsan, 1898

But more than knowledge will be required. In the end, the person who sits the Iron Throne will have demonstrated wisdom in addressing the enduring threats of

Ice and Fire. These concerns, relegated to the periphery of Westeros' cultural consciousness, will come to the fore as ASoIaF progresses. If the supreme leader lacks the primary ability to tap into the truths evident to Bran and Daenerys and other seers, she will have to acquire that knowledge through a trusted seer, but she will also have to make sense of stores of information from several sources, some of which will invariably come to be in disagreement. The leader will need to cultivate an ability to synthesise knowledge into a plan of action; she will have to demonstrate wisdom.

At this point in the story, Jon Snow represents Ice, and Daenerys Targaryen represents Fire (I'm ignoring some quite well-founded theories saying one of these characters represents both Ice and Fire). The Iron Throne, though, seats just one person. The supreme leader of Westeros will need to tame, conquer, deflect, or otherwise address the threats or powers of both Ice and Fire. It seems to me unlikely that the representative of one supernatural power could take the throne unaided. Therefore, I tend to favour someone like Bran Stark as the final king. The second stumbling block to Tyrion's ascension is his demonstrated inability to synthesise raw knowledge into unassailable wisdom. If he can break through the epistemological walls he has created for himself and attain to a more complex and more useful real-world wisdom, Tyrion Lannister could become the single person in Westeros to unite the knowledge of Ice and Fire into the enlightened leadership of the highest office in the Red Keep. Perhaps Tyrion will surprise me. Life, after all, is full of the most delightful possibilities.

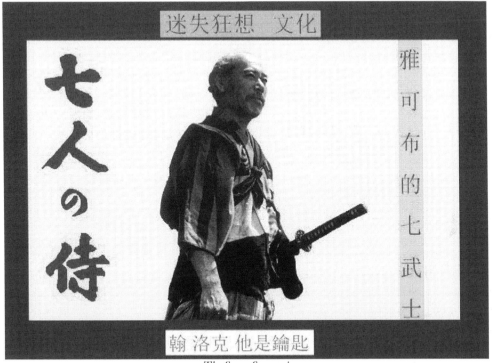

The Seven Samurai
Design by Pearson Moore, 2010

What is the basis for any legitimate claim to the Iron Throne? Tonight we were offered no less than seven theses for kingship, imbued with the full authority of the most highly-placed lords of the realm.

LAW

Lord Eddard Stark
Protector of the Realm
The King's Hand, Lord of Winterfell, Warden of the North

Ned Stark knew he was taking a potentially lethal risk in changing the last words of the King on a legal document. King Robert, on his deathbed, instructed Ned to write that the Protector of the Realm would "rule in my stead until my son, Joffrey, comes of age." Ned substituted "rightful heir" for "son, Joffrey" in the King's last will and testament.

Ned Stark, who lived his life according to the most exacting strictures of highest honour, disobeyed his king. Perhaps he felt he knew Robert well enough to predict the King's wishes. There was no time to explain to Robert that none of Cersei's children were his. If the King knew the children belonged to Jaime Lannister, whom Robert had always held in contempt, surely Robert would have concurred with Ned's substitution.

That there was an already existing order of succession to the throne does not excuse Ned's replacement of the King's words with his own. Any number of considerations might prevent the execution of particular elements of a last will and testament, but the recorder of the will is not constrained in the same way as the executor. The recorder's duty is to transcribe precisely the words of the testator. That Ned did not do this opened up legitimate legal challenge to the authenticity and legal authority of the document. In not accurately transcribing King Robert's words, Ned Stark was contravening the law.

We understand Ned's motivations. Although from a legalistic point of view he was breaking the law, he was attempting to buttress the order of succession, which is a higher, more important article of legislation than any statute guiding the disposition of personal estates. Even a king's personal preference would have no legal bearing on something as important as the order of succession. But we recognise in Eddard Stark's actions a more noble motivation than simple adherence to law.

Law is the foundation upon which any civilisation must be built. A civilisation not girded with the sure, immutable principles of law will become subject to the whims of dictators and the fads of the time, neither of which could be good for the realm and its citizens. I read Ned's deliberate rewording of King Robert's will as a concern for the continuity of the Seven Kingdoms under the rule of law. I don't believe he was interested in the preservation of sterile legislative precedent for its own sake, but as the best and most enduring instrument of a vital and healthy civilisation.

FAMILY

Lord Tywin Lannister
Lord of Casterly Rock
Warden of the West, Shield of Lannisport

Lord Tywin Lannister shared Ned's concern for the continuity of the realm. But at the time of succession, even the highest law of the land would have little or no impact on the proceedings. The nitty-gritty of governing a land as vast as Westeros was all about the realpolitik of flesh-and-blood human beings confronting the requirements and limitations of the time. No one in any position of authority during King Robert's reign worried that he had no legal claim to the Iron Throne. No one outside House Targaryen shed any tears over Prince Viserys Targaryen's exile to a foreign continent, even if he was the legal heir. How did the long-established legal principles underlying the correct order of succession aid Prince Viserys' claims or ambitions? Did the legal order of succession do anything to alleviate the bloodshed during the Sack of King's Landing or at the Battle of the Trident? In fact, looking back as far as history was recorded, did legal authority ever have bearing on the actual succession?

Louis XIV and Family
Hyacinthe Rigaud, 1692

Succession to the throne, whether we look to the history of the Seven Kingdoms, England, France, or any other monarchy, was determined by the health and power of the ruling family. In the end, House Targaryen fell, not because King Aerys was insane, but because his house could not defend him or any potential successors from the royal house. The War of the Roses in 15th century England ended with the ascension of the almost unknown House of Tudor and the installation of Henry VII as King. The Tudors outlasted the Yorks and the other Lancasters, and Henry further strengthened his position by marrying Elizabeth of York, effectively combining the two warring houses under the single red and white Tudor rose.

Law simply has no bearing on the holder of the throne. Robert Baratheon, confronting Prince Rhaegar at the Trident, didn't stop mid-battle when he realised Rhaegar was rightful heir to the crown. He swung his war hammer with all the power his right arm could muster and shattered the Prince's chest. He made sure that Prince Aegon and any other claimant to the Iron Throne was likewise assassinated. As leader of the rebellion, and with the full support of Houses Stark and Lannister, Robert Baratheon ascended the throne. Legal purists in some obscure corner of the realm might have argued that Prince Viserys was the rightful king, but by the time King's Landing had been gutted and the last of the Dragon King's adult heirs had been murdered, any such claims were entirely academic. Robert Baratheon was King because his family was healthy and strong.

"It's the family name that lives on," Tywin Lannister said. "It's all that lives on. Not your personal glory, not your honour, but family." The last king had been a drunkard, and the one before him a mad man. In Tywin Lannister's mind it was time to take the throne out of the hands of those who were clearly incompetent to rule. Since the continuity of the realm depended on the strength of the family holding the throne, the people of Westeros would be best served by a king descending from the healthiest, strongest, and wealthiest house in the land. It was Jaime Lannister's solemn responsibility to become the man he was meant to be, and it was House Lannister's solemn calling to occupy the Red Keep. Historical fact and political reality pointed inexorably to a single conclusion: A Lannister must sit the Iron Throne.

CHARISMA

Lord Renly Baratheon
Master of Laws
Lord of Storm's End, Second in line to the Iron Throne

Lord Lannister's argument does not hold up to careful scrutiny. House Targaryen was the most powerful and durable house in the realm. It stood for three hundred of the most difficult years the continent had ever seen, and yet it prevailed against every threat. The royal house did not fall due to the strength of House Baratheon. The Baratheons were a minor family, with feeble royal lineage, and would never have been compared to the royal lines of Lannister or Stark. No, the dragon lords lost power because their leader, King Aerys, lacked the one feature every leader must have in abundance: Charisma. Lord Renly Baratheon, Master of Laws, friend of the Knight of Flowers, was the most charismatic leader in the Seven Kingdoms. For the sake of the realm, Renly was the one who should have been elevated to the Iron Throne.

We come to know kings by their personalities, and by the way their personalities play out in greater society. If I tell you about Ivan IV, Grand Prince of Moscow, who ruled from 1533 until 1584, you may confess that you have never heard of this obscure tsar. But in fact, you know him quite well, for his most famous title is Ivan the Terrible. Ivan subjugated foreign lands to his absolute authority; those who challenged him in any way were mercilessly executed. He declared that everyone in Novgorod be killed; because of his decree, the city was sacked and burned, and over 60,000 of its inhabitants were murdered. He beat his pregnant daughter in law, causing a miscarriage. When his own son complained about what he had done, Ivan killed him.

We know little about the treacheries of the Mad King, but we know that everyone in the Seven Kingdoms feared the insane unpredictability of the last of the Dragon Lords. The fall of House Targaryen had nothing to do with law, the continuity of a dynasty, or the power of the royal house. The Mad King had to be removed because he was the very opposite of what a charismatic leader had to be. If the people fear their leader, they will eventually depose him. If the people love their leader, there is no law or family in the world that can oppose him, for he rules from a position of unquestioned power and authority.

The Starks wished to enforce laws that no one cared about. The Lannisters wished to rule through sheer force, intimidation, and raw fear. Renly knew that neither of these approaches was sustainable in the long run. To rule with authority, longevity, and positive effect, a king must be loved by the people. Renly Baratheon would be the best king Westeros had ever seen.

KNOWLEDGE

Lockheed SR-71 Spy Plane
Judson Brohmer, U.S. Air Force officer, 1994

Lord Petyr Baelish
Master of Coin

"What we don't know is usually what gets us killed."

Mad King Aerys probably believed up until the very end that people loved him. Prince Viserys had no difficulty believing that entire cities in the Seven Kingdoms were saying prayers for his return to power. Every leader who ever was thinks himself loved by the populace; every emperor parades around naked in what he believes to be the finest garments ever fashioned for a ruler. Charisma is a potent aphrodisiac, but it is, more often than not, an illusion.

The true means of achieving and maintaining power is not through law, family, or false charisma. Real power is maintained through intelligence and asymmetric knowledge. A ruler does not fight fire with fire, but rather uses knowledge and stealth to foil conspiracies and kill enemies. Those who believe in the convenient and stupid fantasy of "honour" think poisoning a "woman's" means of assassination. But poisoning is a stealthy means of achieving superiority over an enemy and must be counted among the most useful weapons in the ruler's arsenal.

"Only by admitting what we are can we get what we want." Littlefinger is no emperor, but then, would a master of spies ever take a position that necessarily depends on unreliable sources of intelligence? Kings and queens are the focus of unscrupulous conspirators and fabricators of all manner of deception; by their very position they are denied the unvarnished truth. True power is concentrated in the masters of whisperers and spiders who control the most powerful commodities in the realm: intelligence, knowledge, and covert information. These are the masters of the realm, the kingmakers whose absolute control of the flow of information can make or break a royal house.

Law and honour are for the weaklings of the world who lack the mental capacity to balance a dozen competing factions. But the weaklings of the world have no business becoming involved in the high-stakes world of crown and coin. The king and his court will inevitably become subject to the single master of intelligence who decides the extent of each person's understanding. Actions are based on knowledge; the master of information decides the actions that will be taken, since he controls the information the decision makers receive.

Littlefinger long ago admitted what he is, and now he will claim his prize: the self-confirmed right to choose the man or boy who sits the Iron Throne.

POWER

Khal Drogo
Great Khal of the Dothraki Sea of Essos

The children ride before they've even learned to walk. Young warriors learn to shoot a bow from a moving horse before they've reached their fifth birthday. They are as fast as the wind and virtually invincible in combat against the slow, slashing, armour-encased knights of Westeros.

Who but the strongest has the right to assume the throne? Lord Baelish can have his secret little birds and spiders. Espionage is useful only for those cases in which an enemy exhibits weakness. What is the value of surreptitious knowledge when it uncovers no weakness of any kind?

Governor Arnold Schwarzenegger
Bodybuilder, Actor, Politician
Stefanie Broughton, U.S. Navy, 2005

The only thing standing between Khal Drogo and domination of the entire known world is the historic reticence to load men and horses into ships to cross the roiling black sea. But we should not confuse traditional hesitation with fear. Khal Drogo fears no man, and he fears no water—not even the salt water that is death to horses.

How have the weak royal houses of the last three hundred years helped the people of the Seven Kingdoms? Weakness leads to attempts to wrest power from the ruling clan, which leads to war, which causes the death of hundreds of thousands. Does not the very order of things demand that the strongest be installed as absolute ruler? Wouldn't such adherence to natural law tend to bring greatest stability and prosperity to all? The failures of House Targaryen, House Baratheon, and House Stark are the inevitable result of reliance on the stratagems of the weak: honour, family values, the charisma of feeble and emasculated men, and the silliness of spiders and whisperers. Weakness has led to the almost continual suffering of everyone in the Seven Kingdoms.

Soon only the weak will suffer their due. The choicest horses, the best land, and the most desirable women go to the strong, to the victors who will rule the land according to the laws of strength and might. All the people shall be united into a single khalasar, all the people of the world will become the herd of the greatest of khals. The time of suffering will end when all bend their knee to the Khal of Khals, to the Stallion Who Mounts the World.

FAIRNESS

Jon Snow
Steward
The Night's Watch

"It's the steward's life for me," Sam said.
"There's honour in being a steward," Jon replied.
Jon Snow could tell everyone of the great honour associated with service as a steward. Because of his great skill, entirely amenable to the demands of life as a ranger, his was a higher calling, a superior station. Until, that is, Jeor Mormont, Lord Commander of the Night's Watch, gave Jon his assignment: "Jon, to the stewards." Only one man was smiling when Jon's assignment was read. Jon was certain Ser Alliser Thorne was responsible for his appointment to the lowest class of men of the Night's Watch.

Maester Aemon: "Jon Snow, Lord Commander Mormont has requested you for his personal steward."
Jon Snow: [Sneering] "Will I serve the Lord Commander meals and fetch hot water for his bath?"
Maester Aemon: "Certainly. And keep a fire burning in his chambers, change his sheets and blankets daily, and do everything else the Lord Commander requires of you."
Jon Snow: "Do you take me for a servant?"
Maester Aemon: "We took you for a man of the Night's Watch. But perhaps we were wrong in that."

That anyone as capable as Jon Snow should end up being assigned the most menial of assignments could only mean he had been intentionally slighted, forced into a service role when he should have been given an assignment commensurate with his rare abilities and reflecting the glory of the great works he was sure to accomplish in the future.

"Stewards are nothing but maids," Jon said. "I'm a better swordsman and rider than any of you. It's not fair."

I feel for Jon Snow, because I have been in his shoes many times. I have been passed over for promotion, losing positions to people less qualified. I have been singled out for punishment, for tax audits, for reprimand, when I have done nothing to deserve these chastisements. Others who have committed offence, have cheated on their taxes, have behaved in any number of undignified ways suffered not the slightest rebuke. It's not fair.

Justice
Maarten van Heemskerck, 1556

If you examine your life, you are likely to find at least a few instances in which life has treated you unfairly. Your accomplishments have gone unrecognised, while those of lesser skill have risen to fame and fortune. You have worked hard on projects, only to have them cancelled or dismissed by those above you. You try to get ahead, but the world conspires against you.

But fairness requires a certain point of view. What I deem manifestly fair will seem irrelevant or unfair to you. What is clearly fair in your mind may seem inherently unfair, unwise, and untenable to another. Our determination to seek what we believe is our due often makes us blind to the many possibilities attendant to any situation.

Jon Snow was blinded by his attitude of superiority and his contempt for others, even for his friend, Samwell Tarly. He did not understand the true reason for his appointment as the Lord Commander's personal assistant, even when the significance was as plain as day to Sam and Pyp.

Jon wishes to believe that fairness is a fundamental constituent of leadership. Not only must a leader be fair, but the factors used in selecting leaders must be fair. Because the selection process in his case was influenced (or so he thought) by non-objective criteria, the process was flawed and unfair, unnaturally biased against him. This seemed to Jon to violate something vital in the structure of the universe. In a perfect world, leaders would be chosen fairly.

Perhaps many facets of the world would change if the universe were perfect. Would David Cameron have risen to #10 Downing if we lived in a perfect world? Surely other MPs had more experience, had better ideas for leading the UK to a more secure and prosperous future. Does anyone believe that Barack Obama had more experience than Hillary Clinton or John McCain? Can anyone, other than the most rabid partisan, claim that Clinton or McCain would have served with less distinction in the White House than its current occupant? If not, then what fairness is there in being given Cameron as Prime Minister and Obama as President?

Life is not fair, and never will be. It is not an expectation that any of us can have. If we do succumb to the common temptation posed by the strange ideal of "fairness", we are most likely to become bitter, hostile, and withdrawn. Why participate in the game when the rules are rigged and everyone playing the game is against us?

Leadership, and the qualifications for leadership, will never be fair. Leaders will always be chosen in a manner that is biased, subjective, and entirely subject to the winds of politics and the whims of those already in power. Jon Snow has much to learn about the way the world works—especially if he aspires to lead.

SERVICE

Lord Jeor Mormont
Lord Commander of the Night's Watch

"You came to us as outlaws: poachers, rapers, killers, thieves. You came alone, in chains, without friends or honour. You came to us rich, you came to us poor. Some of you bear the names of great houses, others only bastard names or no names at all. It does not matter. All that is in the past. Here, on the Wall, we're all one house."

Social standing, wealth, title, criminal background: None of it mattered on the Wall. All men started from the same place, and all claimed the same title: Brother of the Night's Watch.

It might seem from the flavour of Lord Commander Mormont's speech that the Night's Watch was based entirely on an unbiased egalitarianism. All men were treated as equals, every man was offered the same opportunities, and everyone had the same potential for advancement. But this was not the organising principle of the brotherhood. Not at all.

The Vigil
John Pettie, 1884

The key to understanding the structure of the Night's Watch is found in the final words of Commander Mormont prior to giving the new brothers their assignments. "You've all been assigned an order, according to our needs and your strengths." The needs of the Night's Watch and the abilities of the recruits were matched. Assignments were influenced neither by family nor by law. Position within the organisation was determined on the basis of neither charisma nor secret knowledge. Fairness had absolutely nothing to do with any assignment. The single criterion by which men were placed was quite simple: Service. Men were placed in the position in which it was felt they could best serve the needs of the Night's Watch. But there was something more:

"A man of the Night's Watch lives his life for the realm. Not for a king or a lord, or the honour of this house or that house. Or for gold or glory or a woman's love. But for the *realm*, and all the people in it."

Service in the Night's Watch was not service for its own sake. Work can be thought of as bearing inherent dignity and value, but this was not the attitude of the

Night's Watch. Service at the Wall was service of the needs of the entire continent, whether a united government, seven separate kingdoms, or no kingdoms at all.

The best leader is not the person who can most intelligently interpret the law. The ideal leader is not drawn from the most influential family or from the name with longest pedigree. Charisma, physical strength, and the ability to balance competing interests through lies, deception, and espionage have no place in the highest echelons of enduring government. The best leader is, quite simply, the person who is best able to serve the needs of all the people.

SERVICE AND ICE, LEADERSHIP AND FIRE

The Romans Cause a Wall to be Built for the Protection of the South
William Bell Scott, 1857

I hope the ideal of service seems to you a reasonable expectation of leadership. Of the seven theses explored during this seventh episode of Game of Thrones, I believe service provides the strongest basis for competent and just leadership. I think if we were to present these seven ideas to George Martin, he would almost certainly tell us that the Wall has stood for eight thousand years, primarily because men did not stand on honour or accomplishment or fame or glory. The Wall endured because the strongest basis for leadership at the Wall was service.

However, I believe GRRM would also tell us that service does not constitute his ideal for leadership. At the end of this long tale, the person who sits the Iron Throne may well be the individual who is best able to serve the needs of the entire continent—perhaps the entire known world. But I am absolutely certain of this: Specific qualities are required of GRRM's ideal leader, and these qualities have so far not become manifest in any of the leading candidates playing the current game of thrones.

In the end, the song of ice and fire will not be led by the singer most capable of capturing every note high and low, the voice with the most melodious tones or the most captivating phrasing or rhythm. No, the master of this song of ice and fire will be not only singer and performer, but in all ways an accomplished musician. The leader of the orchestra and chorus will be conductor, but more importantly, composer and music theorist. The leader who sits the Iron Throne will grasp not only the nuances of politics, but the deep realities behind the story, the old ways, the Old Gods, the whispers in the weirwoods and the laughter of the children.

There is an eighth thesis, the Martin Thesis, and it is the basis of everything we have seen in seven hours, and will be the basis of everything for dozens of episodes and years to come. We have barely begun the journey, and we have only heard the first tantalising notes of the grand melody to come. I am looking forward to hearing the score, and joining my voice to the song.

Khal Drogo
copyright Dalisa 2011
used with permission

"The Council has determined," Queen Cersei said, "that Ser Jaime Lannister will take your place as Lord Commander of the Kingsguard."

Ser Barristan seethed at the Queen's words. "The man who profaned his blade with the blood of the king he was sworn to defend?"

We believe we understand the full significance and import of this scene. The Queen has dishonoured Ser Barristan, and in so doing, brought dishonour to herself and her house. What other interpretation is possible? Surely a knight stands for honour more than anything else, does he not?

If Season One has had one major theme, that theme has been honour, as best exemplified by Lord Eddard Stark. A man as honourable as Ned Stark would recognise the greatness of another man's honour, and if he counts Ser Barristan Selmy as bearing greater honour than himself, we ought to consider his evaluation to carry more merit than any judgment we might make about a knight's character.

But Ned Stark is wrong. He is wrong to the point of being chained in a dark, disease-infested dungeon, awaiting death. All of us watching this scene tonight were wrong, no less than Ned Stark. Ser Barristan Selmy did not hold honour as the highest of the virtues. Ser Barristan is a representative of perfection, held up for us as an ideal. But which ideal? If he is not honour incarnate, which high trait of humanity does he exemplify?

Tonight's episode was a rich feast of conflicting ideals, all of them higher than honour, all of them mightier than the sword.

MIGHTIER THAN FIVE SWORDS

Somewhere among the millions who call ourselves fans of ASoIaF there is a musician—a composer—who has penned a song in honour of Syrio Forel. "The First Sword of Braavos does not run." Even when he is outnumbered five to one, even when his enemies carry sharp steel and he bears nothing more than a hollow wooden stick, he does not run.

Courage such as this is worthy of song. But Syrio Forel was not the first hero tonight to face a ruthless and heavily armed enemy, naked, alone, armed only with courage and with the certitude of self-confidence and the indomitable strength of conscience.

Probably no songs will be written about Septa Mordane, but songs there should be. If courage can be personified, tonight we witnessed its greatest example in the person of a humble, dignified tutor who knew she faced certain death, but who gave her life so that her pupil might live.

Yet in that moment, as she walked toward death, she must have tasted fear in her throat. She must have known there was no alternative, and that the unspeakable destiny that awaited her at the end of the hall had nothing to do with her courage. Septa Mordane was the supreme example not of courage, not of honour, but of a much higher virtue.

GRRM has been looking at the multi-faceted nature of honour for the past eight weeks. Now he begins to reveal to us something of the nature of courage.

The case of Syrio Forel is fascinating. From the pages of the novel, Syrio Forel's final magnificent fight can be interpreted in any number of ways. From tonight's episode we are confronted with a disquieting truth: He could have grabbed one of the fallen swords, but he did not. He had plenty of time. Instead, he went into grand soliloquies that had no place in the midst of a life-or-death battle. Syrio Forel, for a few moments, became literature's greatest swordsman, Cyrano de Bergerac, a single man fighting off a hundred swords while simultaneously composing a poem about his deed.

Cyrano de Bergerac is a play, Game of Thrones is a television series. Perhaps it is GRRM's intention that we consider Syrio Forel's long-winded speeches merely a stage dramatisation, an amplification aimed solely at embellishing the tension of the moment. I believe there is much more to Syrio's words. In fact, I believe we are obliged to bring the fullest measure of deliberation not only to Syrio's final speech, but also to his actions—to what he did, and what he failed to do. He did not show honour. With Septa Mordane he did not show courage. He showed something much greater. It was for this reason that his speech was necessary, and his refusal to pick up a sword was the most important choice he had ever made in his life.

What did Khal Drogo mean to say when he pushed away the arakh, spun around, and dropped the daggers to the ground? What did Obi Wan Kenobi really mean when he said, "You can't win, Darth. If you strike me down, I shall become more powerful than you could possibly imagine"—and then pulled up his lightsaber and closed his eyes? What did it mean when Jon tried to kill Othor's corpse with a sword but could not? What possessed the defenceless Septa Mordane to face a gang of thugs armed with enough steel to turn her into bite-size pieces to feed the dogs? These are all the same inquiry, really, and they all begin with this simplest of questions: Why did Syrio Forel not pick up one of the fallen swords?

CALLING THE BANNERS

The calling the banners scene was effective. We know that each of the hundreds of ravens released *en masse* from Winterfell represented hundreds of men, each of them pledged to defend the Lord of Winterfell. The original intention, never presented on screen, was nothing short of majestic. As Westeros.org noted:

"Theon's expectation that Robb will be afraid if he isn't stupid was nicely played, as was the gorgeous image of the castle's ravens fanning out to race to the seats of the scores of landholding lords, knights, and others who owe Winterfell their fealty. Well done! It doesn't entirely replace the very cool-sounding, extremely expensive-sounding "calling of the banners" scene GRRM apparently wrote in his first draft—that would have been something to see—but it certainly is a decent substitute."

I agree. The substitution was decent. But it might have been spectacular, as fans of old Yul Brynner movies know (see "The Ride to Dubno" in the 1962 version of Taras Bulba—you should be able to find it on YouTube). If they could do it in 1962, why couldn't they do it in 2011?

Gathering of the Army
unknown artist, Palace of Barcelona, late 13ᵗʰ century

It must have seemed madness to everyone south of the Neck. "Your son—against the Lannisters?" Lysa asked Catelyn. Robb's 18,000 against House Lannister's 60,000; an untested teenage boy against a battle-hardened general who had seen every major battle in the last forty years? It had to seem lunacy.

Action against the Lannisters was fine by "the Greatjon," the elder Jon of the extreme northern House Umber of the Last Hearth, but even he could not imagine a "boy" going up against the seasoned and ruthless Lannisters.

Robb: Galbart Glover will lead the van.
Greatjon: The bloody Wall will melt before an Umber marches behind a Glover. I will lead the van, or I will take my men and march them home.

There were several problems with the Greatjon's statement, and they were only peripherally related to the idea of honour. Fealty was at stake. Robb had to demonstrate courage, and he did so, rising to meet Jon Umber's challenge to his authority.

The end of this scene, in which the Greatjon swore fealty by saying "Your meat is bloody tough!", was virtually identical in flavour to the famous knighting scene from one of the great fantasy films, *Excalibur.*

In the film, Sir Uryenes leads a majority faction opposed to "the boy-king" Arthur's ascension to the throne. He has laid siege to the castle of one of Arthur's supporters. Arthur, barely a squire, jumps from the castle wall and pulls Uryenes from his horse and into the water of the moat, where he commands Uryenes, at sword point, to swear allegiance to him. The magical sword, Excalibur, held firm to his neck, the knight refuses. What happened next was one of the great moments in cinema.

Uryenes: [scornfully] A noble knight swear faith to a squire?
Arthur: You're right... I'm not yet a knight. [Hands Excalibur to Uyrenes and kneels] You, Uryenes, will make me a knight.
Merlin: [Alarmed] What's this? What's this?
Uryenes: [arms shaking, he hesitates and then touches Excalibur to Arthur's shoulder] In the name of God, St Michael and St George, I give you the right to bear arms and the power to mete justice.
Arthur: That duty I will solemnly obey, as knight and king.
Merlin: I never saw this.
Uryenes: Rise... King Arthur.
[Uryenes kneels before Arthur]
Uryenes: I am your humble knight, and I swear allegiance to the courage in your veins. So strong it is, its source must be Uther Pendragon's. I doubt you no more!

King Arthur had "courage in his veins"; Robb Stark had "tough meat". In both cases, an experienced knight swore fealty to a "boy". But much more than fealty was at stake in both cases. *Excalibur* was the story of what it meant to be king; Game of Thrones is going to be a six- or seven-year examination of the qualities required of the one who would rightfully sit the Iron Throne. The questions are virtually identical. I believe the answers will turn out to share strong similarities.

But what is the question?

A QUESTION OF MERCY, A QUESTION OF LISTENING

If neither honour nor courage is the predominant concern of Game of Thrones, what is the central idea? Perhaps thoughtfulness toward others, even one's enemies?

Varys: What madness led you to tell the Queen you learned the truth about Joffrey's birth?
Ned: The madness of mercy. That she might save her children.
Varys: Ah, the children. It's always the innocents who suffer. It wasn't the wine that killed Robert, nor the boar. The wine slowed him down and the boar ripped him open. But it was your mercy that killed the King... I trust you know you're a dead man, Lord Eddard.

Ned had so many opportunities to seize the moment, to end Cersei's ascension to power. He could indeed have saved Robert's life, and his reign, if he had confided the truth of Cersei's poisoning of Jon Arryn, of her attempt to kill Bran, of her incestuous couplings with her twin brother, Jaime. Prudence did not force him to hold his tongue. It was mercy, his thoughtfulness toward Joffrey and the Queen's other children, that led to Robert's death, the threats against his own children, and his consignment to a dungeon cell.

The Eleven-Faced Goddess of Mercy
Unknown artist, 12th century

Eddard Stark chose good and admirable virtues on which to found his life. But he chose the wrong virtues. He instilled the same virtues in his children, meaning that his progeny share in the same deficiencies that are leading House Stark to ruin. The exchange between Bran and the slave wildling, Osha, was most illuminating in this regard.

Osha: You hear them, boy? The Old Gods are answerin' ya.
Bran: What are you doing here?
Osha: They're my gods, too. Beyond the Wall, they're the only gods. Even slaves are allowed to pray.
Bran: You're not a slave.
Osha: [raises her leg and jingles the leg iron attached to her]
Bran: Well, your friend did put a knife to my throat.
Osha: I'm not complaining...just tellin' truths.
Bran: What did you mean about hearing the gods?

Osha: You asked them. They're answerin' you. [She closes her eyes] Shhh. Open your ears.

Bran: It's only the wind.

Osha: Who do you think sends the wind, if not the gods? They see you. They hear you.

Osha challenged Bran's understanding of his faith. He sat at the weirwood rattling off petitions: "Please watch over Robb. And watch over all the men from Winterfell…" We might well imagine Ned Stark praying in exactly the same way—relaying his concerns and desires, perhaps every now and then offering a prayer of thanksgiving for the gods' beneficial intervention in his life.

Most of us who believe in a higher power, I suppose, are no different from Bran and Ned. We send out supplications and give thanks for benefits or graces received. How many of us take the time to listen for an answer to our prayers? Among those who listen for an answer, how many listen for a *question*?

Among the women and men who pray seven or twelve times a day, there are few supplications. Franciscan friars and Buddhist monks and cloistered Benedictines do not go about their days requesting this or that convenience or perceived need. If they request anything at all of their Creator, it is a change in their own perception. "Make me an instrument of Your peace," St. Francis and his followers say. Change my heart, Lord. Make me receptive to Your will. These are the most frequent types of petitions from among the women and men who pray several times each day. But if you asked them what prayer truly is, they would tell you Osha has it right. Prayer is not a process of listing acquisitive hopes and dreams. Prayer, more than anything else, is a process of preparing oneself to *listen*.

Benedictine monks gather two to seven times a day for prayer. During Evening Prayer, they chant psalms and recite short spoken prayers followed by a brief reading from their Sacred Scripture. All of that is a long, ritualised preamble to the focus of their thirty-minute routine. It is the absolute silence that follows the scripture reading that the men look forward to. For it is in that five minutes of perfect silence that they have the opportunity to listen, which for these men is the objective of prayer.

Laypeople in such an environment are like fish out of water. Whether they are among Buddhist monks or cloistered Dominican nuns, the ritualised chants, prayers, and absolute silence have no meaning for them. The silences become uncomfortable occasions of psychological turmoil, not opportunities for focussed contemplation.

You are wondering what prayer has to do with Arya's final lesson from Syrio Forel, or Khal Drogo's decision to drop his weapons to the dust and fight an armed man. In fact, a few sessions of Evening Prayer with Benedictine monks are probably the best preparation for Khal Drogo's type of hand-versus-weapon fighting. The prayer of cloistered monks and the decision to fight steel with wood both require the same frame of mind: attentive listening.

I AM A KNIGHT

Death's Wail
Fritz Rehm, Jugend Magazine, 1897

Last week Ned Stark said no man could question Ser Barristan's honour. Lord Stark apparently did not read my essay on Episode Five, in which I not only questioned Ser Barristan's honour, I compared him to Nazi war criminals.

Ser Barristan Selmy had no honour, and he proved it in this spectacular scene, the focal point and true dénouement of tonight's episode.

The Queen informed Ser Barristan that he would retire, to be replaced as Commander of the Kingsguard by her brother, Ser Jaime. Ser Barristan bristled at the pronouncement. "The man who profaned his blade with the blood of the king he was sworn to defend?"

Many viewing this scene will take Ser Barristan's action of unsheathing his sword, pointing it in direct threat to King Joffrey, and then addressing the King as "boy" to be an example of supreme irony. How could he question the appointment of the "Kingslayer" as Lord Commander of the Kingsguard and less than twenty seconds later threaten the life of the King, then disrespectfully address him as "boy"?

As I wrote in my Episode 1.05 essay, Ser Barristan placed duty ahead of honour. He was able to threaten the King with drawn sword because he was not a man of honour. Ser Barristan was a man of duty. Queen Cersei and the Small Council severed Ser Barristan's relationship to the King. Since Ser Barristan no longer served the King, he was free to threaten him, or even kill him.

While he was Lord Commander of the Kingsguard, no amount of gold, no inducements of any kind could have persuaded him to kill the king he protected with his life. Protecting the King was his duty, but more than that, protecting the King was his duty *because he was a knight*.

Being a knight, as with anything else in life, is an agreement between parties. The office of Knight of the Kingsguard was perpetually binding to both parties to the agreement. That is to say, a knight of the Kingsguard served for life, regardless of the person sitting the throne, regardless of the feelings any member of the Small Council may have expressed about a particular knight. By severing the connection between knight and duty, Queen Cersei was breaking an unbreakable contract. Her action violated something fundamental to the core ideals of the realm.

Listening requires the active and respectful participation of two parties. Listening is a right, not a privilege. As Osha said, "Even slaves are allowed to pray." The gods are obliged to listen and speak. Kings and queens are obliged to listen and speak. There is something in the nature of the gods that precludes anything less than full attention to the wellbeing of every petitioner. But the petitioner must, more than anything else, strive to listen. "Not my will, but Thy will be done." Some petitioners will be required to sacrifice—even to the point of giving up their own lives.

"My tongue lied," Syrio told Arya. "My eyes shouted the truth. You were not seeing...The seeing—the true seeing—that is the heart of swordplay." Swordplay is between two parties. At the risk of severe injury or death, both parties are obliged to see—to listen, as we would understand it in this essay—to what the other person is saying.

ENGAGEMENT

Syrio listened better than anyone around him. He knew what the Lannister guards were truly saying when they told him to hand over Arya because he was fully engaged.

For the rest of her life, Arya will listen and see more attentively than she ever has, for she knows anything less than full engagement will lead to her death.

Khal Drogo could walk into a fight without weapons—even against a heavily armed man—because he was fully engaged.

President Obama Listening
The White House, Washington, D.C., 2010

Listening is engagement. It is immersive giving of self to another. Khal Drogo listened so well, he was so completely engaged in his opponent, that he was aware of every one of his enemy's intentions. The opposing combatant was simply incapable of surprising Khal Drogo with any thrust or feint. Because he listened better than any warrior in the world, the Great Khal walked into the match incapable of losing.

Ned Stark's sin was not honour, or mercy, or justice, or any of the other virtues that defined his being. Ned Stark's great and unforgivable sin was disengagement.

Ser Barristan Selmy was not an honourable man. He was a man of duty, but more than anything, he was a man engaged. If we say the word "knight" in the context of ASoIaF, we should think of one man: Ser Barristan Selmy. He is the definition of duty. He is the definition of engagement. He is the ideal that transcends honour, mercy, justice, courage, and every other piddling quality mistakenly held to be an ideal.

Ser Barristan is a knight. He *is* duty and service. The Queen doesn't know this. She has unleashed on herself and on her house the most terrible enemy anyone could possibly imagine. Just as Khal Drogo needed neither arakh nor dagger to finish off his enemy, Ser Barristan Selmy required neither sword nor knife to defeat his foe.

Game of Thrones does not end this season, because we have much more to learn from Ser Barristan Selmy, and the many other exemplars of listening and engagement: Bran Stark, Tyrion Lannister, Jon Snow, Arya Stark, and the most fascinating woman in Essos, Khaleesi Daenerys Stormborn of House Targaryen, heir to the Iron Throne.

Let us listen. Let us immerse ourselves in the story. Let us *engage*. For engagement, dear friends, is mightier than the sword.

Knight With Sword
Dreamstime Royalty Free Images, 2012

What is the purpose of a bastard sword? Such a weapon confers greater power than a single-hand sword, but as with all longswords, the bastard sword has two polished blades; it cuts both ways. The warrior wielding such a sword must render a decision. Shall I cut forward or back, up or down?

Tonight's episode, *Baelor*, was about the double-edged sword. Every character was given a life-or-death decision. That a concerted effort to choose life for Ned Stark instead resulted in his execution marked the most fascinating event of the episode, not because it disclosed anything of interest about a particular decision, but because it revealed critical properties of choice itself.

Who wields the Sword of Mormont, and the direction she decides to cut, is the most compelling question of Game of Thrones.

LORD FREY'S SWORD

In Catelyn Stark's mind, Lord Walder Frey had a simple choice: Forbid the northern army passage across the bridge, or allow the crossing after extracting a ridiculous toll out of proportion to the cost of giving passage to eighteen thousand men. It was a one-time decision with immediate consequences to the outcome of a single battle. In Lord Walder's mind, the question was also simple, but the proposition centred around the feeling of sharp steel cutting through the brittle bones and tired muscles of his neck. It was a decision that would have enduring consequences for House Frey. Was the likelihood of being branded a traitor by the Crown offset by anything Catelyn Stark might have to offer?

The question was framed quite differently by Lady Stark and Lord Frey, but the final question remained the same: Allow the crossing, or forbid it? Lord Frey would argue that the question of treason preceding the final decision regarding use of the bridge was fundamental to the entire dialogue. To Lady Stark, any demands imposed by Lord Frey were simply the caprices of a lecherous old man. To Lord Frey, his decision had repercussions for himself and for his house for the next three or four generations. Depending on the house that finally took the Iron Throne, House Frey would either prosper magnificently, or suffer attack, execution, and enslavement.

With this life-or-death interaction at The Twins we begin to see the reality that there are many ways to formulate a two-edged question. The manner in which we pose the question is more often than not a measure of the extent to which we have mapped out the most likely series of consequences. However, there are many other considerations that should be brought to an examination of dilemma and choice.

LORD MORMONT'S SWORD

"It's a man's sword. It'll take a man to wield it."

That the sword had been in the Mormont family for five hundred years was not incidental. That Lord Mormont was passing the sword to Jon Snow carried tremendous significance. But the element of greatest moment in this scene was the Lord Commander's preamble to bestowing the longsword: "It's a man's sword."

The Commander of the Night's Watch believed Jon Snow had potential. Of all the young men most recently chosen for the Night's Watch, Mormont chose Jon as his personal assistant. But Jon was not yet a man. "Now, don't think this means

I approve of this nonsense with you and Alliser Thorne. It's a man's sword. It'll take a man to wield it." Jon's knee-jerk, childish response to Alliser Thorne's taunts was sure indication that, even with his skill and tremendous potential, he was not yet a man.

Samurai With Sword
unknown photographer, circa 1860

Mormont gave the sword to Jon in recognition of innate abilities. No one else in the Night's Watch knew the Commander was being stalked by a wight. If not for Jon, Mormont would have been killed, or perhaps would himself have become a wight. But this was not the first time Jon Snow demonstrated unusual capability in determining the true meaning of signs and events. Recall in the direwolves scene from the very first episode that it was Jon who attached significance to the five direwolf pups: "Lord Stark, there are five pups, one for each of the Stark children. The direwolf is the sigil of your house. They were meant to have them." In the original version of the scene, Jon went even further, noting there were three male pups and two female pups, making the correspondence to the Stark children even more meaningful. No one else in the scene made any such connections. Jon must have been demonstrating the same analytic and synthetic abilities at the Wall, but he brought even more. For the last several months he has been teaching and training his fellow recruits. Thanks to Jon, many more men were comfortable wielding dagger, blade, and bow.

The significance to us, as we consider the question of dilemma-based decisions, is that the person posing the question is at least as important as the final form given to the question. The question can have enduring value only if the full range of consequences of the bifurcation are given mature consideration by a wise and tempered mind.

It is more than likely that Jon Snow will ascend to a leadership position in the brotherhood of the Night's Watch. His decisions could determine the life and death of hundreds or thousands of men. Longclaw is the symbol of the great weight of responsibility imposed on those who would pose two-edged command questions, weigh their consequences, and render wise and well-considered decisions.

MAESTER AEMON'S SWORD

What value should we attach to the incoherent ramblings of a blind old man long ago exiled to a forgotten life on the very periphery of civilisation? Should this value be any different than the attention we might give those of the heir to the Iron Throne? We might believe there is great distinction in value, since there is obviously tremendous distinction in potential ramifications. If I perform a kindness for an old man, nothing more concrete than spiritual benefit may accrue. However, if I perform a kindness for the heir to the throne, I may be rewarded with unimaginable power and wealth. In the same way, if I slight a powerless old man, I am not likely to suffer anything more substantive than spiritual torment for my sin. On the other hand, if I in any way slight the heir to the throne, I may simply lose face—or I may lose my head when the new king has me publicly executed.

The question before us is value. The consideration I have so far raised is that of perceived consequence. But are consequences the only possible consideration? I submit that any such limited consideration runs contrary to the demands of the Sword of Mormont. If maturity is required to wield a longsword, it necessarily follows that any sword-edge decision must be based on a dilemma properly understood. A question worthy of consideration can be understood only by those of wisdom and maturity, and these greater faculties must be informed by every factor bearing on the situation. Certainly a logical consequence of any particular action is only one of many factors that must be weighed.

This blind, white-haired old man was quite possibly the only legitimate living heir to the throne. He may have renounced his claim, but the fact remains that his full name was Aemon Targaryen, third son of Maekar I, King of the Seven Kingdoms. Whether he was forced to forswear the crown or gave it up of his own volition, we can be sure that he weighed more than the series of consequences emanating from his decision to remain at the Wall even after the Sack of King's Landing, and the consequences that would have flowed from any decision to involve himself in the political manoeuvrings around the throne.

Allegory of Choice
copyright MaraB. is a brainless s.f., 2006, CC-SA 2.0
photograph cropped by Pearson Moore

Aemon: Tell me, did you ever wonder why the men of the Night's Watch take no wives and father no children?
Jon: No.
Aemon: So they will not love. Love is the death of duty. If the day should ever come when your Lord Father was forced to choose between honour on the one hand and those he loves on the other, what would he do?
Jon: He'd do whatever is right, no matter what.

Aemon: Then Lord Stark is one man in ten thousand. Most of us are not so strong. What is honour compared to a woman's love? What is duty against the feel of a newborn son in your arms? Or a brother's smile?
Jon: Sam told you.
Aemon: We're all human. We all do our duty when there's no cost to it. Honour comes easy to him. But sooner or later, in every man's life, there comes a day when it is not easy. A day when he must choose.

Maester Aemon spoke from the unpleasant experience of having had to choose, at a time when personal or family gain was more obvious than any benefit that might obtain through an opposing action. In his youth he had considered the benefits to the realm of his ascension to the throne. By his own decision, or by the vagaries of the court, he instead ended up taking the Black. Decades later, already an old man, with the Usurper and his coterie of Lannister and Stark swords threatening the capital, Aemon Targaryen was forced to make another decision. He stayed at the Wall.

Maester Aemon brought considerations to his deliberation that would probably have seemed peripheral to anyone else. What of his sacred oath to the Night's Watch? The oath was sacred only among the brothers of the Black. If he became central to a ruling political faction, his former oath would be dismissed or forgotten, and would certainly have had no bearing on the administration of the realm.

The lesson, to those who would wield the Sword of Mormont, is that life-or-death questions must be framed so as to include in their creation considerations that may seem unrelated, peripheral, or inconsequential. Maester Aemon's oath does, in fact, have bearing on the discussion around the politics of King's Landing. The Wall was not put in place after some king's fancy. The Wall has a reason, and the brotherhood of the Night's Watch has a purpose and a value that may exceed even the worth of the Iron Throne. The truly wise bearer of the Sword of Mormont will have to weigh all considerations, not only those raised by partisans, or those obvious at the time.

QUEEN DAENERYS' SWORD

"I have never been nothing. I am the blood of the dragon."
In a few short days we will learn the full depth of Daenerys Targaryen's words. Others march with cold sword or biting arakh; the heir to the Iron Throne marches with flaming sword and the passion of dragons.

Modern science allows us to keep a body alive, even after the patient has been clinically dead for months, or even decades. Those of us old enough to remember the mid-1970s recall the nearly daily reports of court battles over the life of Karen Ann Quinlan, who was kept alive on a ventilator. An autopsy after her death revealed several critical parts of her brain were severely damaged or not at all functional. Nevertheless, for two years the court cases determining her fate dragged on. The more recent case of Terri Schiavo is a reminder that no universally accepted decision has been reached regarding the meaning of human life, nor is there agreement on the efforts that must be made to sustain human life.

When Mirri Maz Duur told the Khaleesi, "There is a spell. Some would say death is cleaner," we saw a woman desperate to maintain her position. But we need to look more closely at her motivations. She did not fear the bloodrider who said when the Khal died she would be nothing. She was not motivated by fear. She was motivated by the person she truly is, by the person circumstance has allowed her to become.

The Sorceress
Georges Merle, 1883

I believe Daenerys Targaryen understood the most likely interpretation of Mirri's words. Khal Drogo would be better off dead. She could keep him alive by her magic, yes, but he would no longer be the person he was. He would become something closer to a human vegetable, an automaton with neither reason nor personality. Perhaps in her heart she hoped for something better, but her heart was not the organ guiding her desire to keep Khal Drogo alive at all costs.

What Daenerys Targaryen brought to her formulation of the sword-edge question was the nature of her identity as a Targaryen, as a trueborn daughter of the dragon. That the character of a wife should have any bearing at all on the life or death of anyone else in the world—even her husband—ought to strike us as nonsensical. Nevertheless, this was the most important element informing her desire to keep the Khal alive.

Daenerys has put forward the question. She realised the attempt to prolong the Khal's life would mean death. Certainly a life as important as Khal Drogo's would require a death no less important. Nevertheless, the questions stands. I will go no farther in defining the question, or the Khaleesi's response to the question she poses. I would say, to those who are interested in a deeper consideration of the question, that you may wish to ponder earlier statements she has made about herself, and about her brother, Viserys. The consequences of her thought, in conjunction with her desire to assert her identity through Khal Drogo, may provide some insight into the most likely evolution of events in the near future.

CAPTAIN MORPHEUS' SWORD

He was captain of the *Nebuchadnezzar*, and expert in all matters related to the Matrix. But he was most famous for the sword-edge dilemma he posed to Neo. The red pill/blue pill dichotomy, one of the most famous ideas to come out of graphic science fiction, is so well known that even the image of a blue pill stamped with the word "facebook", is immediately understood as an attack on the social value of Facebook. Facebook has little social relevance, the image says, because in its electronic pages we can believe whatever we want to believe—about the world, and about ourselves. "I have eight hundred friends. Everybody loves me." It's a wonderful blue-pill illusion. How many of our Facebook "friends" would notice— or care—if we dropped dead tomorrow?

The superficial analysis of Morpheus' words is usually sufficient to our understanding. The red pill represented enlightenment, while the blue pill represented the pleasant bliss of ignorance. But read closely Morpheus' words to Neo: "You take the blue pill; the story ends. You wake up in your bed and believe whatever you want to believe. You take the red pill; you stay in Wonderland, and I show you how deep the rabbit hole goes."

Morpheus was offering more than a strict bifurcation between amnesia and enlightenment. Notice that the blue-pill, Matrix-fed reality would allow Neo to "believe whatever you want to believe." The red pill would not necessarily reveal "reality"; rather, the red pill would force the one committing to this course to remain "in Wonderland". The Matrix is an artificial electronic construct. But is "Wonderland" any more real than the Matrix?

The question is relevant to us, because the question recognises the possible illegitimacy of conditions we attach to the formulation of a proposition. If Wonderland is no more real than the Matrix, what do we achieve by choosing between blue pill and red pill? What will we learn of the world or ourselves through a Wonderland enlightenment? Do we unconsciously impose on our life-or-death questions any conditions or considerations that have no bearing on the question?

Of course, we are equally justified in considering Wonderland to deliver a broader and deeper understanding of reality than any single person could achieve by experience alone. The "White Rabbit" of the television program *Lost* was a recurring motif dealing with realities greater than even the hero of the show could understand (see, for example, the final chapter of *LOST Humanity*; http://pearsonmoore-gets-lost.com/LostHumanity.aspx). That Christian Shephard, the White Rabbit of *Lost*, encompassed the full reality of the Island has become one of the most widely-debated of my positions on the popular television program.

Regardless of how we look at Wonderland, the red pill/blue pill decision again forces us to examine the nature of sword-edge dichotomies.

TEMPLE MASTER DOGEN'S SWORD

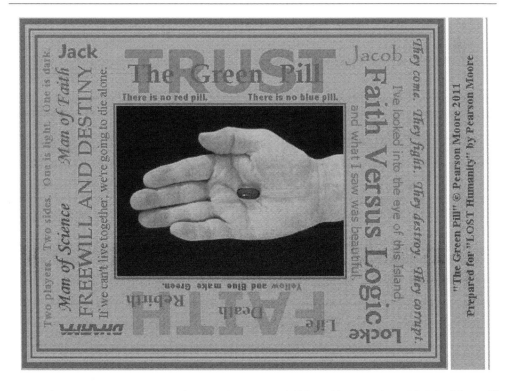

I have come to the conclusion that the red/blue dilemma is artificial. Blue-pill ignorance is not a reasonable choice for anyone seeking leadership. As I noted in last week's essay, Eddard Stark's sin was not a devotion to honour or mercy. Rather, the deficit of character that led to his imprisonment was an unwillingness to engage with his surroundings, at every possible level of his being.

If engagement is the mark of a true leader, the blue pill is never an option. It is a false choice. We need to go further, though, and say that the very presence of the blue pill among the range of choices artificially warps the topography of human volition, closing our mind to possibilities that are required to our complete enlightenment.

A true sword-edge question would carry such moment, and contain within it such breadth of wisdom and depth of consequence that no conditions other than those integral to the question would have any bearing on the final decision. Simply put, the question would contain all parameters necessary to a mature decision. Dogen's green pill, for example, was much more than a poison pill. It contained within itself the essence of life, death, and rebirth (see *LOST Humanity*, Chapters 1, 3, and 12; http://pearsonmoore-gets-lost.com/LostHumanity.aspx). In making life or death decisions, we need to seek paradox, we need to frame questions that transcend the limits of logic, because life and death do not conform to scientific limits. There is nothing theoretical about life or death. These are ultimate realities, and they require knowledge unrestrained by theory or precedent.

The Green Pill is the type of question I believe Daenerys Targaryen sought to formulate this week. I believe the question she eventually poses next week will lead to the radical transformation we will witness with our own eyes at the close of the first season of Game of Thrones. Hers is a question far beyond the confines of logic and science, but founded squarely on her inner awareness of her true identity, which has been the driving force behind her evolution from docile slave of her brother to a woman ready to command armies.

LADY SHAE'S SWORD

The candle flame burns skin in both directions.

Neither Shae's Burning Candle Game nor the Life Experiences Game proposed by Tyrion gave the Lord of House Lannister any additional insights into his new servant-concubine. Her life story obeyed none of the stereotypical progressions Tyrion thought he understood so well. Shae was an enigma because Tyrion lacked the ability to frame questions capable of revealing her inner self. I get the feeling that even a game of Twenty Questions, if Tyrion were questioner, would reveal little or nothing because Tyrion is so completely off-base in his assessment of this woman.

We need to look at this inability of Tyrion to serve as "a fine judge of character" in the context of the greater trends of his life. Tyrion reads whenever he can, but even with his unusual erudition, street smarts, and real-world practical abilities, he remains ignorant of truths that must become integral to those who would survive the coming winter. Recall, for instance, his conversation with Jon on the way to the Wall (Episode 1.02):

Jon: The Night's Watch protects the realm.
Tyrion: Ah, yes, yes, against grumkins and snarks and all the other monsters your wet nurse warned you about. You're a smart boy. You don't believe that nonsense.

Lady Shae holds a sword more powerful than the one wielded by Tyrion Lannister. She is immune to pain, and she understands the mature and informed framing of questions to a degree that has so far escaped Tyrion. She does not pose questions derived of worn stereotype. She brings mature judgment, awareness, and intuition. With Daenerys, she **engages**.

KING JOFFREY'S SWORD

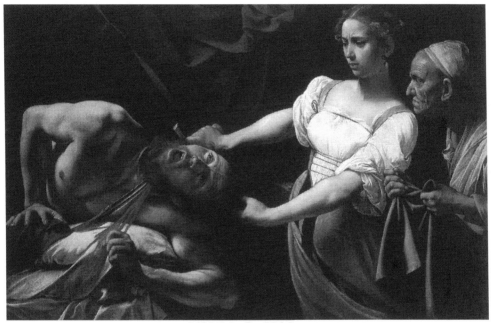

Judith Beheading Holofernes
Michelangelo Caravaggio, 1598

The symbolism of the execution and direwolf scenes of Episode One reached its stunning climax tonight, when Ice, the greatsword that Ned used to execute the deserter from the Wall, was used to end Lord Stark's life in exactly the same way. The highest officials in the realm had been conspiring for weeks to arrive at this singular moment, in which Eddard Stark confessed to crimes he did not commit. The outcome was foreseen by everyone at court: Lord Stark would confess, King Joffrey would exile him to the Wall, and the realm would return to peace. The problem with the plan was that no one informed the King of the necessary outcome.

That Eddard Stark could not be killed was so evident, I suppose, that no one thought the King—even a boy-king—would need to be informed of the absolute necessity of keeping the Lord of Winterfell alive. Lord Varys had been using every trick he had learned as a thespian, visiting Ned on a weekly basis at least, giving him nudges and encouragements as required to surrender his honour, to understand confession as the only means of saving his family from bloody execution at the hands of the Lannisters. The queen had worked hard to bring Sansa into the action plan, forcing her to believe that confession was the only route to her father's salvation.

In the end, Ned Stark had to receive pardon. It was the only way to ensure the dissolution of the northern army. How many of Robb's bannermen would continue to fight for him, after they learned of Eddard Stark's treason, when they heard that King Joffrey was indeed the true heir to the Iron Throne, that all of the former Lord Stark's manoeuvres had been hollow lies aimed at taking the Iron Throne? He was alive to live a life of penance at the Wall only because of the beneficence of their noble King. How many men would follow Lord Stannis Baratheon into battle to take a throne that rightfully belonged to Lord Stannis' nephew, their new King, Joffrey? How many of Lord Renly Baratheon's swords would commit to gaining the throne for him, when everyone in the realm supported Joffrey?

But no one thought to tell the King any of this.

So many important considerations were balanced atop the double-edged greatsword carried by Ser Ilyn Payne. Treason, certainly, was the least of these considerations. Grand Maester Pycelle was instructed to argue for mercy, and he did so tersely but eloquently. The Queen had chosen the venue—the Great Sept of Baelor—which virtually required an attitude of compassion and judgment of mercy. King Joffrey noted Lady Sansa's and the Queen's petitions for mercy. Everything about the scene required a merciful outcome, because the most important issue—the stability of the ruling House Lannister—was predicated on a kingdom at peace, and peace could be obtained only through Ned Stark's confession, contrition, and consignment to the Black.

There were so few pluses in the Execution column that the executioner was not even ready. Littlefinger and Varys must have made it known that no execution was to be carried out. "Be there, just in case, though," they probably said, not because they truly believed there was any chance the boy-king would order execution, but because the unknowing crowd would expect an executioner in their midst, ready to take off the traitor's head. Lord Varys was orchestrating his greatest stage drama, and good drama would require the keeping of appearances.

But everything went frightfully wrong. Perhaps the Queen could have overruled her testosterone-driven son, but not in front of five thousand angry citizens. Not in front of the entire royal court. That would have been more disastrous than Joffrey's execution order, and could only have served to remove the Queen from any semblance of power. She was reduced to shouting in Joffrey's face, "Please, stop this!", but Joffrey only laughed.

The choice was clear to Joffrey: Exercise mercy, like a woman, or exercise power, like a man. He gave no thought to Lord Robb Stark's eighteen thousand, to Stannis Baratheon's thousands, to the tens of thousands of loyal followers of Renly Baratheon, to the hundred thousand Queen Daenerys might someday command. He was a teenage boy, revving the engine of his race-car-red Camaro, asserting his control over powers given him.

We have seen many poorly-drawn questions this season, and many foolish decisions, but Joffrey's command was in a league all its own. With six short words, King Joffrey profaned the Great Sept of Baelor, destabilised the entire continent, and made it unlikely that he would survive into adulthood. We have seen few individuals evincing the qualities of one who would wield the Sword of Mormont. But we now know of at least one person who is entirely unsuited to the rigours of question formulation and decision making. The spiders know when a mad man or an incompetent sits the throne—and they know to move against him. King Joffrey will have to be continually on his guard, because some of his closest advisors and lieutenants will conspire relentlessly to return balance and peace to the Seven Kingdoms—and such harmony will be impossible as long as a powerful child, incapable of wielding the Sword of Mormont, sits the Iron Throne.

David Slaying Goliath
Peter Paul Rubens, 1630

He succumbed to Lord Varys' charms. He sacrificed his honour in exchange for a life of obscurity and shame among the brigands and thieves of the Night's Watch, confessing to crimes he did not commit and had never contemplated. Perhaps King Joffrey understood that one who would so easily surrender qualities of great value was not worthy of the slightest reprieve. Justice was certainly done when Joffrey looked on the frail, weak, and pitiful wreck that had once been a man, and asked for his head.

Perhaps we do not consider the execution just, but didn't Ned Stark demonstrate his weakness and the impotence of a life based on honour when he surrendered to political expediency, hoping but making no provision for the safety of his family? In the end, did he not prove the weakness of his position by basing his choice on fears and dreams rather than on virtues and truths? Can anyone argue the point that Ned Stark's honour proved pointless, useless, and injurious to his family and the realm?

I believe it is indeed possible to look on Eddard Stark's life as a pointless ruin. But this would not adequately take into account the fact that the choice Lord Stark made, and the honour he upheld throughout his life, will continue to guide the course of events through A Clash of Kings, through A Dance With Dragons, and to the end of A Song of Ice and Fire.

FAMILY FIRST

Lord Stark did not fear death. Everything in his behaviour and bearing indicated the truth of his words to Varys: "You think my life is some precious thing to me? That I would trade my honour for a few more years of what... of woe? You grew up with actors. You learned their craft, and you learned it well. I grew up with soldiers. I learned how to die a long time ago." It was only when Varys pointed out that Ned was not the only soul who faced peril, that the lives of Catelyn and all their children were on the line, that Ned's countenance became sober and still.

Eddard Stark did not sacrifice honour for "a few years of woe". Most would agree with Maester Aemon's assessment: "Love is the death of duty." Ned Stark had to sacrifice honour, Maester Aemon would tell us, out of his love for family. The duality is unavoidable; even the best of men—Benjen Stark, Lord Commander Jeor Mormont, even the heir to the Iron Throne, Maester Aemon Targaryen—must at some point make a choice between honour and family.

"If the day should ever come when your lord father was forced to choose between honour on the one hand and those he loves on the other, what would he do?" We believe we know the answer: Lord Stark chose family over honour. He sacrificed a lifetime of devotion to principles greater than any individual so that he could save his daughters, sons, and wife. This is certainly the conventional wisdom, the centrepiece of discussions in these days following the amazing events of Episode 1.09. I have to say, with greatest respect for the learned wisdom of Maester Aemon, and in admiration for the many sacrifices he has made, I disagree with the Night Watch's great sage.

Lord Eddard Stark sacrificed much at the Great Sept of Baelor. He lied. He gave up his life. But he did not sacrifice his honour. In fact, his choice saved his family, saved his honour, and saved the realm.

THE MANY FACETS OF CHOICE

Choice
Image: FreeDigitalPhotos.net 2012

We look at Ned in the dungeon, we hear Varys' words, and we sense a dilemma. If Ned spoke the truth about Joffrey's lineage, he and his family would be executed for treason. If instead Ned told a lie, he and his family would be spared, but he would be sentenced to a lifetime of living with the lie, never being able to undo the damage he had done by subjecting Westeros to the tyranny of Lannister rule. Ned contemplated two pans of a scale balanced on a sword's thin edge. There were only two choices, and therefore only two possible outcomes. But this is not the thinking that Lord Stark brought to the choice. There was no dilemma. Maester Aemon brought nothing to the discussion. In fact, Lord Varys brought nothing to the discussion.

Eddard Stark had long, endless days to contemplate his situation and the multitude of possible outcomes. He had considered all of them, even something as remote as the Master of Whisperers assisting in his escape from the dungeon. He had thought through every possible scenario, not once, but dozens of times, each time adding solid insights and variants of possible outcomes to his deliberations over probability. Any choice he may have been presented was drawn from the vast array of possible outcomes he had already observed and watched play out in his mind's eye.

One of the scenarios he doubtless considered at length was the "dilemma" between confession and fearless proclamation of Cersei's incest and Joffrey's illegitimacy. Of course, in his long thoughts on the matter, he never considered the choice to present a dilemma. These were merely two of the myriad possible outcomes of his imprisonment. The key to understanding Ned's position here is that he would have thought through every possible ramification of a particular action. He would have considered likely manoeuvres before the final choice, and he would have catalogued likely and less likely outcomes in both the immediate and long-term futures.

Any choice involving the fearless proclamation of Joffrey's illegitimacy had limited potential for desirable outcome. Lord Stark would have been forcibly silenced, his crimes recited in public, and he would have been executed on the spot for treason against the crown. His family would have been located and executed in the field or brought to King's Landing for a show trial. Lord Stannis or Lord Renly may yet have called bannermen and taken up swords, but they would have done so from a position of weakness, in the knowledge that House Stark had already attempted a coup. House Lannister, the wealthiest house in the realm, would have stood firm with House Baratheon and most of their bannermen, and would have presented a firm front to weak and disorganised opposition.

On the other hand, if Ned chose to tell the lie of Joffrey's legitimate ascendency to the Iron Throne, he would accomplish much more than simply saving the lives of daughters, sons, and wife. His family would never believe that he had plotted a coup. A lifetime of service, duty, and honour made any conclusion that he had conspired to take the Iron Throne laughable and entirely outside the consideration of any reasonable person acquainted with the sterling authenticity of Lord Stark's life. Ned counted on this. He knew his family, at the very least, would understand he had committed no act of treason. With his son, Robb, close to adulthood and now Lord of Winterfell, and with the wisdom and knowledge provided by Catelyn, House Stark would be in excellent position to add its forces to those of Lord Stannis, and probably House Arryn's and House Tully's as well, to make a concerted and sustained attack on House Lannister's illegitimate claim, whether through diplomacy, incitement of the people, or outright war. In fact, in such a scenario, it would have seemed entirely unlikely that Eddard Stark would have spent more than a few months, or at most a couple of years, at the Wall before his son or Lord Stannis came to release him from his oath.

THE UNBEARABLE WEIGHT OF HONOUR

By now most readers will be fuming. "The whole point of Ned's dilemma was that he was blinded by his honour," you say. "If not for Lord Varys' intervention and well-placed suggestions, Ned would have shouted out the truth at the Sept of Baelor, blind to the horrible consequences of maintaining his honour." Superficially, I agree. This was the surface-level dilemma that Ned faced. But this is the dilemma we perceive, as outsiders. We must place ourselves in Ned's position, breathe in the dank, diseased air of the dungeon, feel the cold, biting iron of the shackles on wrists and ankles, feel the endless monotony of darkness, the unrelenting cold of a dark and evil place. This is not a position of hopelessness for a man of resolve and action. Rather, it is a position of sober contemplation, a place to bring every advantage of experience and knowledge to decisions of lasting consequence.

If we accept the testimony of all participants as carrying equal truth and merit, I believe we must conclude that Eddard Stark was indeed blinded by honour. However, if we do so, we consign A Song of Ice and Fire to the mediocrity of ordinary fantasy. Game of Thrones, then, is nothing more than a collection of episodes of Law And Order, or CSI Miami, where sword and bow replace revolver and rifle, and golden armour replaces police uniform and detective suit. But this is not the type of story we seek to understand.

Honour Guard
Funeral for Smokey Smith, Parliament Hill, Ottawa, Ontario, 2005
Ernest Alvia Smith was awarded the Victoria Cross in 1944
photograph by Spiegel898, released to PD 2008

Cersei: "A king should have scars. You fought off a direwolf. You're a warrior, like your father."
Joffrey: "I'm not like him. I didn't fight off anything. It bit me and all I did was scream. And the two Stark girls saw it, both of them."
Cersei: "That's not true. You killed the beast. You only spared the girl because of the love your father bears her father."
Joffrey: "I didn't. I—"
Cersei: "When Aerys Targaryen sat on the Iron Throne, your father was a rebel and a traitor. Someday, you'll sit on the Throne and the truth will be what you make it."

There is no "truth" in Game of Thrones. There is no reliable narrator. If we believe Eddard Stark to be the only reservoir of unvarnished truth and honour, we are not watching carefully enough. If you are watching Game of Thrones because you believe it tells the true tale of a fantasy land, that good will always prevail, that gallant princes become fair and just kings, you are as blind as Sansa Stark, accepting a necklace from her beloved in such syrupy, fantasy-induced stupor that she was in danger of fainting from glorious excess of emotional bliss.

Watch again the very first episode, just 47 minutes into the epic. Take in the complexity of Ned's facial expressions as he listens to Maester Luwin and his wife, Catelyn. Note the conflict evident in the hand rising to rub his beard, the conflicted thoughts that race through his mind in this moment of decision. These are not the resolute expressions of a man whose honour is the only force guiding his steps toward a single goal.

Catelyn: Your father, and brother, rode south once on a king's demand.
Luwin: A different time. A different king.

The superficial truth is that Ned's deliberations in this scene were informed by the knowledge of the terrible outcome of the Mad King's summoning of Lord Rickard Stark to the trial of his son, Brandon. Both Stark men died at King's Landing, murdered in the Throne Room by the King himself. However, in order to give this amount of weight to Ned's consideration of these murders—and to the fear for Ned's life expressed in Catelyn's invocation of this parallel to an unhappy past—we need to believe that Ned feared death. However, we have already dispensed with this, in accepting the truth of Ned's words to Varys in the dungeon. "I grew up with soldiers. I learned how to die a long time ago." Ned's view on the matter could have been no different in Winterfell. If death was necessary, so be it.

Review the "dancing lesson" at the end of Episode 1.03. The training swords made the dull sounds of wood striking wood—until, that is, we began to see and hear the scene through the eyes—through the conflicted memory—of Eddard Stark. When we saw the scene through his eyes, we also heard the scene. We heard the sound of sharp steel striking razor-sharp blade. We were witness to battles long since fought.

Why the conflict? Why the surfacing of memories, if not because of conflict, if not the result of unmitigated desire for an alternative outcome? Lord Stark, watching his daughter receive lessons in swordplay, was not thinking of her, but of some event in the past that troubled his mind and brought a frown to his face. We need to ask ourselves during this scene why a man guided solely by honour would ever feel regret. A man with pre-determined priorities has no sleepless nights, never searches his mind for alternatives to past mistakes, never feels the awful pain of regret.

Lord Eddard Stark had regrets. He was not guided by honour alone.

THE BASTARD

Of course, we say. We know the answer: Ned regretted the indiscretion that led to the birth of his bastard son, Jon Snow. He lived daily with his wife's scorn, with her hatred of the boy Ned wished he could make his own by inheritance, title, and privilege. That Jon's life was so miserable was due entirely to the early sacrifice of honour that had gained Ned nothing more than an afternoon's pleasure. This youthful indiscretion had earned a lifetime of pain and hardship for himself, his wife, and Jon, and had brought dishonour to one of the great houses of the realm. Is it any wonder that from that moment on, Eddard Stark never again compromised his honour?

We need to ask ourselves, then, why a moment of sexual indiscretion would summon to his mind regrets around battles of old. Did his fathering of a bastard boy lead to a swordfight? Did Catelyn's recollection of Rickard Stark's death in Episode 1.01 cause Ned to remember the shame of having had sex with someone other than his wife?

Both of these are non-sequiturs. The regrets Lord Stark felt had nothing to do with having fathered a bastard. What, then, was the source of Ned's inner conflict?

THE GRAND CONSPIRACY

The Conspiracy of Julius Civilis
Rembrandt van Rijn, 1661

The greatest battle of Lord Eddard Stark's life was unquestionably the Battle of the Trident, 283 AL, fought approximately 17 years before the beginning of the present story (GoT time, not ASoIaF time). This conflict was the decisive battle of the war, in which the rebel armies of House Stark, House Baratheon, House Arryn, the Riverlands, and the Stormlands defeated House Targaryen and Dragonstone, taking Westeros and the Iron Throne.

If this was indeed the battle dredged from the recesses of Ned's mind during Arya's sword training, why would he have any regrets around the memory? His friend, Robert Baratheon, was installed as king. Winterfell had been House Baratheon's primary support, and House Stark had benefitted greatly from Robert's close friendship over the years since the Stag began wearing the crown. What regrets could Ned have possibly had over an outcome that brought such bounty to his clan and to his closest friends? Even if Robert had turned out to be a whoring drunkard, I'm quite certain Ned would have said in all honesty that Robert's reign was much better for the health of the realm than the madness of King Aerys. If the battle was the source of Ned's angst, what could possibly have been the spark that triggered it?

The most notable personal achievement of the Battle of the Trident was not Ned's, but Robert's. Robert, as head of the rebel armies, went head to head with the commander of loyalist forces, Crown Prince Rhaegar Targaryen. Prince Rhaegar, whom Robert hated more than any man ought to be able to hate another, had abducted and almost certainly raped Robert's beloved Lyanna.

This is just about all we know from Game of Thrones, the television series. From the novel, however, other interesting facts are known. After the Battle of the Trident, Ned secured King's Landing for Robert. He learned that three loyalists knights of King Aerys' Kingsguard had gathered at the Tower of Joy, presumably to protect whatever lay inside. Ned gathered six rebel soldiers and confronted the three loyalist knights. They fought to the death; only Ned and one of his close friends, Howland Reed, survived the fight. Ned rushed into the tower to find the single occupant he reported seeing: his sister, Lyanna Stark, moments from death. As she lay dying, she made a deathbed request of her brother. "Promise me, Ned," she said, after telling him this deepest of secrets. Apparently Ned promised to keep the secret, for he never revealed its contents to anyone. The nature of the secret is recorded nowhere in the five volumes of A Song of Ice and Fire.

Ned recounted to Robert the history of Lyanna's last moments as the two of them looked on her statue in the Stark crypt:

"'I was with her when she died,' Ned reminded the king... He could hear her still at times. *Promise me*, she had cried, in a room that smelled of blood and roses. *Promise me, Ned.* The fever had taken her strength and her voice had been faint as a whisper, but when he gave her his word, the fear had gone out of his sister's eyes. Ned remembered the way she had smiled then, how tightly her fingers had clutched his as she gave up her hold on life, the rose petals spilling from her palm, dead and black."

Whence the rose petals? I will discuss their significance in the final chapter of this book. For now, a better question might be, why were three knights of the

Kingsguard—*men whose sole function was to guard the king*—fighting to the death to protect whatever lay inside the Tower of Joy?

I attended college during the 1970s. Even in those heady days of the Sexual Revolution, a man learned that rape is an interesting concept. If a woman said "yes", a testosterone-driven young man could proceed, and the couple might experience the greatest joy two people can share. If, however, the woman said "no", the man had to stop immediately—mid-sentence, if necessary. He had to remove himself from anywhere near the woman, for to proceed under those circumstances was to court prison time—in some states, even the death penalty. If the woman invites intimacy, courts of law refer to the act as consensual sex. If, on the other hand, she does not wish to have sex, the act is called rape. The state of the woman's mind, her attitude toward the act, determined its legitimacy.

State of Mind
Image: FreeDigitalPhotos.net

Robert Baratheon thought Rhaegar a rapist. But Robert had not been with Lyanna immediately before or during her "abduction". Lyanna was betrothed to Robert, Rhaegar was wed to Elia Martell. But Lyanna was the prettiest girl in the realm. Rhaegar, of course, was the most handsome prince in the land. The two of them were alone after her "abduction" for many long months.

There are some—well, tens of thousands, actually—who believe Ned, Lyanna, and his friend, Howland, were not the only three individuals in the Tower of Joy as Lyanna lay dying amidst the smell of blood and roses. If she had been wounded in battle, why did not the men outside tend to her wounds? Whence the blood?

The blood, many people believe, was due to the presence of the fourth person in the room. That fourth person, it is said, was Rhaegar's newborn son. We don't know the name Lyanna gave her son, but most likely the name she chose was Jon. He would have been known as Jon Targaryen, First of His Name. We know him as Jon Snow, bastard son of Eddard Stark.

Why did Ned Stark feel troubled, why was his soul tormented by his memory of the Battle of the Trident? Because it was during that battle that his best friend, Robert, killed his beautiful sister's lover and father of her son, Rhaegar Targaryen. It was because of that fateful death in a river that Ned was entrusted with the greatest secret anyone had ever been asked to hold.

SECRETS MAINTAINED, TRADITIONS UPHELD

The Triumph of Truth
Mussini Luigi, 1848

No one other than George R. R. Martin knows the full truth of the events that occurred in the Tower of Joy in the year 284 AL. We don't know that Lyanna was Jon Snow's mother. However, we do know the truth of the aftermath of Robert's rise to power and his wife's usurpation of the Iron Throne. The secret Lyanna entrusted to her brother, Ned, is apparently safe. Only Howland Reed, still alive as far as we know, was witness to the dramatic events inside the Tower of Joy. The identity of Jon Snow's mother, even if she was not Lyanna Stark, likewise remains a secret to all.

Eddard Stark was the unhappy recipient of at least two, and possibly three, secrets that had the power to radically realign power in Westeros. The final words of the woman who had last been with the crown prince, the identity of Jon Snow's mother, and the identity of Joffrey Baratheon's father were state secrets that followed Ned Stark to the grave. He kept the secrets entrusted to him; not even the prospect of imminent death could cause him to betray the trust Lyanna and Jon Snow's mother had placed in him. His word to Lyanna and to his son, Jon, was unbroken: He never sacrificed his honour by betraying their trust. Maester Aemon was wrong, you see; in putting family before himself, he was not sacrificing his honour. Rather, he was upholding his honour. There was no dilemma, no knife-edge decision. Ned Stark protected his family and protected his honour in the same action at the Sept of Baelor.

By making the decision he did, every one of Ned's children survived the terrors that killed everyone else in his household at King's Landing. Bran lived to dream again. Catelyn lived to help Robb lead. Arya lived to dance—and fight—again.

Ned's son, now Robb Stark, First of His Name, King In the North, became a fierce defender of House Stark, upholding every good and noble and honourable tradition Ned had ever tried to instill in him. He became a perceptive and talented general, employing tactical genius to defeat the greatest army in the realm.

Ned's (adopted?) son, Jon Snow, regardless of the circumstances of his birth, became a leader among the fabled men of the Night's Watch. He brought honour to Ned's house and its ancient traditions when he knelt before the weirwood tree to take his vows before gods and men.

Ned Stark died, but death did more to maintain the honour of family, house, and kingdom, than anything he might have accomplished in life. Everything that was good and virtuous and honourable in Ned Stark's life was maintained, and even strengthened, in his death.

Here, then, a tribute in words, a testimony of praise, to the good and honourable Lord Eddard Stark, the nobility of his life, the triumph of his death.

Daenerys Targaryen
copyright Dalisa 2011
used with permission

Ser Jorah: I know what you intend. Do not.
Daenerys: I must. You don't understand.
Ser Jorah: Don't ask me to stand aside as you climb on that pyre. I won't watch you burn.
Daenerys: Is that what you fear?

What do we understand, and what do we fear? Do we understand the trouble brewing beyond the Wall? Do we fear the blue-eyed wights? Do we understand the power of fire? Do we fear the dragons it spawned? We flee. We seek refuge from our fears.

An elephant fears a mouse because it does not understand. Ser Jorah feared Daenerys' transformation to ash because he did not understand. The morning after the funeral, he should have run. He should have sought refuge from his fears. No one understands dragons. No one understands a woman reborn in fire.

Trembling, he bowed down. Not because there be dragons. Not because a queen was reborn. There are greater fears than things not understood. Ser Jorah bowed down, he trembled and did not run, because he knew she understood what no one can understand, and from this frightful knowledge he had no place to flee, he had no refuge from fear.

REBIRTH

An Appeal to Osiris, god of rebirth
unknown artist, circa 1500 B.C.

Arya was reborn as Arry, Robb was reborn as King In The North, a tavern singer was reborn as a mute, and Tyrion was reborn as Ruler of the Seven Kingdoms. Perhaps we should have understood the forebodings of Daenerys' rebirth as queen of dragons, but who among us could have imagined Sansa's rebirth as woman with a backbone?

Yoren used his knife to save a life in the critical minutes after Eddard Stark's execution.

"I'm not a boy," Arya said.

"You're not a smart boy, is that what you're trying to say?" Yoren asked.

Arya's survival depended on her complete transformation. She could not act like a boy but think herself a girl. She had to think, act, and dream the life of a boy, or she would be turned over "quick as spit" by boys looking for a pardon, or she'd be raped and then betrayed. No lord would protect her anymore. She didn't even have a father or family to whom she might appeal for mercy. She was on her own, because "nobody gives three shits." Her new life would centre on "a long way to travel, and in bad company."

There was a time when kings and high lords would have sought her as future mate to a favoured heir, when the fate of battles or political manoeuvres might have hinged on her disposition toward a particular faction. But no more. Her father dead, the most powerful and wealthiest house in the realm pledged to kill her brother and exterminate her house, she was a child without a family, without protection, without legal recourse of any kind.

The cutting of hair is not merely a practical matter. In many societies, and especially in established religious orders, the cutting of hair is symbolic of leaving behind the old life to take on a new life among those formally segregated from ordinary society.

We think Arya's fate too much for a young girl. We mourn for her. But if anyone in House Stark was prepared for this turn of events, it was Arya Stark. We need not mourn her loss of high standing. Recall Ned's words to her in Episode 1.04: "You will marry a high lord." Arya, taking a short break from her "dancing" lessons, thought for a moment, but then said, "No. That's not me." Indeed. No girl in the realm was more comfortable marching long distance on foot, a sword at her side.

Those not familiar with the history of medieval Europe—the closest historical parallel to the social structure of Game of Thrones—may believe that GRRM has gone too far in depicting a high lord going out of his way to provide his daughter formal lessons in the use of the sword. While rare, such practices were not unheard of. Accounts of women leading men in battle can be found among the histories of the time. Joan of Arc is perhaps the most recognised military leader of fifteenth century France, for example.

There is a special place in my heart for girls like Arya. In fact, the heroine of my first novel, "Cartier's Ring" (http://pearsonmoore.net/default.aspx) picked up a bow and arrow at about the same age that Arya first picked up a sword. Myeerah became one of the most honoured and recognised leaders of her country; I expect a similarly honoured outcome is possible for young Arya.

COURAGE BORN OF FIRE

I did not include Sansa Stark among the "grotesques" (see my essays on Episodes 1 and 2, and also my essay on the thesis of Game of Thrones), only because she did not match Tyrion's definition. I don't believe she has yet demonstrated that she counts herself among the disabled, disadvantaged, and despised of the world, but she has taken a huge step in that direction. More importantly, in this episode she began to give up her childish, romantic notions of chivalry and honour. There is no honour in King Joffrey's evil heart, and Sansa finally recognises this.

This episode was not about the qualifications for inclusion in the sisterhood of the damned. Rather, this installment was about birth and rebirth. In the Sansa scenes, I feel obliged to conclude we saw an instance of birth rather than rebirth. We have never before seen in Sansa's character anything beyond the childish imposition of an idealised understanding of the world. The shock of her father's cruel and unnecessary execution and the daily evidence of Joffrey's repulsive personality and malignant spirit have shocked her into a more realistic evaluation of her predicament. Many of GRRM's characters begin moving out of childhood at an early age. Sansa is relatively old to begin her transformation, but she is probably well within the safe limits for the harsh world of Westeros.

She had no strategy for dealing with the sudden awareness of evil in her midst. Her impulse to push Joffrey off the side of the ramp to his death was ill advised. If she had succeeded in her momentary whim, her severed head would have adorned the wall of the Red Keep, and she would have consolidated Cersei's power as Regent to her younger son's reign as King. The power structure would only have become more entrenched within House Lannister, and her death would have accomplished nothing substantive for anyone other than Cersei.

Cosette
Emile Bayard, illustration for Les Misérables, circa 1885

If she is to be counted among *les misérables*, she will have to embrace the need to study and learn. There is no evidence of any thirst for knowledge in her personality or in her upbringing. She memorised the facts relating to the Targaryens' long reign, but only because her septa required this of her. She was never disposed toward any understanding of history, because she had already created her own world, which until her father's execution was sufficient to her needs.

But Sansa Stark is awake now. She knows where she is, and she is beginning to understand who she is. Most of all, she has found within herself a bit of the courage of her mother and father, and she demonstrated that courage—foolish and unfocussed as it was—in standing up to Joffrey.

Joffrey: I'll tell you what. I'm going to give you a present. After I raise my armies and kill your traitor brother, I'm going to give you his head as well. **Sansa:** Or maybe he'll give me yours.

The Hound showed her an ordinary kindness that may have extraordinary implications. In giving her a hankie to daub the cut on her lip, he prevented her from exercising her desire to push Joffrey off the ramp. We know from previous episodes that Sansa has a place in Sandor Clegane's heart, and we know his is one of the few chivalrous hearts in a dark and bloody world. But the question we must ask ourselves, after witnessing his quite precisely-timed offer of assistance, relates to his deepest sympathies: Did he know Sansa intended to push Joffrey off the ramp? And if he did, was it his intention to protect Sansa from herself? Going a bit further, if he was aware of Sansa's intentions, could this be a sign of his willingness to enter into conspiracies against House Lannister?

THE KING IN THE NORTH

In less than five minutes, Arya Stark descended from the heights of landed and honoured Lady of House Stark to the depravity of a homeless and orphaned boy on the streets of King's Landing. Also in less than five minutes, her eldest brother ascended from marginalised rebel leader to King In The North.

If Arya's transformation was bewildering to her, it was even more bewildering for us. We are marching into strange territory never before explored in network television. Killing off the main character in the first year of a series is simply not done. In fact, in the 63-year history of network television it's never been done—until last week.

But this strange new, unexplored territory is not without boundaries and rules. Tonight we saw the beginnings of a new equilibrium, with some of the story's most forceful characters focussing all of their prodigious energies on the speedy re-establishment of order in the Seven Kingdoms. Of course, we should not expect any such speedy realignment, but we should feel quite certain that the women and men caught up in this game of thrones are no different from the rest of us in the ways that are important to a story well told. In fact, the strangest events of the evening contained within themselves some of the sturdiest and best understood elements of traditional fiction.

One such event was the elevation of Lord Robb Stark to the Throne of the North. It was an historic instance of rebirth, as the North had not been a kingdom since before the reign of House Targaryen. But as with every instance of rebirth portrayed tonight, it had its origin in seeds planted many episodes before, and it followed an orderly procession consistent with the rules of Westeros.

The Greatjon did not proclaim Lord Robb as King In The North on a whim. Robb had not only taken on and defeated the most powerful and well-funded army in the Seven Kingdoms, he had done so through strategic planning and tactical genius. Because of his bold military initiative, Jaime Lannister was in chains and half of the Lannister army had been killed, injured, or forced to flee. In a short matter of weeks Robb demonstrated greater leadership than anyone in Westeros had seen since Robert's Rebellion.

Robb's spontaneous acclamation as King by every major house in the North made sense in light of his spectacular leadership on and off the field of battle, but it was also a reaffirmation of the northerners' feeling of being distinct from the pampered southerners ("What do they know from war? Or the Wolfswood? Even their gods are wrong."). Robb's ascension to the throne means there is to be no return to any allegiance to King's Landing, at least as long as there is a Stark in Winterfell. But this fact was not the result of any unilateral action by the houses of the North. Indeed, Tyrion noted to his father's lords that King Joffrey determined Robb's course of action by executing Ned Stark. The proclamation that Robb is King In The North was merely a formalised declaration of House Lannister's understanding of the current political situation.

DWARF REBORN AS GIANT

The Dwarf and the Giant
Georges Méliès, 1901

The first indication that things have changed for Tyrion came from his father Tywin's hand. When Tyrion reached again for the carafe, his father prevented him from taking it, in an almost perfect recreation of the scene from Episode 1.08. But this time, he poured the wine for his son and offered a rare complement: "You were right about Eddard Stark."

When Tywin announced that Tyrion was to make haste to King's Landing, to "serve as the Hand of the King in my stead," we heard no rejoicing from Tyrion's lips.

"Why not my uncle? Why not anyone? Why me?"

"You're my son."

Tyrion understood Tywin's appointment as an honour, and one he could not have expected from his cold and calculating father. But he understood the enormity and near impossibility of the challenge awaiting him in King's Landing. Joffrey was undisciplined and prone to hasty and rash judgment. His sister, Cersei, was the most power-hungry person in Westeros. Asserting himself over his sister and his siblings' bastard boy-king was fraught with lethal peril. Cersei slept with her own brother, and now with her cousin, her husband's former squire. There were no taboos for her. I don't imagine Tyrion would have had any illusions about the implications. If she were willing to perform any vile deed to maintain power, would she consider the murder of her own brother somehow beyond contemplation?

Tyrion has always had to work harder than anyone else just to survive. He understood the appointment to the second highest office in the land as possibly the most determined assault on his survival that he has yet had to face. In fact, the only bit of happiness Tyrion found that evening was not in the honour of being chosen Hand of the King, but in his decision after leaving the Commander's tent to defy his father and bring Shea with him to King's Landing. That evening, among the sullen and beaten men of the Lannister army, one woman's heart danced with joy.

GRAND MAESTER JANUS

Acting the forgetful and decrepit old fool is hard work, especially when a spry old man would rather be screwing docile young maidens a quarter of his age. When Ros left Grand Maester Pycelle's house, the man jumped up, did quick calisthenics to relieve his body of the self-imposed rigours of feigned old age, bounded across the room, threw on his maester's cloak, made sure everything was suitably wrinkled and drab, drew out his muscular chest, looked himself over one last time, then hunched his shoulders, bowed himself down, and slowly shuffled out the door.

It must be strange for all of them: Pycelle, Baelish, Varys. "A man from another land, despised by most, feared by all. But they carry on, "whispering in one king's ear and then the next." Littlefinger and Varys again expressed their admiration for each other. "A grasper from a minor house with a major talent for befriending powerful men—and women," was Lord Varys' assessment of Lord Baelish. But any of the three of them might have expressed the same or similar words of admiration for any of the other two.

So there they stand: Pycelle, Baelish, Varys. "In mutual admiration and respect, playing our *roles*, serving a new king. Long may he reign." Thespians, all three, and more skilled at their craft than the most acclaimed of actors on any stage. But they hardly stand "in mutual admiration and respect." I have to believe that Pycelle and Varys would be among the unfortunates, under any reign of King Littlefinger, who would regret anything they might have done to impede his ascension to power, who might instead have simpered and bowed to him, rather than sneering at him. "It's hard for them to simper and bow," Baelish said, "without heads."

I get the feeling, though, that both the Spider and the Littlefinger would rather take the route Grand Maester Pycelle has found advantageous over the last sixty-seven years: sit at the foot of power, rather than seeking the Iron Throne itself. Schemers always aim their dastardly deeds at the king, not at his lieutenants. The three of them serve whomever sits the throne, unaffected by the ravages of time, power, or politics. "Long may he reign," Littlefinger said. He did not speak facetiously, though his prayers for a long reign had nothing to do with the boy-king's health, and everything to do with the greater wealth and power that derives of political stability.

FATHER ICE

The politicians have had their say for most of Season One. In the final eight minutes of the season, we finally saw the beginning of this Song of Ice and Fire. Jeor Mormont, Lord Commander of the Night's Watch, opened the door through the Wall and led all of the men of Castle Black through to the other side.

"Beyond the Wall," Lord Commander Mormont said, "the rangers are reporting whole villages abandoned. At night they see fires blazing in the mountains from dusk until dawn. A captured wildling swears the tribes are uniting in some secret stronghold—to what ends? The gods only know. Outside East Watch [they] discovered four blue-eyed corpses. Unlike us, they were wise enough to burn them. Do you think your brother's war is more important than ours?

"When dead men and worse come hunting for us in the night, do you think it matters who sits on the Iron Throne?...I'll not sit meekly by or wait for the snows. We need to find out what's happening. The Night's Watch will ride in force against the wildlings, the White Walkers, and whatever else is out there."

Tonight, we heard the first stirring bars of the song that will play—if the gods are good and just—for several years to come.

Father Frost (Дед Мороз) of Belarus, 2010
photograph by Yogi555, released to PD 2011

MOTHER FIRE

Courage. Strength. Freedom.

Daenerys Targaryen's naked form has rarely been used to indicate sexuality. In her first nude scene, she was the naked and vulnerable slave of Viserys, King of Westeros. In her second nude scene, she was the naked, vulnerable slave of Drogo, Khal of Essos. But in her final nude scene, she was slave to no one, vulnerable to nothing. She was reborn, naked and invulnerable, a primordial exemplar of feminine courage, strength, and freedom.

"Blood of my blood," Ser Jorah's oath on seeing his phoenix queen rise from the ashes of Drogo's pyre, may not mean much to those who have not yet read GRRM's novels. The significance is deep. "Blood of my blood" is the bloodrider's oath. It means the bloodrider is the khal's blood brother. The bloodrider will defend the khal to the death. If the khal should die, the bloodrider will go on living long enough to avenge the khal, and then end his own life, in battle or through suicide.

The oath meant that Ser Jorah recognised Daenerys not as queen to a khal, but as Khal in her own right.

It is important to note that dragons did not bring Ser Jorah Mormont to his knees. No one understands dragons. Viserys Targaryen was no expert in dragon lore, but he did get one thing right. "Brave men," Viserys' whore said in their bath, "killed the dragons." Viserys told her she misunderstood. "The brave men didn't kill dragons," he said, "The brave men rode them. Rode from Valyria to build the greatest civilisation this world has ever seen." It is never the dragons to which strong men bow. It is to the courage, strength, and freedom of those who ride the dragons that those of lesser understanding must always bend the knee. Only those who understand dragons can become their masters. Those who become masters of the most feared creatures in the world become the rulers of that world.

The three dragons that clung to Queen Daenerys' naked body could have been stomped to death by the weakest among the new Khal's followers. Even when the dragons reach maturity, they will offer no sustained or overwhelming threat to the life of people in Westeros. Dragons were killed in the past, and they will certainly be killed in the future.

The true threat is created by those who honour the power of the dragons' master. Daenerys now enjoys virtually unlimited power, because no resident of Essos with a mind to think is going to put herself in opposition to a woman who commands dragons and armies. The Queen will stand at the head of the most committed vanguard of bloodriders the continent has ever seen, and her host will number in the hundreds of thousands. Three dragons could probably not take even a single city. But three dragons and two hundred thousand fiercely loyal soldiers could rule the world.

The most powerful weapons in GRRM's fantasy world are not ice or fire, White Walkers or dragons, magical incantations or intimidating spells. The most powerful weapons are those cultivated and nurtured most assiduously by the weakest among us: by the slaves, the dwarfs, the bastards, the tomboys, the women who are not recognised for who they are but forced to become the toys men would like them to be. The most powerful weapons in the world of Westeros are those that are honoured and admired by the grotesques: Courage, Strength, Freedom.

"You will be my khalasar. I see the faces of slaves. I free you. Take off your collars, go if you wish, no one will stop you. But if you stay, it will be as brothers and sisters, as husbands and wives...I am Daenerys Stormborn of House Targaryen, of the blood of Old Valyria. I am the dragon's daughter, and I swear to you that those who would harm you will die screaming."

Liberty Leading the People
Eugène Delacroix, 1830

Daenerys Targaryen stood naked before her khalasar. Anyone with spear or bow could have pierced her unprotected body and killed her. But when she stood naked and entirely vulnerable before them, they could no more raise a hand against her than they could against their own mother or father. She was mother to them, because she was to them everything that is good in the hearts of women and men.

It is the bold assertion of who she is, not the accoutrements of weapon, shield, and armour, that render her invulnerable.

In stepping into the flames, she demonstrated the courage that everyone wants to believe good and virtuous people possess. In resisting the flames, she showed the strength that all of us yearn to call our own. In emancipating every slave in her midst, she evinced the dedication to liberation that all women and men wish to see in their leaders. Daenerys Targaryen is Courage. She is Strength. She is Freedom.

This song of ice and fire goes to the heart of our identity as human beings. It is the greatest of songs—and we have heard only the few chords. I look forward to savouring every stanza and verse.

Furious Dragon
copyright Mac m 13 2008, CC-SA 2.5

"I am the blood of the dragon."

We heard her give passionate voice to these seven words in the ninth episode of Season One. We believe we saw the full manifestation of her statement in the final scene of the season, when Daenerys Stormborn of House Targaryen, unharmed by fire and smoke, rose from the ashes of Khal Drogo's funeral pyre. She had the strong constitution of a dragon, able to withstand any trial by oven heat or open flame. If we believe this, we are incorrect in our assessment. Daenerys did not say, as her brother often proclaimed, "I am the dragon." Daughter of dragons, mother of dragons, yes. But herself a dragon? Much more is contained in her proclamation than anything as simple as physical or spiritual connection with beings of fire. In fact, her words point to something much grander in scope, something to

237

be sensed not through the visual appreciation of her ascension from the ashes, nor even through experience of the heat and smoke that surrounded her winged progeny. These seven words, in fact, form the first verse of A Song of Ice and Fire.

BLOOD OF MY BLOOD

Band of Brothers, 101ˢᵗ Airborne in Iraq
Signaleer, U.S. Army, 2006

Ser Jorah Mormont's words, "Blood of my blood," spoken as he knelt before his new fire-born queen, were the final words uttered in the first season of Game of Thrones. The words provided the strongest possible ending to the first set of episodes because they expressed a thought central to every event of significance in the series. From a narrow consideration of Dothraki culture alone, we would be justified in drawing from Ser Jorah's statement the fact that he is merely uttering the bloodrider's oath. He has formally accepted Daenerys as his overlord and khal, and has pledged his life to her using the bloodrider formula. But in the greater context of Daenerys' behaviour in the hours during Khal Drogo's impending death, and her actions after his demise, the words carry more profound significance.

Blood is not a mere physical or biological material for George Martin. Nor is it symbolic of something else. It is, rather, a perfection, an essence in itself, that points to itself and provides the origin for ideas of lesser value or entities of lesser ability. We know this from long acquaintance with Martin's peculiar way of talking about blood. "You are a Stark. You might not have my name, but you have my blood." I know of many ways to interpret Ned Stark's parting words to Jon Snow, and I will discuss the possible meaning of at least one of those interpretations in another chapter. But for the purpose of this chapter on Daenerys Targaryen, I believe Lord Stark's words can be used to shed light on the deeper significance of Daenerys' bold proclamation in Episode Nine.

Jon Snow did not bear Ned Stark's name. He had no right to title, position, inheritance, nor any privilege deriving of highborn status. He was nothing more than a bastard, his social standing known to any who heard his name. Yet Lord Stark maintained "You are a Stark." Let's take a closer look at the context of Ned's final words to Jon.

They were at the great cairn just west of Winterfell. Jon and Tyrion Lannister, led by First Ranger Benjen Stark, were to ride north, to the Wall. Lord Stark, now Hand of the King, was to lead a contingent of House Stark and bannermen south to King's Landing. As Ned glanced ahead to his younger brother, Benjen, he turned to Jon and said, "There's great honour serving in the Night's Watch. The Starks have manned the Wall for thousands of years. And you are a Stark. You might not have my name, but you have my blood." Jon had made a decision to carry on the Stark tradition of serving at the Wall. Though both Benjen and Ned knew the Night's Watch to be populated by the lowest of criminals and social vermin, they nevertheless maintained that service at the Wall was perhaps the highest calling in the realm. Thus, Jon was not only a Stark, but he was upholding the most meaningful tradition of the ruling house of the North. He was a Stark, and he was carrying on the noblest service any Stark had ever performed.

That Jon did not bear Ned's name was immaterial, because "you have my blood." In fact, it was blood, not a name recognised to others, that meant Jon Snow was a Stark. Being a Stark, behaving as a Stark would behave, and carrying on the traditions of House Stark, were the proofs of standing. Certainly no such proofs were required; no one would argue that Sansa Stark was not a Stark, but she did not behave as a Stark, nor did she uphold Stark traditions. Her needlework was beyond compare, and she could bat doe-eyes at princes better than any lass around, but these abilities did not place her in the category of women like Catelyn Tully or Arya Stark, whose courage and resolute intent to live by the Words ("Winter is coming") marked them as exemplars of House Stark. Nor can we say that any such proofs were sufficient. Theon Greyjoy, ward of House Stark, certainly demonstrated courage in the rescue of Bran Stark, and he gave prudent and well-considered advice to Robb Stark, but Theon Greyjoy could never be a Stark. Theon was of House Greyjoy—he was the blood of House Greyjoy, to use Martinesque terms. Jon, though, had Ned Stark's blood. He was the blood of House Stark, and he proved this in his decision to serve at the Wall. For Ned, Jon's decision was nothing more than the latest proof of the boy's true standing. Ned knew of Jon's close spiritual kinship with the most Stark-like of his children, Arya and Bran. He watched as Jon tutored Bran in archery and so many other disciplines a young lord of House Stark would be expected to master. He knew of the strong bond between Arya, and later, when he learned of Arya's hand-made sword, Needle, he must have known its true origin, and he approved, even to the point of hiring the realm's most famous swordsman as her tutor.

It is blood that defines a person's true identity. Perhaps Lord Greyjoy would disown his son, label him a Stark, and have nothing further to do with him. Even if House Stark admitted Theon into the house with full honours and full rights of inheritance, he could never be a Stark because he had no Stark blood. Blood determines identity, destiny, and any course a person might wish to pursue. It is the final arbiter of human value. The name "Stark" has lesser value than the blood-reality of being a Stark. Ned Stark can say, "You are a Stark. You might not have my name, but you have my blood" because the name is of no consequence. It is the inner reality, the blood-reality, of being a Stark, of being Stark blood, that determines who Jon truly is.

Thus, "blood of my blood" means much more than an oath to protect a khal, even to death. It means "Your essence is my essence. The reality you are at the highest level, at the level of blood-reality, is the reality that determines who I am. I define myself, at the very essence of who I am, in terms of who you are at the highest level of your being." This is the true meaning of the bloodrider's oath. In the context of the final scene of the season, though, the oath is subsidiary to the bold reality of Daenerys' new-found identity as Blood of the Dragon.

THE DRAGON

Bronze Dragon
by RoShin circa 2011, Clker.com Royalty-Free Images

"I am Daenerys Stormborn of House Targaryen, of the blood of Old Valyria. I am the dragon's daughter."

These words, too, convey more meaning than direct translation allows; the full appreciation of significance can be drawn only from a full consideration of context.

Superficially, Daenerys was heir to the Iron Throne, forged in the fiery breath of the great dragon, the Black Dread, Balerion. By declaring herself of the House Targaryen, now the only surviving member of that ancient ruling clan, she proclaimed herself inherent ruler over those gathered around her at Khal Drogo's funeral, but also heir to the great continent across the Narrow Sea, Westeros.

This is a bold statement, to be sure, but it is neither more nor less than anything her brother, Viserys, had been reciting since his fifth name day. We know the history. We know Robert Baratheon, assisted by Lord Eddard Stark and Lord Tywin Lannister and their houses and bannermen, ruthlessly sought out and executed every member of House Targaryen he could find. Viserys and Daenerys, by accident of place and time, happened to escape the Usurper's fury, living only because of the good graces of people like Magister Illyrio Mopatis of the Free City of Pentos, who provided free apartments, perhaps in the hope of future rewards from the king-to-be.

But Daenerys was not addressing herself to the former glory of her ancestors' accomplishments. "I am the dragon's daughter" is not merely a statement of legitimacy, of rightful claim to the throne. Daenerys made the statement only after prefacing her words with a fresh, bold declaration of purpose: "You will be my khalasar. I see the faces of slaves. I free you... If you stay, it will be as brothers and sisters, as husbands and wives." With these words, her reach extended far beyond anything she could have claimed as "the dragon's daughter". Before a crowd of Dothraki slaves and warriors and bloodriders, she claimed the title of Khal.

THE NEW KHAL

But she was to be no ordinary khal. Not only was she the first woman to arrogate the title as her own, she did so under terms no khal before her would have accepted. Everyone in her khalasar was to be not slave, but free. This was a radical concept to those gathered around their fallen leader. Why would they ever follow a woman? And how could such a delusional, cursed, diseased woman, whose unborn child was killed by a sorceress's magic, proclaim anyone's freedom, or lead anyone to anything beyond suffering and death?

Yet she stood at the dead khal's pyre, quite sure of herself, speaking to those she considered among her khalasar. Her boast of being able to confer freedom on those who had lived as slaves did not constitute her most radical departure from Dothraki culture. In fact, her claim of status as their khal was not as bold as the idea she planted during her speech.

The most startling claim she made, the statement that every member of the khalasar would have questioned immediately, was the coupling of "You will be my khalasar" with "I am Daenerys Stormborn of House Targaryen." The justification for their identity as khalasar—as followers of this new female khal—was Daenerys' identity as Lord of House Targaryen. That is, this new dragon-khal proclaimed the primacy of blood over strength.

The idea that anything, whether conceptual or concrete, could gain ascendency over raw physical strength was a radical and probably entirely unacceptable idea to everyone listening to Daenerys. They must have felt assured of their assessment of her insanity when she calmly stepped into the flames and her clothing began to burn away from her body. Surrender to the flames must have been seen as proof of the sheer insanity of her strange boasts—that she, a woman, was a khal; that blood transcended and superseded muscle.

Genghis Khan
unknown artist, circa 1550

But even the Dothraki had it in their minds, though probably in parts of their psyche they preferred to ignore, that blood was stronger than muscle. They had their medicine, magic, and mythology, but they recognised one particular strain of magic—blood magic—as more powerful, and therefore more terrible and frightening, than anything the Mother of Mountains would allow them to practise. Blood magic, the Dothraki knew, was more powerful than physical strength, for it brought logic or chaos to the primal forces of life and death. Anything that conferred its own order on the most powerful forces in the universe—a force that even life and death must obey—had to take precedence, even over physical human strength. Deep in their hearts, the Dothraki knew blood was stronger and had deeper meaning than muscle.

Even so, the Dothraki preferred to place their trust and faith in the power of human strength. When Daenerys, facing the reality of Khal Drogo's impending death, argued that she had nothing to fear, that her son was destined to be the Stallion Who Mounts the World, Ser Jorah set her straight. "This isn't Westeros," Ser Jorah said, "where men honour blood. Here they only honour strength. There'll be fighting, after Drogo dies. Whoever wins that fight will be the new khal. They won't want any rivals. Your boy will be plucked from your breast and given to the dogs." Thus it was, thus it had ever been.

Strength trumped any other aspect of human existence, even when the triumph of physical power led to the suffering and death of multitudes. Daenerys, devoid of the strength provided by her khal, would become as weak, and therefore as meaningless, as the most feeble and unproductive cripple among the dependent hordes of the khalasar. Thus it was, thus it had ever been.

When Daenerys rose from the ashes, though, the slaves in the khalasar were forced to re-examine their beliefs. Perhaps they were, after all, not slave but free. Perhaps this woman who withstood flame and heat and smoke was truly their khal. Perhaps her blood, which gained strength and life from burning fire, was after all stronger than muscle.

But we have not yet begun to understand the full meaning of the proclamation of her identity. "I am the blood of the dragon." Indeed. It is the boldest statement any human being could make, for it is uttered from a position of complete weakness and naked dependence.

THE SISTERHOOD OF THE DAMNED

"I am the dragon's daughter," she told her future followers. It was a strange claim to make, and seemed to be contradicted only hours later, when the sun rose on the smouldering cinders of Drogo's pyre. The three dragons born in fire did not cling to her as to a daughter, but as to a mother. Daenerys was nurturing leader—mother—to the three dragons. She knew before she entered the flames the outcome that awaited her. Ser Jorah tried to talk her out of "throwing herself on Drogo's pyre", fearing the flames he was certain would kill her. "Is that what you fear?" she asked. She knew she had nothing to fear, that the heat would bring life to her and to the petrified eggs. She knew, even before she kissed Ser Jorah's cheek, that she was to be mother to dragons.

Yet she chose to be known as daughter to the dragon. A figure of speech, you say. She referred to the dragon, the sigil of her house, to mean House Targaryen. "Dragon's daughter" meant simply that she was descended of House Targaryen. When she added the definite article ("the dragon's daughter" rather than "a daughter of the dragon"), she indicated she was the only remaining member of the royal house. At most, we might say, by asserting identity as sole living member of the royal house, she was claiming to be rightful heir to the Iron Throne, and she assumed to herself the full power of House Targaryen.

Certainly we can consider her words in this way. However, I believe an even stronger possibility present in her words.

In the novel, *A Game of Thrones*, Daenerys Targaryen had just turned fourteen when she said, "I am the dragon's daughter." She was a child, yet she assumed the power and privilege of a fully-grown male who had defeated every man who challenged him—she claimed for herself the title of khal. Now, the television series took some liberties, giving Daenerys a full-blown speech, when the novel gave her only a few words. But why would the writers of the screenplay choose to portray her as calling herself "daughter"? Why would she fix the image of herself as helpless child in the minds of those she wished to convince of her super-human omnipotence?

Maria Palaiologina, Khaness of the Mongols, circa 1250-1280
unknown mosaic artist, 14th century

I believe her speech was not so much intended for her future khalasar as it was for us. Benioff and Weiss, I believe, created Daenerys' speech to convey yet again the Martinesque notion of the Sisterhood of the Damned, or as Tyrion Lannister framed the group, it is that collection of castaways comprised of "Cripples, bastards, and broken things." (GoT 1.04) Daenerys was daughter of the dragon, with the emphasis not on dragon, but on ***daughter***. She was among the grotesques, whom the world had damned and condemned. With Jaime Lannister, the world would just as soon forget the Sisterhood of the Damned, or deliver "a good, clean death" to its members. Tyrion, remember, disagreed with his brother—and the hasty assessment of the "civilised" world. "Speaking for the grotesques," Tyrion said, "I'd have to disagree. Death is so final. Whereas life... ah, life is full of possibilities."

We can see a frail daughter as having attained the full measure of her weak and susceptible present state—or we can see her as embodying the fullest measure of unlimited potentials. The young, the cripples, the dwarfs, the bastards, and all who are damned because of gender, race, stature, or beliefs, represent the greatest potential for growth. Crippled Bran could not shoot a bow, track a deer, or even convey himself from one location to another. But on a horse, he could do all of these things. In fact, because the horse allowed him to do these things, and he was aware of the limitation, he could train himself to become more proficient in any of these skills than those able to develop hunting abilities using their own legs.

In Martin's world, no less in ours, it is the grotesques who are most aware of their limitations, but also most aware of their infinite potentials. The greatest president of the 20th century was not the athlete and sportsman, Dwight Eisenhower, but the polio victim and cripple, Franklin Delano Roosevelt. With his powerful yet reassuring voice, with his resolute courage in the face of the greatest assaults on his country, Roosevelt became the most meaningful symbol of human strength the United States had ever witnessed. Roosevelt was routinely depicted as a boxer, runner, weightlifter, or other athlete in newspaper cartoons. The cartoonists would almost certainly have been shocked to learn that this most exalted symbol of courage and strength could not even move his legs.

It is this ability to construct real strength out of the most difficult physical situation that Martin has called upon for his most favoured characters. GRRM has chosen as his mouthpieces those characters on the periphery of the story. The bastard, Jon Snow, and the weak little girl, Daenerys Targaryen, were at the geographical boundaries of his world—at the Wall and across the Narrow Sea, on Essos—and they were at the periphery of social acceptability. Jon was the despised bastard of a great lord, and Daenerys was powerless sister to the "beggar king", Viserys. Both of them, because of their full membership in the Sisterhood of the Damned, have realised their limitations, and they have embraced their infinite possibilities.

I AM THE BLOOD OF THE DRAGON

Now, finally, we can begin to grasp the full significance of Daenerys' claim. "I am the blood of the dragon." She was rightful heir to the Iron Throne. She embodied all powers and privileges and ancient claims of House Targaryen. She was Supreme Khal, greater even than Drogo. She was daughter of the dragon, mother of the dragon, protector of all who would call themselves free. She was all of these things, and many more, too. But most of all, she was the origin. She was the blood—the highest reality—the aspect of existence that controlled even life and death. But even this—even blood—was of lesser import than Daenerys Stormborn's identity as origin of all possibilities. She was the most important member of the Sisterhood of the Damned, by definition most aware of her real limitations and most aware of her unlimited potentials. It was her informed, bold, unwavering assertion of the full truth of herself as infinitely possible that rendered her naked, frail vulnerability stronger than thickest armour. She stood naked, susceptible to any who would assault her with bow or spear, yet invulnerable because of the boldness of her claim. The fire did not make her strong. The dragons did not give her courage. Her strength was human fortitude itself—stronger than muscle, more enduring than blood. Her courage was the heroism of every age—unflinching, even when logic and common sense demanded acquiescence. Hers was a freedom informed by blood that drew life from fire, by muscle and bone tempered in flame.

Water, they say, is the most lowly of all things. It seeks the lowest places, fills the dark and abandoned crevices that no other substance will deign to penetrate. Yet water is the most powerful of all forces known to humanity. Water can destroy cities in an instant, can level mountains in a day. Daenerys Targaryen was the weakest of all characters in Game of Thrones: a feeble, powerless, pitiful, naked girl. But because she was the weakest, she was also the strongest, the most powerful, the most courageous, and the first voice to sing the lusty, enchanting, rapturous harmony that is A Song of Ice and Fire.

The Iron Throne
from the original photograph copyright Pop Culture Geek 2011, CC-SA 2.0
modified by Pearson Moore, 2012

The second book of A Song of Ice and Fire is called *A Clash of Kings*, and with good reason. Joffrey was not Baratheon, but Lannister. In fact, neither of the boys born to Queen Cersei was of royal blood, and neither had any claim to the throne. The rules of succession appear to be clear, but in a land called "The Seven Kingdoms", in a place which has never known true unity even under the dragons of

House Targaryen, we should not be surprised that deep disagreements are to be found regarding the legitimacy of claims to the throne. Already, the houses of the north have rejected not only Joffrey, but Lord Stannis and Lord Renly as well, proclaiming Lord Robb Stark the King In the North.

Seven claimants to the throne represent four major houses. All of them can present bona fides substantial enough to bring legitimacy to their claims. Only two claimants, though, have taken an oath to defend the entire realm; every other pretender, potentate, or prince has pledged himself not to the people of Westeros, but to his own house. Can any of these men, committed to a personal agenda, move beyond provincial interests and petty desires to serve the common good?

JOFFREY BARATHEON

Many will consider this name ineligible for consideration among those bearing legitimate claim to the Iron Throne. After all, his own mother admitted that he was Jaime's, not Robert's son. Therefore, we might conclude, the question has been settled: Joffrey has no claim. In reality, Joffrey may have stronger claims than we realise.

Human relations are built more on emotions, perceptions, and desires than on facts, truths, and logic. While it may seem a human preference for comfort should have little or nothing to do with politics and rules of succession, we need look no further than recent history in our own world to see that political reality does not always adhere to rules, facts, and truths. For instance, the United States Supreme Court, in December 2000, halted the counting of votes in Florida as part of Bush v. Gore, in which the court eventually ruled in favour of plaintiff, George Bush. Subsequent ballot counting, underwritten by a large group of non-partisan news organisations and completed in September 2001, revealed that presidential candidate Al Gore won the Florida vote by between 60 and 171 votes (http://en.wikipedia.org/wiki/Florida_election_recount), and therefore should have been elected president. But the citizens of a large majority of states voted for Bush in numbers sufficient to declare Bush the winner in that state. Bush had the support of the judiciary. Thus, even though Al Gore won the popular vote and should have won in the Electoral College, George Bush was declared winner and was essentially appointed to the presidency.

Especially in the western world, we like to think ourselves adherents of logic and the rule of law. We find the interesting propensity of human beings to organise societies on the basis of emotion rather than law to be shocking, even when we see evidence of this in our own world. Fiction does not often hold up for us a mirror of this interesting tendency, but I am aware of at least one recent instance in popular television. In Mad Men, near the end of the first season, one of Don Draper's underlings, Pete Campbell, learned that Don Draper was not Don Draper. He assumed the name during the Korean War. His real name, Campbell learned, was Dick Whitman. Pete tried to extort a promotion out of the knowledge, but Don called Pete's bluff, and marched him into the office of Sterling Cooper's senior partner, Don's boss, Bert Cooper. Cooper listened attentively to the entire story, in which Pete revealed the vast extent of Don's deceit. At the end of it all, Bert said, "So what. It doesn't matter. Don Draper is the best ad man I've ever known."

King Ananda Mahidol Rama VIII
unknown photographer, circa 1920

Joffrey was born to Cersei Lannister. King Robert affirmed him as his son and rightful heir to the Iron Throne, both at his son's birth and to his Hand, Ned Stark, at his deathbed. We know already that Robert disliked but endured the fact that he was surrounded by "those yellow-haired shits", the Lannisters. But he loved his yellow-haired son, and regretted that he had not spent more time with the boy. What would Robert have decided, if at his deathbed, Ned had told him of Cersei's incestuous infidelity, and Joffrey's status as bastard to the Lannister twins? It is not at all difficult to imagine that Robert might have said, "So what. It doesn't matter. Joffrey's been a fine son and he'll make a noble king."

We can argue all we like that the rules of succession trump even a king's wishes. But Joffrey had the full support of House Lannister and all their bannermen, including House Clegane and its powerful knight, Ser Gregor ("The Mountain"), and its devoted strongman, Sandor ("The Hound"). Joffrey could call upon the might of his house, and its vast wealth, to uphold his claim. In what way would this have been any different than the manner in which King Robert maintained his claim on the throne? Until he sat in the iron chair, he was a rebel, the Usurper of the rightful king, murderer of the rightful heir to the Iron Throne, and lord of a minor house. He had no "right" to the crown; he took it by force of arms. That Joffrey was empowered to do the same only meant he was continuing the tradition his mother's husband had begun. How can we maintain that Joffrey had to follow rules the previous king had never been obliged to obey? Why should Joffrey be singled out to adhere to an unreasonable standard to which no previous king had been bound? Is there any real legality in such an arbitrary imposition of strange political whim? Joffrey, by tradition and popular acclaim, was true and rightful Protector of the Realm and King of the Seven Kingdoms.

TYRION LANNISTER

Any claim Joffrey might have had was specious, to be knocked down by even the weakest syllogistic argument. Tyrion had a stronger claim; thanks to his father, Tywin, he will be given the opportunity to validate that claim in the second season.

Tywin recognised his son, Tyrion, as the most level-headed and capable man in House Lannister, and placed him as temporary Hand while he went about the business of defending the realm from its enemies. Tyrion was almost certainly one of the most learned men in Westeros, his attention given to books whenever he had a free moment, preferring the written word even to whoring and drinking, if some of his contemporaries are to be believed.

As Eddard Stark demonstrated, the Hand of the King is entitled to question the legitimacy of any claimant to the Iron Throne. Lord Stark, unfortunately, inhabited the wrong side of the Westeros power equation; Tyrion the Imp was bound by no such impediment in his clear mandate to rule with the full power vested in his office. He was perfectly positioned to place himself or any other suitable claimant onto the throne.

Tyrion ought to be able to demonstrate Joffrey's lack of temperament and unsuitability to rule. Anyone in House Lannister, including the Queen herself, recognised Joffrey's decision to execute Lord Stark as unwise and having potentially deadly effects to the health of the realm and society. The validity of their extreme reservations could be seen already in the civil war being fought at the border with the northlands of King Robb Stark. Without question, Joffrey will continue making ill-advised and dangerous decisions from the throne. The weak position of the Red Keep, the tenuous situation of the entire realm, and the demonstrably poor decisions resulting from Joffrey's childish thinking rendered him unsuited to the task of protecting and administering the Seven Kingdoms. It ought to be a simple matter for Tyrion, with the backing of House Lannister, to declare Joffrey insane, illegitimate, and unsuitable, and to replace him with the next person in line to the throne, Tommen Baratheon.

All of this could be done in accord with existing succession law. Such a move would probably require some careful engineering, but it would raise none of the concerns posed by either Robert's forcible taking of the throne from House Targaryen, nor even the issues posed by Joffrey's illegitimacy. Joffrey was the lawfully accepted and installed King; Tyrion's manoeuvres would use that fact as a starting point for any changes that might be made regarding the occupancy of the land's highest office.

The advantage, of course, is that Tyrion would remain the appointed Hand, and young Tommen, barely out of toddlerhood, would not come of age for nearly twenty years. During that entire time, Tyrion would remain as Hand, Regent, Protector of the Realm, and *de facto* ruler of the Seven Kingdoms.

While Tyrion enjoyed no traditional claim *per se*, what he did have, in far greater measure than anyone else in Westeros, was an ability to understand issues from several different points of view, comprehending even the most intractable of difficulties with a profundity born of constant stimulation and building up of his hungry and passionate intellect. No other such determined yet practical source of wise rule was to be found anywhere in the realm. An unbiased observer would certainly be incapable of arguing Tyrion's lack of suitability to rule, or that his rule would confer on the Seven Kingdoms anything less than the most ideal situation for peace, stability, happiness, and growth. For the sake of everyone in Westeros, Tyrion Lannister **must** become *de facto* king. This claim has to be understood as trumping all others.

STANNIS BARATHEON

There is but one true, legitimate claimant to the Iron Throne. Others may make a claim, but any such assertion must eventually find its illegitimate premise in the idea that Might Makes Right, that a ruler governs strictly through the imposition of force sufficient to crush any opponent. But a kingdom founded on illegitimate principles cannot claim to represent anything noble or even worthwhile in our humanity. Unless a kingdom is based on the rule of law, there can be no law, and therefore there can be no universally recognised and accepted code of conduct. Without laws, there is no kingdom, no mechanism for the establishment or enforcement of justice, no peace, no stability, no order. There can be only the continual seeking after power so as to take by force what nature intended to be inherited by lineage and blood. In fact, when a country has made a decision to welcome chaos rather than expecting lawful behaviour, there can be no king.

Charles V
Tiziano Vecelli (Titian), 1548

The rule of law must prevail, and therefore the king must be legitimate, presented the crown according to the orderly rule of succession. All of the children of Queen Cersei were the illegitimate offspring of her twin brother, Jaime, therefore they were not eligible to ascend the throne. According to the Seven Kingdoms' laws, if the king had no offspring, the eldest brother of the dead, deposed, or displaced ruler became king. The eldest brother was Lord Stannis Baratheon, ruler of Dragonstone, Lord of House Baratheon, and Lord Paramount of the Stormlands.

The practical benefits of respecting and maintaining the line of succession are enormous. The only house that could gain from the ongoing presence of the bastard, Joffrey, on the Iron Throne was House Lannister. But Lord Tywin's house was already the richest and most influential house in the Seven Kingdoms. By also taking the throne, Lord Tywin, Queen Cersei, and their minions were ensuring the development of a radical imbalance that could only lead to the rapid loss of peace, stability, and health throughout the realm. Anyone with eyes to see and ears to hear—and not just a few tavern singers—would know that Joffrey was illegitimate. It would not be long before virtually everyone in the kingdoms would suffer extreme deprivations or limitations on movement, speech, or trade due to Joffrey's capricious and dangerous wielding of power. He thought he served Westeros, but in reality he served only those interests favoured by his mother, and those whims that came to mind whenever he fancied belligerence over benevolence.

On top of his legal right to the throne, Lord Stannis distinguished himself in a number of ways normally considered essential attributes of a competent leader. During Robert's Rebellion, he and his forces held Storm's End during a long siege by loyalist forces. Robert gave him Dragonstone, the traditional land held by the heir to the throne, and Lord Stannis administered the territory with fairness and prudence. In his capacity as Master of Ships, Lord Stannis during the Greyjoy Rebellion trapped and destroyed almost all of Greyjoy's ships, thus bringing a practical end to the rebellion and ensuring his brother's uninterrupted reign from the Red Keep. A keen military mind, both on land and at sea, Lord Stannis had abilities and force of character proven time and again over the decades. Perhaps no one could ever meet the perfect standards set by everyone, but Lord Stannis Baratheon, in addition to being the only true heir to the throne, was seasoned in battle, trusted by his people, and more than capable of addressing any challenge a king might face. Lord Stannis was the only true, legitimate, and practical claimant to the Iron Throne.

DAENERYS TARGARYEN

Legitimacy is always relative to some higher standard. Stannis Baratheon could certainly claim the Iron Throne according to rules established half a generation before. But the rules governing lawful succession would have excluded him and any of the members of his house when the Targaryens held the throne. Those same rules had stood for nearly three hundred years, since Aegon the Conqueror united the Seven Kingdoms and forged the Iron Throne. Unity, peace, and centuries-long order under the rule of law were Targaryen inventions. Religion gained significance under Baelor the Blessed, the first of his name, and the ninth of the dragon kings. Time itself was measured according to a Targaryen clock, with the years meted out by their distance in time from Aegon's Landing (AL).

Myeerah of Hawk Clan, Matriarch and Warrior
painting by Peter Ortiz, 2011
commissioned by Pearson Moore for Cartier's Ring

The higher standard by which the veracity of Stannis Baratheon's claim must be evaluated is the Targaryen Standard. The history of Westeros, to future generations, will note a sorry period of less than a generation, during which time a deranged, sex-crazed drunkard, the Usurper, Robert Baratheon, raped and pillaged his way to King's Landing, executed the Crown Prince, sacked the city, burned the Red Keep, and had one of his wife's henchmen stab the King in the back. This cowardly pretender and his wife's illegitimate bastard son sat the Iron Throne—the Targaryen Throne—for a few years before sanity, peace, order, and legitimacy returned to King's Landing. History will record that wrongs are eventually righted. Sooner or later, the only rightful heir to the throne, Daenerys Targaryen, will return to the Red Keep. She'll bring the dragons back, too.

Stannis Baratheon was despised by his own people. The entire House Lannister, after Lord Tywin sent Ser Gregor on his campaign of burning, looting, and destruction, was hated by everyone in the Seven Kingdoms. But lives of misery were not created only by those considered evil. Even the houses otherwise deemed noble, such as House Stark, took in slaves and unpaid servants. Theon Greyjoy, for instance, was a "ward" (a polite way of saying "slave") of House Stark. Slavery was legal, widely practised, and universally condoned throughout the Seven Kingdoms.

Under Daenerys Targaryen every citizen would experience the broadest possible latitude in actions both public and private. She abhorred the practise of slavery; we have every indication, based on her own statements, that she would outlaw the holding of individuals as property or against their will. In Season One we saw her take extraordinary, dangerous action, moving against the Khal's closest lieutenants, commanding them to end their brutal acts of raping and enslaving those they had conquered. Perhaps the realities of the world will one day cause her to modify her thoughts on the admissibility of slavery, but even so, everything we have so far experienced regarding the quality of her leadership indicates her reign will be based more on the needs of those she rules than on any personal caprices she may wish to exercise. Who among the pretenders to the throne has expressed genuine concern for the lowest among the people, the slaves, the conquered masses, the poor without voice or strength of arms? Queen Daenerys empathised with all of them, if for no other reason than she *was* all of them. She was slave to her brother, conquered by the Baratheons, the poor sister of the "beggar king", Viserys.

Not only was Daenerys Stormborn the only possible heir to the throne, she was the only leader born to nobility who would bring dignity, peace, and true stability to every house, every village, and every child, woman, and man inhabiting the lands she ruled. Hers was the only true claim. Hers was the only *humane* claim.

ROBB STARK

The dragon lords enjoyed perpetuating the fiction that they were the true-born and natural overlords of Westeros, that only they were suited to rule the kingdoms. Rule they did, but only because King Torrhen Stark, the King Who Knelt, accepted Aegon the Conqueror as his king, gave up his crown, and became the first Lord of Winterfell. It was a three-hundred year experiment that ended with the universal declaration of Lord Robb Stark as King In The North.

King Robb Stark
copyright Dalisa 2011
used with permission

Aegon the Conqueror, the first of the dragon kings, styled himself "King of the Andals and the Rhoynar and the First Men". The title had only symbolic meaning, for the Targaryens had no relation to the First Men. The Starks, on the other hand, were the direct descendents of the First Men, the lords of the north, and the guardians of the faith of the Old Gods. Lord Eddard Stark was a devoted follower and practitioner of the Old Ways.

For eight thousand years the Starks had led not only from Winterfell but also from the Wall. The King In The North assured the safety of the entire continent by maintaining the proper staffing of the Night's Watch as his highest priority. The honour associated with the throne was derived not of its position of pre-eminence, but entirely of its significance as the post of highest responsibility. Honour, duty, responsibility, and above all, service to the realm were the expectations of the King In The North. "The man who passes the sentence should swing the sword," Ned told his son, Bran. Even the lowest of criminals were granted the king's respect.

Thus were the enduring, good, and honourable characteristics of the world formed by the Starks into the image of the First Men.

The Targaryens, the Baratheons, and now the Lannisters would claim the throne, but they did not accept any requirement to serve, protect, and maintain the health of those in their charge. For three hundred years the Night's Watch had been neglected. The only things that had been served in that time were the rulers' insatiable and unreasonable desires.

The claims of House Targaryen and House Baratheon amounted to nothing more than the childish desires of selfish, power-hungry ne'er-do-wells whose continued occupation of positions of authority could only further corrode the social order created and maintained by House Stark for over eight thousand years. The only legitimate claim was that of the house that selflessly served the continent since even before recorded history. Robb Stark was the only man fully entitled to sit the Iron Throne.

RENLY BARATHEON

A common characteristic of pretenders' claims was the benefit to society of a particular person's ascension to the throne. Thus, Daenerys Targaryen would abolish slavery, or Robb Stark would reinstate the humane practises of yore, or Tyrion Lannister would listen to all sides of an argument and carefully weigh the evidence before rendering a decision, and so on. All of these "benefits" were presumably intended to serve the interests of the people of Westeros. I suppose I ought to consider a ruler who makes available for purchase three types of chocolate superior to the ruler who thinks to provide only one type. And I ought to be grateful for the choice. But suppose I don't like chocolate. Suppose I couldn't care less whether chocolate were available for sale. And what if I don't care whether the queen keeps slaves, or the king worships the Old Gods, or Tyrion Lannister is slow to administer justice in his hear-everything court?

If a king is to be chosen on the basis of the benefits he brings to the people, who is the determinant of these benefits' value? Does any agency of king or court have the ability to determine the value of benefits? Are not the people themselves best equipped to determine the benefits they would most wish to enjoy?

If we pursue this line of thinking, we see immediately that the king most suited to lead the people is the man noble of spirit and kind of heart who is most loved by the people. Stannis Baratheon, despised even in his own house, would never be granted legitimacy by the people he sought to rule. Anyone from House Lannister or House Targaryen would likewise be despised, and feared. Tyrion Lannister would become a focal point not only of the people's fears, but he would be an object of derision.

Especially in a time of civil war, the Seven Kingdoms needed unity, stability, and a clear route to lasting peace. These objectives would best be obtained by raising up a king universally loved and admired by the people. The only legitimate claim is the one brought by the people themselves, and that claim is best satisfied by Lord Renly Baratheon, Lord Paramount of the Stormlands, brother to Robert, beloved of the people.

JON SNOW

Jon Snow
copyright Dalisa 2011
used with permission

There is yet a seventh possible claimant. His is perhaps the strongest claim of all, yet to all appearances, the claim is not only weak, but absurd. How could a lowly bastard ever hope for high office, let alone ascension to the Iron Throne? In order to understand this strange possibility we need to examine the weight of evidence drawn from many layers of history. We need to delve into the recent events of not less than three houses, the politics of the Royal Targaryen Court, the functioning of several military and political entities during the time of the Targaryens, and most of all, we need to gain access to the mind of Lord Eddard Stark. We will do so in the chapter titled "A History of Westeros".

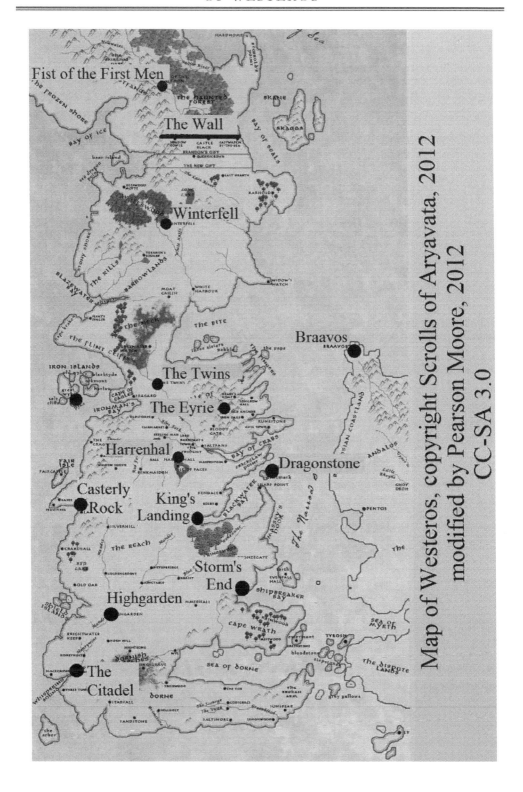

Fist of the First Men

The Wall

Winterfell

Braavos

The Twins

The Eyrie

Harrenhal

Dragonstone

Casterly Rock

King's Landing

Storm's End

Highgarden

The Citadel

We will never know the history of Westeros.

This statement may seem disappointing. It may induce other, even stronger emotions. But we need to ask ourselves this question: What do we seek in this history of Westeros? Do we seek abstract knowledge of time and place? Do we seek independently-verifiable truth of events and persons as they occurred and lived? Westeros is a fictional place, and perhaps instinctively we couch our desire for the full truth of its history in the recognition that any information we might obtain will come through the pen of George R. R. Martin. He is the single author; our ever-hopeful minds tell us we can count on him to reveal every fact of Westeros' history we need to fully understand A Song of Ice and Fire.

Would that this were true. We need to study the bits of information available from Westeros' past, and I will present in this chapter some of the bits I consider most important to a deeper understanding of ASoIaF. But in the end, we will have to make up our own minds about the significance of events and historic personages to the greater story. GRRM will not tell us. And he will never reveal which events are "true" and which are "false". Every event we consider will contain a complete truth from one perspective, but will represent the vilest of falsehoods from another, equally valid perspective. The most important truth to be gleaned from the history of Westeros is that we must become actively involved in piecing together its meaning. I hope to assist in the effort, and I begin my attempt with this chapter.

I am going to spend some time developing the idea of perspective, and why this is essential to understanding GRRM's work. After surveying these ideas in subjectivity, I will begin digging into Westeros history, beginning with the assassination attempts on Bran Stark and Daenerys Targaryen, the death of Jon Arryn, and the three-hundred-year reign of the Targaryens, with a special focus on the end of dragon rule in Robert's Rebellion. Finally, I will turn my attention to the ancient history of Westeros, in the time of the Andals and the First Men.

PERSPECTIVE FROM WITHIN

GRRM does not directly put together the story we know as ASoIaF. He creates characters, each of which has a unique personality, history, objectives, and behaviours, and then he sets them loose to tell us about the other characters in the scene, and how the characters interact with each other to bring about or conclude events. More often than not, because of conflicting objectives, characters disagree with each other. Even more interesting for us, they often disagree not about objectives, but in their understanding of the situation they're in, or the significance of events leading to the situation. This accurately reflects real human interaction, as anyone who has committed to a life partner can attest. My wife and I sometimes disagree on objectives, but more often than not any conflict over goals finds its origin in our disagreement over the meaning of earlier events in our marriage or even occurrences from before our wedding day.

I do not speak here of misunderstanding. My wife's understanding of events is as valid and "true" as mine is. She emphasises certain aspects of interactions, while

I emphasise the essentiality of other aspects of the interaction, often unrelated to facets of the event she considers most important. We gain a glimpse of the conflict under discussion in the bathtub scene between Viserys and his paid female companion:

Whore: "Your Grace."
Viserys: "Yes, my dear."
Whore: "They call you the last dragon."
Viserys: "They do."
Whore: "You have dragon's blood in your veins."
Viserys: "Well, it's entirely possible."
Whore: "What happened to the dragons? I was told that brave men killed them all."
Viserys: "The brave men didn't *kill* dragons. The brave men *rode* them. Rode them from Valyria to build the greatest civilisation this world has ever seen."

Kannon Riding a Flying Dragon
Sesson Shukei, 16ᵗʰ century

Men killed dragons, but earlier in history, men also rode dragons. The question of whether bravery is more fully expressed in the riding or in the killing is not an abstract or meaningless query. In fact, if we believe with Viserys that bravery, and every other good and noble virtue to be found in the hearts of women and men, is best expressed in a reality in which dragons are subjugated and transformed into the willing agents of Westeros' rulers, we are obliged to believe that the Iron Throne was unjustly taken by the Usurper, Robert Baratheon. If, however, we believe the only good dragon is a dead dragon, we are probably more inclined to consider that Robert Baratheon, Eddard Stark, Jon Arryn, and Tywin Lannister fought the good fight in removing the Mad King from the throne.

But our take on Westerosi lore is not the only position we must consider when evaluating significance. In the above dialogue from Episode 1.04, both the servant girl's and Viserys' biases are products of their upbringing and the individual filters they have applied to their own experience. When GRRM writes characters, he does not impose artificial constraints on them; he allows them to observe, comment on, and participate in the scene in the way their consciences dictate. They will not remark on actions they consider uninteresting or irrelevant. When they observe the actions around them, the way they record those events for us will be filtered through their limited and biased understanding.

There is no "reliable narrator" in A Song of Ice and Fire. No provision is made for an "objective" narrator in the television series, either. What we see is filtered through the characters' perceptions and psyches. As much as many believe Tyrion Lannister represents George Martin's "true" voice, I'm pretty sure if we put the question to Mr. Martin, he would confess that not even Tyrion Lannister presents unbiased views. As a test of this, ask yourself whether White Walkers and dragons truly exist in Westeros and Essos. Tyrion believes in neither. In fact, Tyrion belittled Jon Snow for pledging his life to the Night's Watch to protect the realm from "grumkins and snarks and all the other monsters your wet nurse warned you about." Tyrion also believes in and repeats the common wisdom that dragons existed hundreds of years ago, but they have been extinct for many generations, since long before the Targaryens' reign came to an end.

Regardless of anything else we might wish to believe regarding the "truth" of events depicted in Game of Thrones, we must always keep in mind that everything we see is filtered through characters' flawed, biased, and partially obscured perceptions and sensibilities. The characters are embedded within the scenes. They are irretrievably and inseparably integral to events. Every perspective to which we are privy is a limited orientation from within the scene, and from within the character noting the observations.

OBJECTIVITY

The inherent inability to perceive the "truth" of ASoIaF may irritate or disappoint, but no appeal is possible. We should not hope that GRRM is telling only part of the story, that somehow every question will magically be answered by a reliable narrator or authoritative character, or by the author himself, before we reach the end of the story. This will not happen. I suppose the scientist in us rebels most energetically at such a statement. What about the objectivity of truth? If we investigate a matter in a logical, scientific manner, will we not automatically arrive at the truth?

It is indeed the scientist in us that provides the best means of understanding fiction. There is, of course, no entity bearing any resemblance to "truth" in the long experience of science. Science catalogues observations and connects them by means of syllogism, induction, deduction, and scientific method into the ideas we know as theories. But these theories are never presented as facts, and they should not be understood as such. Truth is never discussed. As we parse every observation and split every hair, we eventually come to one of the invariant principles of scientific investigation: We cannot know everything.

Observation itself imparts to the object under consideration some change that renders the entire situation biased. The witch in Scene Four, in the dungeon, is wearing a green dress, clearly visible in the light of her minions' torches. We know from another character to beware the sorceress dressed in green, for she will kill the prince. We see her ascend the steps out of the dungeon, wielding a long dagger. As she comes into the light of day, in the courtyard, she conceals the dagger and draws close to the prince. We fear for the prince's life, but then we realise something important has changed. Her dress, once a brilliant green in the dungeon, is now a solid blue in the light of the sun. Is this a trick? Some magic conceived to confound or confuse the prince?

The Heisenberg Uncertainty Principle
German postage stamp, 2001

There is no trickery here. No magic incantations were performed to change the colour of the dress. In fact, the dress has not changed at all. Yet the colour has most assuredly changed, and changed dramatically. How is this possible?

The perception of colour requires not less than three entities: The object we wish to observe, the light source we use to illuminate the object, and a detector (in this case, our eyes). Neither object nor detector has changed. The source of illumination, though, is quite different between dungeon and courtyard. A burning torch emits radiation (light rays) in a certain spectral range and intensity. Both the spectral range and the intensity are different—in fact, enormously different—in sunlight. The light of the torches is rich in light wavelengths that reflect off the dress as green light. On the other hand, the wavelengths that reflect as green are poorly represented in the radiation (light) from the sun, to the point that we see no green at all in the dress once the witch emerges from the dungeon. We see only a rich blue, because sunlight is deficient in light that reflects as green, and rich in light that reflects as a deep blue.

As I stated earlier, science tells us that the act of observation itself imparts a change to the object that biases our interpretation of facts. We cannot say that the witch's dress is "really" green or "really" blue. We can say only that our detector (our eyes) perceives a green colour in the presence of torch light, but a blue colour in the presence of sunlight. By imposing a particular illuminant source (torch light or sunlight), we are biasing the observation toward green or toward blue. If we are going to observe, we may do so only in a biased manner.

We cannot even accept the variability of colour as the only aspect of the situation that must remain the result of subjective observation. In most situations, in fact, if we are able to gather one particular type of information, we may be entirely incapable of gathering other information. For instance, the Heisenberg Uncertainty Principle says we cannot simultaneously know both the position and the momentum of a subatomic particle. This may seem esoteric, but it really is entirely applicable to our study of Game of Thrones.

Think of a scene illuminated by candlelight, fireplace, and a match. The prince lights a match and we see a woman dressed in green suddenly raise a dagger. The prince, scared out of his wits, drops the match, and the scene is plunged into darkness. We hear rapid footsteps and see a bald man, the intensity of his eyes made fierce in the distant light of a fireplace. We see a torch, fear in the bald man's eyes, his muscles taut, ready to pounce, we hear running feet, we see the silhouette of a richly-dressed man, a woman raising a black dagger, the man turning, stopping, raising his arms in front of himself. For an instant, we see the man's face—it is the prince! We hear a scream as the silhouetted knife jabs into his shadow. A character lights a match, and we see him: The bald man, dead on the floor. The prince, holding the match, laughs. The witch in green, beaming into his eyes, draws her head back and cackles into the night air.

In the jumble of activity in the scene above we were not able to simultaneously discern the physical position and the intentions of all the characters. The Heisenberg Uncertainty Principle is as applicable to fiction as it is to particle physics.

THE ASSASSINATION ATTEMPTS ON BRAN STARK
AND DAENERYS TARGARYEN: FIDELITY OR PERFIDY?

We would like to believe we have unbiased, true information about the events we witnessed transpire over the course of ten episodes. But even here, we should remain aware that objectivity is not possible.

The Attempted Assassination of President Andrew Jackson
Endicott, 1835

In light of the common wisdom that Tyrion Lannister was responsible for the second attempt on Bran Stark's life (recall the assassin's knife belonged to Tyrion), and the conversation between Lord Varys and Magister Illyrio Mopatis we overheard in the dungeon storeroom (Episode 1.05), we have two strong suspects outside House Lannister. Lord Varys is originally from the Free Cities, and may indeed have a greater affinity for the Magisters of Essos than for the rulers of Westeros. Illyrio Mopatis has clearly been trying to curry favour with the Targaryens, even resorting to a gift of dragon eggs, which evidently cost him a considerable fortune to procure. Why *wouldn't* these two men conspire to weaken House Baratheon so the Targaryens could reclaim the Iron Throne? Couldn't they have been the masterminds behind the second attempt on Bran's life? Why didn't we envision this possibility prior to Episode Five?

In these revelations we believe we may finally have attained some purchase for our desire to implicate the guilty party. We caught the Master of Whisperers red-handed, guilty of devising a crime so cruel it would force an overwhelming response even from a man of honour such as Ned Stark, conspiring to create a war between House Lannister and House Stark that would topple the royal house and allow Viserys Targaryen, the "beggar king", to become their tool in controlling not just Westeros, but the entire world.

Littlefinger confided to Varys that he was aware the Master Spider had been "escorting a certain *foreign* dignitary (Magister Illyrio)." Lord Varys seemed unconcerned that Littlefinger knew of Varys' meeting with the known benefactor of the Targaryens. In the delicious throne room scene in Episode 1.05, we saw Littlefinger's confrontation with the master spy, we saw Lord Varys' face fall, as if acknowledging guilt, but then Lord Renly appeared and announced the Small Council meeting. Lord Baelish was surprised, but Lord Varys was as smooth as ever. "Disturbing news from far away," Varys said, turning to Littlefinger as he walked toward the council chamber. "Hadn't you heard?" And then the revelations at the council itself:

Lord Stark: [To King Robert] "You want to assassinate a girl, because the Spider heard a rumour?"
Lord Varys: "No rumour, my Lord, the Princess is with child."
Lord Stark: "Based on whose information?"
Lord Varys: "Ser Jorah Mormont. He's serving as advisor to the Targaryens."
Lord Stark: "Mormont. You bring us the whispers of a traitor half a world away and call it fact."
...
Lord Varys: "I understand your misgiving, my Lord, truly I do. It is a terrible thing we must consider, a vile thing. Yet we who presume to rule must sometimes do vile things for the good of the realm."

By all appearances at the Small Council meeting, the Master of Whisperers was prepared, in fact eager, to bring an end to any possibility of the Targaryens' re-ascension to the Iron Throne. He was the most forceful proponent of the initiative to assassinate Daenerys Stormborn, calling the meeting of the Small Council to notify them of the news of her pregnancy, which he learned from Illyrio Mopatis, long before Lord Baelish accused Varys of treason.

Which appearance is correct, then? Would Lord Varys simultaneously work to strengthen Daenerys Targaryen (in his clandestine meeting with Magister Illyrio) and to destroy the Princess (during the Small Council meeting)? A third possibility presents itself, from the early portion of Littlefinger's throne room discussion with the Master Spider:

Baelish: "You look a bit lonely today. You should pay a visit to my brothel this evening. First boy is on the house."
Varys: "I think you're mistaking business with pleasure."
Baelish: "Am I?"

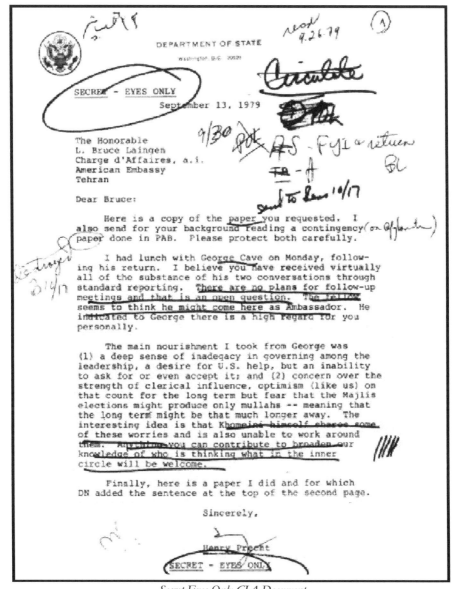

Secret Eyes-Only CIA Document
seized from the U.S. Embassy in Tehran by Iranian students, 1979

Of course, Littlefinger is not confusing business and pleasure. Not at all. Everything he discusses with Varys can be understood in at least two different ways. He disputes the idea that he is mistaking business for pleasure. With these words, Varys knows to listen for the underlying sense of Littlefinger's words.

Baelish: "All those birds that whisper in your ear. Such pretty little things. Trust me: We accommodate all inclinations."

That is, Littlefinger is telling Varys that his talks with "all those birds" (spies from various locations, not only spies of which the King may approve) are fine. Littlefinger will not divulge his knowledge of Varys' illicit discussions ("We accommodate all inclinations.").

Varys: "Oh, I'm sure. Lord Redwyne likes his boys very young, I hear."
Baelish: "I'm a purveyor of beauty *and* discretion, both equally important."

Littlefinger is telling Varys that even an extreme position—perhaps even a desire to commit treason—may be something he would overlook. It struck me during this conversation that he may have been promising more, that perhaps he was in fact offering to assist Lord Varys in treason.

Varys: "Though I suppose beauty is a subjective quality, no?"

That is, the enticements to treason may vary from person to person.

Varys: "Is it true that Ser Marlin of Tumblestone prefers amputees?

The real question, as Littlefinger heard it, was this: "Suppose, Lord Baelish, that the plan I have in mind would do grave harm (amputation) to the realm? Would you consider any such plan acceptable?

Baelish: "All desires are valid to a man with a full purse."

Translated, Littlefinger told Varys his plan depended on the amount he was willing to pay.

Varys: "And I heard the most awful rumour that a certain lord with a taste for fresh cadavers... it must be enormously difficult to accommodate that inclination. The logistics alone... to find beautiful corpses before they rot."

The question, rephrased: "Are you sure you're with me on this, Littlefinger?"

Baelish: "Strictly speaking, such a thing would not be in accordance with the king's   laws."
Varys: "Strictly speaking."

In other words, Littlefinger was saying, "Varys, you misunderstand me. I would never commit treason." Lord Varys' response was equally bold: "I laugh at you, Littlefinger. How could you have ever thought I would be manoeuvring against the king?"
But the question of treason, at the fore of Littlefinger's thoughts during his throne room discussion with Varys, had to be resolved, and it was for this reason

that Littlefinger probed further, using less veiled language, referring directly to Varys' meeting with the Magister from Pentos. Varys in turn insinuated that Littlefinger may have his own propensities toward treason, thanks to his lifelong desire to bed Catelyn Tully ("Everyone's well aware of your enduring fondness for Lord Stark's wife"), but Littlefinger brushed off Varys' clumsy accusation, drilling home his knowledge of Varys' meeting with the Targaryens' wealthy patron from across the Narrow Sea.

The throne room meeting ended in a stalemate, with neither Varys nor Littlefinger able to determine the other party's inclination toward any treasonous act. What this intriguing scene did give us, though, was the truth that even a single individual among the myriad players in this very complicated game of thrones could have multiple, competing allegiances and motivations. It is entirely possible, for instance, that either Littlefinger or Varys, or both of them, seek wealth and power without regard to the person sitting the throne. In the greater scheme of trying to make sense of even the immediate history of Westeros, we should understand from this important meeting, and others between Varys and Baelish, that simple lines of cause and effect probably are not in play. We will have to pay close attention, and weigh a considerable number of often conflicting bits of evidence, before we can determine the true inclinations of any particular player in this fascinating game.

HISTORY SINCE THE DEATH OF JON ARRYN

What of the death of Jon Arryn? We saw Jaime and his sister, the Queen, carrying on in a most jovial manner at his funeral. We know he was murdered, most likely using the Tears of Lys, a poison which leaves no trace. Lady Lysa Tully, Jon Arryn's widow, was willing to risk her life to inform her sister, Catelyn, that the Lannisters had murdered her lord and husband. We know that Ser Hugh of the Vale, who had been Lord Arryn's squire, was only consecrated a knight days before his death opposite Ser Gregor Clegane at the jousting tournament in honour of Lord Stark's appointment as Hand, and that he mysteriously had enough money to pay for a full suit of armour. The implication is clear: Cersei and Jaime conspired to bribe Ser Hugh to murder Lord Arryn in such a way that the death could not be traced to anyone.

But there are some troubling complications that leave a considerable level of doubt in our minds. For instance, we know the movers and shakers of Westeros considered poison a weapon of "women, cravens, and eunuchs". The clear implication is that a man of honour, or indeed, even an ordinary criminal, would never descend so low as to resort to poison. We know there is honour in Westeros, even among thieves and criminals, even when the blood is hot and the cause is just. Jaime Lannister, for instance, confronted Lord Stark outside Lord Baelish's brothel (Episode 1.05). He challenged the King's Hand to a one-on-one sword fight over Lord Eddard's unjust imprisonment of Tyrion. Jaime knew that Tyrion had done nothing wrong, and he was angrier than he had ever been. Nevertheless, he showed restraint, fighting an honourable and fair fight with the Hand. When Ned began to take the upper hand in the battle, one of Jaime's men intervened, stabbing Lord Stark in the leg. Jaime's disgust was evident, and he could not honourably continue fighting. Even though he would have been justified in killing Lord Eddard, honour prevented him from doing so. He admitted to his father, Lord Tywin, "It wouldn't have been clean." To Jaime, even in his aroused state of anger, honour was more important than settling a score. In fact, honour was more important to him than it would have been to an ordinary knight under the circumstances. As Lord Tywin said, "I suppose I should be grateful that your vanity got in the way of your recklessness." That is, killing Lord Stark would have been preferable to upholding Jaime's perverse sense of honour (which his father called "vanity").

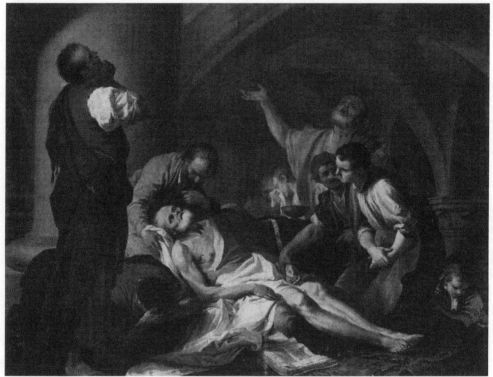

The Death of Socrates by Hemlock
Giambettino Cignaroli, circa 1760

The conclusion that Jaime held honour the highest among the ideals to which he subscribed can and should be questioned. We should never forget, for example, that Jaime—a knight of the Kingsguard—stabbed King Aerys in the back. This treasonous treachery, as dishonourable an act as can be imagined, became the most infamous deed of Robert's Rebellion. The moniker "Kingslayer" meant not simply "one who slays kings" but rather "one who slays kings in perfidy and dishonour". However, Jaime admitted to despising the title given him by history. My understanding, in light of what I have seen of the Kingslayer's behaviour, is that Jaime regrets the manner in which he took the king's life. If presented again with any such opportunity, I believe he would acquit himself in bold but honourable fashion.

If Jaime had an inordinate, overwhelming sense of honour, as appears to be the case based on his behaviour in a number of situations, how could he ever have condoned a scheme in which one of his enemies would be dealt with using a means considered beneath the dignity of even common criminals? That is to say, how can we believe that Jaime was in any way involved in the murder of Jon Arryn? And if he was not involved, could his twin sister, with whom he shared matters intimate and profound, have had anything to do with Jon Arryn's death? And if neither of them was responsible, who is the guilty party?

THE REIGN OF THE DRAGON KINGS
AEGON THE CONQUEROR TO AERYS II ("THE MAD KING")

William the Conqueror at the Battle of Hastings
Frank Wilkin, circa 1830

Many of the norms we understand from our acquaintance with Game of Thrones had their origin only in the last three hundred years, with the arrival of the first of the Targaryens on the eastern shores of Westeros. The Targaryens' story is in some ways unique, in other ways it contains the same range of events, pedestrian and extraordinary, afflicting every royal house. However, the aspects of the Targaryens' story unique to Game of Thrones are the parts that excite me the most; I believe it is these concerns that have the greatest bearing on the history of Westeros.

Time in the Seven Kingdoms, as it is now measured, had its beginning with the landing of Aegon the Conqueror at the humble outpost that has risen to become the kingdom's capital, King's Landing. This seems a particularly appropriate event to mark the beginning of modern times. Most germane to the time After Landing (AL) is the fact that the entire civilised portion of Westeros was united under a single ruler for the first time. Thus, the time prior to the reign of the Dragon Kings was a long period of disunity, border disputes, and other struggles causing endless wars and misgivings between kingdoms. The Pax Romana allowed by a single ruler led to unprecedented prosperity, to the point that the treasury under the last king, King Aerys II, was overflowing with gold.

Before we consider some of the more mundane (but still interesting!) facts around the Targaryens' reign, I believe we should spend some time looking at the events surrounding the Wars of Conquest, for it is in this sequence of events that we see physical juxtapositions I believe are critical to understanding Game of Thrones.

THE ESSENTIAL GAME OF THRONES

I believe at its heart Game of Thrones is a story of the importance of peripheries. As adults, we learn that which is peripheral is unimportant. We have limited abilities to concentrate, and little patience for multiple, competing demands on our time, so we let go of any concerns we consider minor. As a scientist with thirty years of experience, and as a HazMat first responder and incident commander with fifteen years of training and drilling in emergency response, I am well-schooled in processes based on triage. I am trained to respond first to imminent threats to health and safety. Only after I have responded to the heart of the immediate threat do I assign resources to mitigate and contain longer-term threats. Finally, I ignore anything that I judge does not require my immediate attention. I might get around to addressing these very low-level concerns, but if not, I'll assign them to someone else and then walk away. This pattern of behaviour is something perhaps any of us would acknowledge as an entirely proper system of addressing adult concerns. I believe it is this way of dealing with the world that George Martin questions unrelentingly in A Song of Ice and Fire. At its core, ASoIaF disputes the efficacy and integrity of the modern way of dealing with adult responsibility.

Some adults are trained to be hyper-vigilant regarding activities at borders and peripheries. Military strategists, for example, bring extraordinary concern regarding the importance of flanking manoeuvres and the essentiality of preventing the enemy from outflanking one's own forces. Individual soldiers are trained to be aware of movement or unusual presence at the periphery of their own vision, and in any out-of-the-way (peripheral) location that may be used to obscure a threat. A dip in the landscape, areas of thick vegetation, a mound of dirt, even a crack in the asphalt, may contain lethal threats. Soldiers, commanders in the field, and strategists far from the front lines are often called upon to perform dozens of acts of triage every minute, frantically seeking every bit of sensory and computer information available to them, weighing the evidence, and assigning likely threat levels to everything within their field of vision, range of hearing, or satellite, airborne, and remote monitors.

Other professions require hyper-vigilance. We think of police officers, firefighters, air traffic controllers. We call these "high stress" occupations, recognising that a continual attitude of readiness, and the need to evaluate everything on a split-second basis, for hours or days or weeks on end, is so taxing to the psyche and mind that few can endure such an existence.

GRRM, I believe, is telling us that the cost of vigilance is not too high. In fact, the cost of awareness is the true cost of existence as a human being. The costs of complacency, inattention, and premature triage, on the other hand, are too great to the satisfactory propagation of human societies.

ATTACK FROM THE PERIPHERY

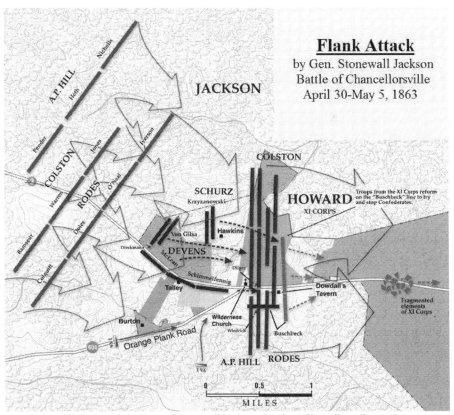

Flank Attack by General Stonewall Jackson, Battle of Chancellorsville, 1863
map prepared by the U.S. Park Service

The Targaryens were not of Westeros. They were shepherds and farmers and other lowly practitioners of the most elementary aspects of subsistence civilisation.

Their distant origin was in the Freehold of Valyria, an entirely inconsequential (peripheral, again) part of the eastern continent, Essos. Far out on the Valyrian Peninsula was a largely uninhabited, and therefore unimportant, ring of volcanoes called the Fourteen Fires. Yet the Fourteen Fires contained the instrument that would raise House Targaryen to the pinnacle of the ruling class of Westeros.

We can consider the Targaryen Valyrians as representing a feature of the world five times removed from the minds of the rulers of Westeros. The immediate concerns of a ruler's own kingdom carried greatest importance. Next in the hierarchy of concern came the worries associated with other kingdoms in Westeros. Anything happening on Essos was of little practical concern. The reason for this was that the Dothraki were the most prominent race on the continent. They were scared of salt water (or anything else that could kill a horse), and therefore posed no threat to anyone on Westeros. Compared to the Dothraki, the Targaryens, in their quaint shepherd dress, herding their little herds, were such a low-level concern as to remain practically unheard of in the great halls of power. Of even lower concern were any events that might occur on a distant ring of volcanoes. Who cared what happened out there?

The "adult" order of concern could be outlined like this, beginning with the element of greatest concern, the ruler's own kingdom:

1. Kingdom
2. Westeros
3. Essos
4. Valyria
5. Valyrian Volcanoes (the Fourteen Fires)

If I put myself in the ruler's position, I can easily imagine believing the kingdom's concerns five times more important than anything happening outside my country's borders. Since Essos presents no threat to my kingdom or to Westeros, I can again imagine considering Essos five times less interesting than the other kingdoms of Westeros. Perhaps my only interaction with a resident of Essos would be arranging for trade routes or greeting the new ambassador from Pentos. I might spend four days a week addressing concerns of my kingdom, one day a week dealing with inter-kingdom business affairs or potential threats, and less than one day a month thinking about anything having to do with Essos. As for Valyria, perhaps I would attend a play or hear second-hand information from a travelling dignitary every few months. And the Fourteen Fires? Probably I've never even heard of them, unless as well as being monarch I am also a cartographer.

The world, according to our imaginary king, would look something like this:

Map of Westeros
Copyright Pearson Moore 2011

The king would draw a long vertical line between Westeros and Essos; everything to the east of the line would have little or no influence on his thoughts. He would draw an identical vertical line west of the continent. He would draw a line at the Wall to the north; why worry about anything north of the Wall when the centuries-old structure would protect the rest of the continent? He'd also draw a line at the border with Dorne in the far south; who cared about those strange Rhoynar folk so far away?

But our imaginary king would have done well to maintain Essos and Valyria at the fore of his thoughts, for it was at the Fourteen Fires that the lowly Targaryens discovered dragons. The Targaryens didn't think the dragons inconsequential. Rather, they risked lives—and probably lost many lives—to become the dragons' masters. And when they had accomplished this feat, they became the masters of the world.

The Targaryens were no more broad-minded than anyone else when time came to subjugate the Seven Kingdoms. When the proud people of the north, under King Torrhen Stark, finally yielded to Aegon's armies, it must have seemed the complete unification of the continent was at hand. Six Kingdoms had bowed to the invading Dragon King. I imagine Aegon probably had it in his mind by that point that the conquest of Dorne would occur almost without a fight.

One of the major lessons of the Wars of Conquest was that Dorne was never taken. Dorne remained a completely independent kingdom well into the second century of Targaryen rule, standing strong and firm, facing the dragons that invaded and threatened their land. To this day, the Rhoynish people in Dorne retain their own laws and a way of life very different from anywhere else in Westeros. The culture, history, and pride of Dornish people gave them the strength to resist, even when dragons levelled entire cities, even when enormous armies marched.

The lesson to the Targaryens, and to us, is that no lines can be drawn on any maps. We may think Dorne unimportant, under-populated, weak, and ready for conquest, but in fact, it was the strongest, proudest, and most resilient of the Seven Kingdoms. The warlords of Nazi Germany were defeated in less than six years. But they were a high-visibility threat. The warlords of Afghanistan are not so visible; they reside more toward the periphery of our thoughts. As a result, after over ten years of war, the Americans and their allies have not yet defeated the Taliban and Al Qaeda guerrillas in Afghanistan.

DIVERSITY, NOT ASSIMILATION

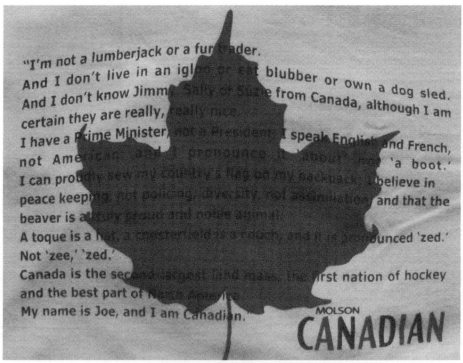

"I'm not a lumberjack or a fur trader.
And I don't live in an igloo or eat blubber or own a dog sled.
And I don't know Jimmy, Sally or Suzie from Canada, although I am certain they are really, really nice.
I have a Prime Minister, not a President. I speak English and French,
not American. and I pronounce it 'about,' not 'a boot.'
I can proudly sew my country's flag on my backpack. I believe in
peace keeping, not policing, diversity, not assimilation, and that the
beaver is a truly proud and noble animal.
A toque is a hat, a chesterfield is a couch, and it is pronounced 'zed.'
Not 'zee,' 'zed.'
Canada is the second largest land mass, the first nation of hockey
and the best part of North America.
My name is Joe, and I am Canadian."

MOLSON
CANADIAN

The Molson Rant, March, 2000
photograph copyright Pearson Moore 2012
Line Eight says, "diversity, not assimilation"

If creation of artificial hierarchies of concern is antithetical to Martin's thesis in Game of Thrones, I believe the creation of stereotypes is another target for his unrelenting attack. We cannot speak of any group as if it were homogeneous or monolithic. Less so can we assign to any member of that group qualities we believe pertain to the group as a whole. At best, we make ourselves look foolish; at worst, we endanger ourselves and everyone we might wish to protect. This is one of the major lessons to be gleaned from a detailed study of the history of House Targaryen.

Despite their tendency toward incestuous liaisons and marriages between brother and sister, the Targaryens, individually and from one monarch to another, were as different as human beings could possibly be. There were squabbles and moments of unity, times of peace and periods of war within the house. Some of the leaders and their households were saints, like Baelor the Blessed; others were scoundrels and disrespectful, self-centred scum. During the time of Rhaenyra, for example, some Targaryens believed a woman could sit the Iron Throne, while others were prepared to risk their lives to prevent any such abhorrent event from occurring. Can a bastard take the throne? In the eyes of King Aegon IV, who loved his bastard sons, such a possibility was not at all unthinkable, but when he legitimised the bastards, his children by the queen were more than a bit upset, and when one of the bastards, Daemon, claimed the throne, he caused a civil war.

These isolated events illustrate the diversity of opinion within House Targaryen regarding just two or three matters relating to the order of succession. A close study of the Targaryens' reign would allow us to compile entire catalogues of the broad diversity of thought and behaviour that characterised individuals within the house. We would find little unanimity in philosophy, or action, or abilities. As we know from our own experience of GoT, some Targaryens, such as Viserys, could feel pain from a flame held thirty centimetres away from his skin, while other Targaryens could find complete comfort in a blazing conflagration.

Stereotypes are incorrect, damaging, and dangerous. King Aegon thought of the proud Dornish people as nothing more than stereotypical Westerosi, who would fall to their knees at the first sight of fire-breathing dragons. He was incorrect, and his damaging, childish assessment led to the unnecessary suffering and death of thousands in his army. Ser Jorah was incorrect in assuming Daenerys could not endure smoke and flame. He applied a useless stereotype regarding the normal range of human capability. He did not understand Daenerys to be an unusual individual, even when he heard reports of the Princess taking baths in scalding water, even when he knew she had handled red-hot dragon eggs without suffering the least harm. If he had been observant and open to *possibilities*, he would have realised she could suffer no harm on the funeral pyre. More than anything, he should have considered the princess as an individual, a person unique in herself. This is a way of thinking GRRM demands of us as we make our way through Game of Thrones.

My apologies to Joe for the section title. I don't live in an igloo or eat blubber or own a dogsled, either. And I don't know Jimmy, Sally, or Suzy. It's on YouTube. You'll like it. Joe's rant is all about stereotypes, and he destroys each one of them, while at the same time selling several million cases of beer. Not bad for a guy standing at a single microphone on a lonely stage. You can see the Molson Rant here: http://www.youtube.com/watch?v=BRI-A3vakVg.

ROBERT'S REBELLION

These are the sections veteran ASoIaF readers have been waiting for. Where does Pearson stand on the question of R + L = J? Confused by the question? You won't be by the time you finish these next sections.

THE MARRIAGE OF PRINCE RHAEGAR

The Wedding of Prince William and Catherine Middleton
copyright Robbie Dale 2011, CC-SA 2.0

Robert Baratheon did not initiate the rebellion that now bears his name. He and his best friend, Eddard Stark, were typical young men of their time, training in the art of war, doing their best to absorb the lessons in diplomacy and tact as relayed to them by their guardian, Jon Arryn, Lord of the Eyrie. They would become the decisive players in the rebellion, but they were peripheral to the events that eventually demanded their engagement.

The rebellion began not with a young man's lust for power, but with political manoeuvres, grudges, and mismatched priorities. It began, really, with a promise to a prince, and the political moves that nullified the promise.

The time was the late 270s, something over twenty years before Game of Thrones began. Cersei Lannister was probably the prettiest girl Crown Prince Rhaegar Targaryen had ever seen. She was the daughter of the Hand of the King,

Tywin Lannister, lord of the wealthiest and most influential house in the Seven Kingdoms. Rhaeagar's father, King Aerys II, knew of his son's infatuation with the beautiful, young blond-haired girl, and gave every indication of their impending betrothal. Rhaegar must have been counting the days.

The wife of Lord Martell of Dorne had been trying for years to marry off her frail daughter, Elia. Though the girl was often in poor health, she had no lack of suitors, probably because Dorne had always been considered one of the most powerful kingdoms in the land. The Martells, with the help of Dornish bannermen, had been the only house to stand up to the Targaryens, and Dorne had remained an independent kingdom well into the second century of the Dragon Lords' rule. Dorne became the last of the seven kingdoms to fall under the domain of the Targaryens, and only then through marriage and diplomacy. But young Elia refused every suitor her mother sent. The Lady of Dorne was left with a frail daughter who would soon be considered an old maid. If she were not married off soon, the daughter would become an embarrassment to House Martell.

It must not have occurred to Elia's mother until quite late that House Martell bore considerable influence with the royal house. When she began manoeuvres in the royal court, she was probably surprised at the success of her endeavour: King Aerys accepted her proposal, and he promised that her daughter, Elia, would become Prince Rhaegar's wife.

Rhaegar must have been incensed. Did everything in his life have to revolve around politics and the appeasement of minor houses jealous of the dragons and their friendship with House Lannister? Why did Rhaegar—heir to the Iron Throne—have to subsume his love of Cersei Lannister to accept an arranged political marriage to some sickly, prudish woman from the sun-baked land of Dorne?

Rhaegar eventually accepted his father's will. Even princes and kings, he probably realised, had to bend their desires to political reality. Rhaegar and Elia had two children together, though Rhaegar must have wondered if the frail young mother would be able to endure a third pregnancy.

THE TOURNEY OF HARRENHAL

Lord Tywin, of course, was seething. He was the Hand of the King, by rights entitled to greater respect and discretion than anyone else in the realm. The king had virtually promised Rhaegar to Cersei, and now Aerys had reneged on the commitment. Before he could demonstrate his displeasure to the king, though, something wonderful happened. Cersei's twin, Jaime, distinguished himself in a major battle. Only fifteen years old, he was knighted on the spot. The news travelled to the Red Keep, and the king realised he had it in his power to calm Lord Tywin with a magnificent show of gratitude to the Hand's eldest son. Lord Whent of Harrenhal had been seeking some way of showing off his house and his young daughter; Jaime's success in battle gave the king the perfect excuse to stage a tournament—in fact, the greatest tournament the realm had ever seen—at

Harrenhal, in Jaime's honour. House Whent would feel honoured, the king himself would appoint Jaime to the Kingsguard, and most importantly, Hand of the King Lord Tywin would smile again.

The tournament was a magnificent affair spanning several days of pomp, revelry, grand melees and spectacular jousts. The great feasts were exquisitely prepared, the entertainers were amusing, and every contest was well represented by the most capable young men of every house. The king made another momentous mistake, though, virtually nullifying every gain he might have made by the expensive show of deference to Lord Tywin. Aerys did indeed bestow Jaime with a white cloak, installing him as honoured member of the Kingsguard. But rather than allowing the young knight to participate in the tourney, King Aerys dispatched him to King's Landing to guard the queen and young Prince Viserys. Either because of the king's presumption of elevating Jaime without Tywin's consent, or because the king refused Jaime's participation in the tournament, Lord Tywin resigned as Hand.

THE GARLAND OF BLUE WINTER ROSES

Blue Rose
Copyright Noumenon 2006, CC-SA 3.0

One man at the tourney distinguished himself above all others. As winner of the jousting tournament, it was Crown Prince Rhaegar Targaryen's privilege to bestow on the woman of his choice the title of Queen of Love and Beauty. As he rode toward his wife, Elia, the crown of blue winter roses in his outstretched hand, many in the large crowd must have been smiling. Some of them knew the Crown Prince had not been pleased with the arranged marriage, but here he was, about to bestow the greatest honorary title of the tourney on his bride. She was not unattractive, after all. Bedecked in her finest dress, most expensive jewels, and striking finery, she was a rare sight.

We don't know what Rhaegar's thoughts were as he rode forward, carrying the crown of blue winter roses before him. His father had determined that he could not claim the beautiful young Cersei for himself. Did this mean any fair maid was off limits?

We don't know if he scanned the crowd, seeking out a beautiful woman, or if he had one in mind already. Drawn as he was to Cersei's rare beauty, it is not difficult to imagine that he fell in love the very moment he laid eyes on the prettiest girl at the tournament. That Lyanna Stark was already betrothed to Eddard's close friend, Robert Baratheon, meant nothing to the Crown Prince. Who was Robert Baratheon, anyway, but an unimportant teenager from a minor house, promised a beautiful young woman only because Baratheon's best friend was Lyanna's second-eldest brother. Why should a boy like Baratheon, almost a commoner, be allowed to claim such beauty for himself? Why should an undistinguished boy have claim to a girl like Lyanna, when the heir to the throne had to make do with whatever sickly political tokens his father saw fit to send the prince?

Everyone must have wondered what was happening when Rhaegar rode right past his wife and headed toward the Stark seats, his eyes locked on the beautiful dark-haired daughter of Lord Rickard Stark. Many must have gasped in horror or in shock when he extended his armour-clad hand and bestowed Lyanna Stark with the wreath of blue winter roses, crowning her Queen of Love and Beauty.

Her older brother, Brandon, must have been confused as never before. Lyanna would have felt a thrill unlike any other she had ever experienced. Out of all the fair young maidens at the event, the dashing young Crown Prince, in his expensive black armour studded with red rubies, had chosen her above all others— even above his own wife—as the most lovely, most beautiful woman of the tournament.

ABDUCTION AND MURDER

About a year later, news came that Rhaegar and Lyanna had disappeared together. House Stark understood this unannounced move as an abduction. King Aerys had been making one strange pronouncement after another from the throne, and now the Mad King's son was taking advantage of his father's insanity to commit acts of theft and rape out of everyone's sight. Brandon Stark demanded an audience with the king to protest the Crown Prince's crime and demand his sister be returned unharmed. The king heard Lord Stark's eldest son, then had him bound and imprisoned and sent a raven, demanding Lord Rickard Stark's presence at Brandon's trial for treason. Lord Rickard dutifully complied with the king's demand. The Mad King gave Brandon and Rickard a "trial", then had both of them mercilessly and horribly murdered before everyone's eyes in the throne room.

Nazi show trial of Erwin von Witzleben
unknown photographer, July 21, 1944

Jon Arryn's two wards, Eddard Stark and Robert Baratheon, were beside themselves with such anger as few men ever display. It was anger of the type that is not assuaged even by extraordinary acts of appeasement. Land, titles, or position would not diminish this anger. The Mad King had publicly murdered Eddard Stark's father, Warden of the North, Lord of Winterfell, direct descendent of the King In The North. He had publicly murdered his brother, heir to Winterfell. He had abducted his beautiful sister, and took Robert's bride-to-be away from him, to feed the unclean desires of the insane ruler's horrible, perverted son. Lord Jon knew the boys' fury was justified, and he joined them, calling the banners to face off against House Targaryen.

THE BATTLE OF THE TRIDENT

As the bannermen and knights of House Stark, House Baratheon, House Tully, and House Arryn fought their way toward King's Landing, the Crown Prince came out of hiding—without Lyanna—bringing with him the full force of the royal armies, headed by House Targaryen, House Martell, and the minor houses loyal to the king. The Battle of the Trident, at the main ford of the Green Fork of the Trident River, occurred in 283 AL. The forces were evenly matched, but Robert

Baratheon, leading the rebel armies, had not yet been beaten in battle. His greatest weapon was not the long-handled war hammer, but a deep, unquenchable fury, directed like a bolt of lightning against the arrogant young prince, the devious criminal and rapist who held the only woman Robert had ever loved. Robert drove his destrier straight toward the knight dressed in black armour and red silk, parried the prince's sword thrusts, and pounded his hammer into the prince's chest, delivering the full force of his anger to crush the prince's chest, killing him instantly.

House Lannister, led by Jaime, marched to King's Landing, apparently to protect the king. Jaime gained the king's confidence, and when Aerys turned his back, the boy thrust his sword into the king's back, earning for himself the title and the legend that would dog him for the rest of his life. Jaime began the Sack of King's Landing, burning to the ground anything he believed had belonged to the Targaryens. House Clegane and members of Jaime's horde began slaughtering everyone in House Targaryen, including Prince Rhaegar's two children. Prince Viserys and Queen Rhaella, pregnant with Daenerys, were secreted off to Dragonstone. By the time Lord Eddard arrived at the Red Keep, the Targaryens were all dead or presumed dead.

THE TOWER OF JOY

Ned learned that a few stalwart loyalists, all of them members of the Kingsguard, had fled to a building called the Tower of Joy. Ned gathered six of his bravest friends and rode to the tower. They found the white-cloaked knights there, weapons drawn, apparently protecting the tower and whatever lay inside. The opposing sides clashed; only Ned and his friend, Howland Reed, survived the battle.

When Ned climbed the tower steps, he found one woman, unguarded, helpless in a bed of blood, clutching old, darkened rose petals in her hand. The woman was his teenage sister, Lyanna, and she was minutes from death. As the dried rose petals fell from her fingers, Lyanna implored her brother to perform an important act—her deathbed wish—and she made him promise he would do it. Ned agreed, and he never divulged the secret he had heard from her lips.

The blood, the rose petals, and Lyanna's secret are mysteries of the highest order. But the mystery of the Kingsguard is no less important. Why were men pledged to protect the king instead protecting a dying woman—a woman not even of the royal house?

There are many plausible scenarios that might explain each of these puzzles individually. However, one particular explanation that has gained currency over the last fifteen years has been able to reconcile almost all of the details of the Tower of Joy mystery.

The R + L = J theory is quite simple. Lyanna, this theory says, was not alone in the tower. Next to her, in the "bed of blood", was her newborn son, who was later to be called Jon Snow. But he was no ordinary baby. This boy was the only living son of Rhaegar Targaryen. He was possibly a bastard, but just as likely, he was a true prince. Rhaegar was not limited to a single wife, and it is entirely possible that he married Lyanna. This would explain the knights in white, weapons drawn, willing—almost eager—to sacrifice their lives. For all they knew, Prince Viserys and the queen were already dead. The newborn child, whose birth had caused his mother's death from loss of blood, was the only living son of Prince Rhaegar, and thus heir to the throne. The knights of the Kingsguard were carrying out the function they were sworn to perform, even to death: They were protecting their king.

The old, blackened rose petals—her most prized possession, the things she refused to relinquish, even during the pain of childbirth—indicated the importance to her of the person who gave her the flowers so long ago, during the great Tourney of Harrenhal. The rose garland was the first gift from the man she truly loved, Prince Rhaegar Targaryen. The secret, of course, was the baby's identity, and the promise Lyanna extracted from her brother was to take the boy, make him Ned's own, never to divulge the secret of who he was, and who he might become.

ANALYSING THE THEORY

The Elopement
John Collet, 1764

The R + L = J theory explains many, but not all, of the strange events that occurred during Robert's Rebellion. It has about it an air of authenticity and legitimacy, explaining as it does some of the greatest mysteries of the rebellion, and bringing huge importance to the young squire currently pledged to the Lord Commander of the Night's Watch.

Opponents of the theory will point out that several other women are plausible mothers to Jon Snow. If Ned Stark had indeed fathered a bastard child, he would have demonstrated the same kind of youthful indiscretion that caused Jaime to murder a king in a most undignified and dishonourable fashion. It was indiscretion of the order that Rhaegar displayed when he abducted and raped Lyanna. All of these dishonourable acts could be seen as part of a larger motif of wisdom gained through painful experience.

I agree with those who oppose the theory that Eddard Stark could have had a wandering eye. There are no true saints in Game of Thrones; I don't believe Lord Stark was without sin. I have read many of the counter-arguments, and I find several of them quite convincing.

I believe any sound theory regarding the mysteries of the Tower of Joy, the death of Lyanna Stark, the birth of Jon Snow, and the true nature of Eddard Stark must unify all of the far-flung elements of the story. It is not nearly enough, I feel, to say that Jon Snow is rightful heir to the Iron Throne. What if he is? How does this impact the events north of the Wall, or south of the Storm Lands? How does it affect the Dothraki and House Lannister? What does it say about the future, and the past? Any theory, whether it postulates Lyanna loved Rhaegar or despised him, whether Jon Snow is Ned's bastard or Crown Prince, must unite all of these elements into a coherent explanation.

I did not provide a detailed chronology of Robert's Rebellion, with special emphasis on the Tourney of Harrenhal and the mystery of the Tower of Joy, because I found the idea that Rhaegar and Lyanna loved each other to be untenable or a concept without merit. In fact, I bring to the discussion thoughts not frequently juxtaposed with those around the events of Robert's Rebellion. Those thoughts go back thousands of years, and they are more often than not delivered to us through the eyes of a ten-year-old boy (or seven to nine years old in the novels). Game of Thrones is a story of peripheries, both geographical and chronological. The greatest mysteries of Robert's Rebellion, I believe, are part and parcel with the greatest secrets of the most distant past. I feel we must travel to that time of long ago, breathe in the air, rub the dirt into our fingers, and know, deep inside, what it all meant.

ANCIENT TIMES

Osha: "You hear them, boy? The Old Gods are answerin' ya."
Bran: "What are you doing here?"
Osha: "They're my gods, too. Beyond the Wall they're the only gods..."
Bran: "What did you mean about hearing the gods?"
Osha: "You asked them; they're answerin' ya. Shhh. Open your ears."
Bran: "It's only the wind."

Osha: "Who do you think sends the wind, if not the gods? They see you, boy. They hear you. Your brother will get no help from them where he's goin'. The Old Gods have no power in the south. The weirwoods there were all cut down a long time ago. How can they watch when they have no eyes?"

St. Francis Communing with the Animals
Unknown artist, circa 1860

Bran has eyes to see, but Osha told him in this scene in the Winterfell godswood that he needed ears to hear, too. Of all the characters, Bran is most tuned into the world around him, sensing the reality throughout Westeros not only through his own senses, but through scents and sounds known only to direwolves, through the sights seen only by three-eyed ravens. He is too young to understand, but also too young to dismiss these deepest of realities as meaningless dreams. His older siblings routinely dismiss not only dreams, but the pleroma of life as they experience it with their own eyes and ears and fingers. As he grows into adulthood, the greatest danger Bran will face is not a grumkin or snark or even a White Walker. The greatest danger—to himself and to the world that desperately needs his insight—is that he will succumb to the normal path of development and learn to relegate his dreams and visions to the toy bin along with the other discarded facets of a forgotten childhood.

All of us, not only Bran, enjoy opportunities to commune with nature, or the past, or the other aspects of life that go beyond the immediate and the mundane.

Mantras and experiences of spiritual ecstasy, for instance, are instruments of spiritual travel, but they provide no lesser provision for travel through space and even through time. The greater aspects of reality do not change, and to commune with these higher truths is to achieve insights obtainable through no other medium, and to connect the present reality with pasts and futures that are no less real.

Bran's life experiences connect him with his past. He sits before the weirwood, as every generation of Starks have. But he experiences nature and the past as no Stark has for thousands of years.

"Old Nan says the children [of the forest] knew the songs of trees, that they could fly like birds and swim like fish and talk to the animals," Bran said. (AGoT, Ch. 66, Bran)

There is no small bit of irony in Bran's words, since he carries inside himself the very same abilities. Ironic, too, that Maester Luwin dismissed Bran's words as soon as they passed his lips. "And all this they did with magic," he said. "I wish they were here now." If only the learned Maester Luwin understood the true nature of the boy sitting at his side. Bran Stark was a direct descendent of the First Men, but he had in him enough of those Children of the Forest that he heard what direwolves heard, saw what ravens saw.

Bran asked Maester Luwin about the Children, insisting the knowledge was important to him. Indeed. Nothing was more important.

The boy's tutor told him that in the beginning, only the Children had populated Westeros. "They were a people dark and beautiful, small of stature, no taller than children even when grown to manhood... Slight as they were, the children were quick and graceful. Male and female hunted together, with weirwood bows and flying snares. Their gods were the gods of the forest, stream, and stone, the old gods whose names are secret. Their wise men were called *greenseers*, and carved strange faces in the weirwoods to keep watch on the woods." (AGoT, Ch. 66, Bran)

The First Men, the ancestors of House Stark and the great houses of the north, didn't come to Westeros until twelve thousand years before Aegon's Landing. The First Men cut down the face trees, preferring farms to forests. There could have been no greater sin in the minds of the Children of the Forest, since the weirwoods were the gods' eyes. Without the gods' knowledge and guidance, the Children could not continue living. The Children went to war with the First Men. "The wars went on until the earth ran red with blood of men and children both" and the two sides eventually signed a solemn truce.'

The Pact was so successful that the First Men began to adopt the customs of the Children, even going so far as to begin worshipping the Old Gods. The period during which the Pact was in effect was called the Age of Heroes (AGoT, Ch. 66, Bran).

The Pact was enough to hold the peace for four thousand years, until the next wave of immigrants, the Andals, a race of fair-haired men, appeared on the shores of Westeros. The Andals eventually conquered all of the kingdoms except for the Kingdom of the North, ruled by the Starks. They brought their own gods, the

Seven, and they killed the Children of the Forest wherever they found them. That was when the Children fled to the north. "North of the Wall... That's where the children went," Osha said. (AGoT, Ch. 66, Bran)

Bran on his own will not be able to bring an end to the adults' game of thrones. At the very least, though, he may open to the narrow-minded people around him new understandings of their connections to the world and to each other. If he can do this, he may be able to incite them to contemplation of a new way of life not based on privilege and power, but rather founded on the connection of one living being to another.

Surely the Children and the First Men counted among their numbers not only wise seers, like the Children's greenseers, but leaders of vision as well. In the second season of Game of Thrones, if the television series again hews close to the novels, we will learn of such leaders: The one who led the Children and the First Men against the White Walkers, and another leader promised to generations in the distant future, when the long winter comes again. "Winter is coming," the Starks tell us. Every sign from the north indicates the winter will be long, hard, cruel, and deadly.

The Vision of St. Eustace
Antonio di Puccio Pisano (Pisanello), circa 1440

I believe the key to winning the game of thrones, to bringing a happy conclusion to A Song of Ice and Fire, will require that the final ruler to kill the White Walkers, tame the dragons, and sit the Iron Throne be a leader of rare vision. She will see through the eyes of direwolves and eagles. She will hear the thoughts of First Men, but feel and understand the wisdom of Children, too. The secret of the Tower of Joy and the final outcome of Robert's Rebellion will be understood to have begun the final trek toward a lasting peace. That peace will not be attained unless it fully integrates Bran's power, which is more than anything else the power to listen to the wind, to see through the eyes of the forest, to surrender the artificial complications of adult life, to become as Children again.

Every member of the Sisterhood of the Damned, every one of Tyrion's army of Grotesques, will be called upon to work together to solve the problem. Those among the able-bodied who say "Give me a clean death any day," will fight those they consider among the damned. In the end, if they do not join forces with the cripples, bastards, and broken of the world, they will perish. For it is the cripples, bastards, dwarfs, and sword-fighting girls who have been given the grace to see, hear, and feel what only the greenseers know: We are all Children, we are all damned, we are all among the grotesques of this world. Every one of us is called to enjoy the innocence of childhood, and the endless, fascinating, delirious pleasures and possibilities of life. In the end, the person sitting the Iron Throne will be able to say, with the lusty resolve of Tyrion Lannister, "I *like* living."

Printed in Great Britain
by Amazon.co.uk, Ltd.,
Marston Gate.